A History of the Universe in 100 Objects

DOCTOR WHO

A HISTORY OF
THE UNIVERSE IN
100 OBJECTS

JAMES GOSS AND STEVE TRIBE

DESIGNED BY
PAUL LANG

ORIGINAL ILLUSTRATIONS BY
PETER McKINSTRY

BBC
BOOKS

10 9 8 7 6 5 4 3 2 1

Published in 2012 by BBC Books, an imprint of Ebury Publishing.
A Random House Group Company

Doctor Who is a BBC Wales production for BBC One.
Executive producers: Steven Moffat and Caroline Skinner

Daleks created by Terry Nation.
Cybermen created by Kit Pedler and Gerry Davis.
Silurians created by Malcolm Hulke.
Autons and Sontarans created by Robert Holmes.

The Random House Group Limited Reg. No. 954009

Addresses for companies within the Random House Group can be found at www.randomhouse.co.uk

A CIP catalogue record for this book is available from the British Library.

ISBN 978 1 785 94048 4

Commissioning editor: **Albert DePetrillo**
Editorial manager: **Nicholas Payne**
Designer: **Paul Lang**
Original Illustrations: **Peter McKinstry**
Jacket design: **Two Associates** © Woodlands Books Ltd, 2012
Production: **Phil Spencer**

Printed and bound in China by **C&C Offset Printing Co., Ltd**

To buy books by your favourite authors and register for offers, visit www.randomhouse.co.uk

BBC Books would like to thank the following for providing photographs and for permission to reproduce copyright material. While every effort has been made to trace and acknowledge all copyright holders, we would like to apologise should there have been any errors or omissions.

What you're holding in your hands is probably wrong. As wrong as a Dalek master plan or altering a fixed point in time. This book is wrong. You can tell just by holding it in your hands. It's as wrong as *The Worshipful and Ancient Law of Gallifrey* (whatever that might or might not have been).

Doctor Who tells a story from before the universe began right through to its very end, and sideways into several others. Along the way, the TARDIS has landed on hundreds of planets (some quite frequently); the Doctor has met thousands of people (usually in the wrong order); he's saved millions of lives. It is a story that cannot be summed up, without barging into wibbly-wobbly, timey-wimey contradictions, or barrelling into madly contradictory – but incontrovertible – evidence.

So... We have tried to sum up the Doctor's universe via 100 objects, some very small, some extraordinarily big. (And don't make the mistake of thinking an object needs to be inanimate; many of our objects are very, very alive...)

We used an exhaustive and fool-proof selection process. The resulting list ran to a couple of thousand really rather brilliant Who-y objects. We couldn't decide what to throw out, and we knew that readers aged 9 to 950 wouldn't ever agree with our list. And then we realised – that's part of the fun.

The very arbitrary nature of some of the objects is designed to provoke you. Why did we choose Object 048? Surely no one knows what Object 082 even looked like? And, even when it looks as if we've been carefully comprehensive, you'll discover that we've left something out. It is because this book is wrong. As wrong as the Rani's Killer Bees, or the Borad's plan to find a wife.

We hope that following the story of these 100 objects becomes a treasure hunt across the universe – as mad, fun and infuriating as hunting for the Key to Time itself (see 003. The Key to Time). On the quest, you may find yourself exploring well-trodden territory, or poking around in the obscure backwaters of a forgotten world – but hopefully, along the way, you'll have exactly the same reaction as Susan Foreman did when she couldn't help becoming engrossed in the first book ever to be shown in *Doctor Who* and commenting 'No, that's not right...'

001

The Urns of Krop Tor

BEFORE TIME

Before light and time and space and matter, before the cataclysmic explosion in which this universe was created, life as we understand it could not have existed. Yet a tiny planet in the drifts of the universe held evidence of a conflict that was lost and won before the Dawn of Time.

The Disciples of the Light rose up against the Beast, a creature of all evil. After a mighty battle, they imprisoned it in a pit beneath the heart of a planet in an impossible orbit around a neighbouring black hole. The scriptures of the Veltino later named this world Krop Tor ('the bitter pill'); the black hole itself was a mighty demon that had been tricked into devouring Krop Tor, only to spit it out again because it was poison.

Two expeditions mounted by the Torchwood Archive in the 42nd century established that the planet was kept in perpetual geostationary orbit around the black hole K 37 Gem 5 by a power source with an inverted self-extrapolating reflex of six to the power of six every six seconds – enough power to fuel an empire. Krop Tor generated a gravity field which held the planet in constant balance with K 37 Gem 5 and projected a gravity funnel out into clear space. The power source was apparently located ten miles below the surface of the planet.

The Torchwood Archive's second expedition constructed Sanctuary Base 6 on the surface of Krop Tor and drilled down to 'Point Zero', discovering a seemingly endless chasm beneath a metal seal covered with unintelligible symbols. This Pit held the Beast – it was here that the Disciples of the Light had chained the creature. They had filled the Pit with air, allowing anyone venturing down there to survive, and they covered the walls with rock art depicting their battle against the Beast. It was a warning – and a trap.

Knowing that the Beast was as devious as it was powerful and might one day make contact with a frailer mind and escape the Pit, the Disciples of the Light devised the perfect prison. In front of the Beast, and just beyond its reach, were two Urns: these were the source of the gravity field holding Krop Tor in orbit. Smashing the Urns would liberate the Beast, but would also cause the gravity field to collapse instantly. If the Beast escaped its chains, Krop Tor would fall into the black hole, taking the Beast with it.

THE NAME OF THE BEAST

Some may call him Abaddon... Some may call him Krop Tor... Some may call him Satan... or Lucifer... or the Bringer of Despair... The Deathless Prince... The Bringer of Night...

> *The Impossible Planet*

I am the sin and the temptation and the desire... I am the pain and the loss and the death of hope...

> *The Impossible Planet*

I am the rage and the bile and the ferocity. I am the Prince and the Fall and the enemy. I am the sin and the fear and the darkness... I shall never die. The thought of me is forever. In the bleeding hearts of men, in their vanity and obsession and lust. Nothing shall ever destroy me. Nothing.

> *The Satan Pit*

The Beast seems to have been at the root of the horned devil image in the myths and legends of a million worlds throughout the universe: from Satan on Earth to the Kaled God of War. Confronted by the Doctor, the Beast claimed to be not a single devil from any one religion, but the darkness behind the demon figure in all religions.

Able to reach out from the Pit and influence lesser beings with its mind, the creature took control of Sanctuary Base 6's complement of Ood servants, turning them into the Legion of the Beast. It also possessed SB6's archaeologist, Tobias Zed, so its mind might escape in the humans' fleeing rocket, even as its body burned up as Krop Tor fell into the black hole.

DAMAGED GODS

THE DOCTOR: I've seen fake gods and bad gods and demigods and would-be gods...

FAKE GODS

THE DOCTOR: Having failed to persuade the Ancient Greeks besieging Troy that he was the Roman god Zeus, the First Doctor was then accepted as a Trojan god by Cassandra's handmaiden Katarina. She believed the TARDIS was his temple.

THE DOCTOR AND DONNA NOBLE: Following the volcanic eruption of Vesuvius, Lobos Caecilius and his family were rescued from the destruction of Pompeii by the Tenth Doctor and Donna. Resettling in Rome, Caecilius later adopted them as his family's household gods.

BARBARA WRIGHT: Mistaken for a divine reincarnation of the high priest Yetaxa, the First Doctor's companion attempted to save the Aztec civilisation by ordering an end to human sacrifice. She failed to convince the Aztecs, who didn't expect the Spanish Inquisition.

POLLY WRIGHT: Pretended to be the voice of the living goddess Amdo, in order to rescue the Second Doctor from execution in Atlantis. Amdo was represented in her temple by a statue of a hybrid of a fish and a woman, with a concealed loudspeaker system allowing 'the voice of Amdo' to be heard.

THE MENOPTRA: Worshipped as gods by the malformed subterranean Optera on the planet Vortis. The Optera were simply the Menoptra's own descendants, after generations of subjugation by the alien Animus and its servants, the Zarbi and the Venom Grubs.

KROLL: A giant squid, worshipped as a god by the Swampies of Delta Magna. When human colonists arrived, the Swampies were resettled on one of Delta Magna's moons, along with a couple of specimens.

XOANON: A damaged shipboard computer which had been badly reprogrammed by the Fourth Doctor. It recreated its split personality by dividing its human crew in two – primitives (Sevateem) and the technologically advanced (Tesh). The Sevateem feared the Doctor as the baby-eating 'Evil One' who had, they believed, falsely imprisoned their god.

BAD GODS AND DEMIGODS

THE GREAT VAMPIRE: Last survivor of a vampire race purged by the early Time Lords. He was stirring from his centuries-long sleep beneath a Great Tower when the Doctor and Romana encountered and destroyed him on a planet in E-Space.

AZAL: One of the mighty Daemons from the planet Daemos, who thrived on the faith of lesser species. Having guided and shaped humanity's development at several crucial stages in history, Azal spent centuries dormant inside his miniaturised spaceship until he was summoned back into being by the Master.

THE CAILLEACH: The Druidic Goddess of War and Magic, but actually Cessair of Diplos, an intergalactic war criminal. Her other disguises during her 4,000 years on Earth included Lady Morgana Montcalm, Mrs Trefusis, Senora Camara, and cottage-owning cycling enthusiast Miss Vivien Fay.

SUTEKH: Also known as Set, he was imprisoned in a mastaba in Saqqara by his fellow Osirans after he destroyed their home world Phaester Osiris and left a trail of havoc across the galaxy. The Osirans, an old and technologically advanced race, were accepted as gods by the people of Ancient Egypt.

THE NIMON: A distant cousin of the Minotaur, they descended on planets and set themselves up as local gods. Which was fine, until they had sucked the inhabitants and their worlds utterly dry and had to head off, via an artificial black hole, to start again on a whole new world.

THE MINOTAUR: A distant cousin of the Nimon, they descended on planets and set themselves up as local gods. Which was fine, until the inhabitants grew secular and imprisoned the creature in the God Complex.

THE GODS OF RAGNAROK: Powerful beings named Raag, Nah and Rok, who inhabited a realm linked to our universe. They caused the deaths of mortal sentient creatures such as humans for their own entertainment. The Seventh Doctor encountered them at the Psychic Circus on the planet Segonax.

WOULD-BE GODS

OMEGA: The Gallifreyan stellar engineer, whose apparent sacrifice during the planned detonation of a supernova gave his people their power. Omega in fact survived – sucked through a black hole to become the god of his own antimatter universe.

THE TIME LORDS V. THE ORACLE: To the people of Minyos, the early Time Lords were gods who gave them technology that all but destroyed their race. A small group of Minyan refugees ultimately forgot their Minyan heritage and started worshipping their computer, the Oracle.

MONARCH: King of the Urbankans, he believed that if he travelled back in time to the creation of the universe he would meet God, i.e. himself. His plan to achieve superlucent travel involved visiting Earth at regular intervals to remove mineral resources and cultural representatives.

THE MASTER: Frequently had aspirations of godhood, but was rarely taken for an actual deity. The people of Sarn, however, mistook him for Logar, their fire god, believing his shiny skin denoted his godliness. (In reality, it denoted his struggle to possess and control the android Kamelion.)

WENG-CHIANG: A Chinese god. When 51st-century war criminal Magnus Greel time-travelled to 19th-century China, he was accepted as Weng-Chiang by local peasant Li H'sen Chang. Chang was soon in London with his sewer-dwelling god – famous magician by evening, abductor of women by night.

THE KROTONS: Worshipped as gods by the local Gonds, these were two survivors of a crashed spaceship. Their plan to breed 'high brains' among the locals by suppressing knowledge backfired, leaving them stranded.

THE EMPEROR DALEK: Having escaped the end of the Last Great Time War, the Emperor Dalek rebuilt his species from sifted human genetic material, eventually declaring himself the God of all Daleks. He wrongly believed himself immortal. The Ninth Doctor speculated that the Emperor had been driven mad by hiding in the darkness for centuries.

002

Tegan Jovanka's Lipstick

EVENT ONE: THE BIG BANG

vent One was the creation of the universe. Falling backwards through time towards the very beginning of existence, the TARDIS became caught up in a massive inrush of hydrogen. Inside the ship, the crew were initially oblivious until the newly regenerated Fifth Doctor noticed 'carmine seepage' on the walls of the TARDIS. He was swiftly corrected by his companion Tegan Jovanka. It was her lipstick – she had been using it to mark the TARDIS walls as she navigated its corridors – and it was melting. The TARDIS crew realised this was caused by the extraordinary levels of heat outside the ship, and had to act quickly to escape being caught up in the Big Bang.

THE BIGGEST EXPLOSION IN HISTORY

Space-time came into existence at the instant of this explosion, 13.7 billion years ago, and the universe expanded from a singularity. In the first 0.00000000000000000000 000000000001 seconds, the universe expanded more than 1,000,000,000,000,000,000,000,000,000,000,000,000,000,0 00,000,000,000,000,000 times in a process known as 'inflation'. After inflation, the expansion slowed but, as it continued to grow ever larger, the universe also cooled massively – after a millionth of a second, it had cooled from 10,000,000,000,000,0 00,000,000,000,000 degrees Celsius to just a thousand billion degrees (approximately). After about three minutes, it was so cool (a billion degrees) that the process of nuclear fusion could begin and the first atomic nuclei were formed from protons and neutrons. A quarter of an hour later, the temperature was just a few hundred million degrees, and it was no longer hot enough for nuclear fusion to occur – there had been time for only the lightest elements, such as hydrogen and helium, to form.

The post-explosion expansion and cooling continued for 377,000 years, until the universe was several million light-years wide and temperatures were down to 3,000 degrees, allowing combinations of electrons and atomic nuclei to make the first atoms. Over the next few billion years, with the universe still perpetually expanding, stars formed and grouped into galaxies, and planets began to form around some of them (see 005. Racnoss Webstar).

In *Castrovalva*, the TARDIS is said to be heading for 'the creation of the galaxy' in a 'hydrogen in-rush'. Galaxy formation is still not well understood by cosmologists but it would probably have involved a fairly gentle collapse of vast (mostly) hydrogen clouds over millions of years, rather than a violent 'hydrogen in-rush'. Accelerating backwards through time this might appear (speeded up and in reverse) as a hydrogen out-rush...

A hot topic in cosmology at the moment is how the supermassive black holes at the centres of galaxies come about. An ordinary black hole forms when a massive star reaches the end of its life and explodes as a supernova. These 'stellar mass' black holes can contain dozens of times as much matter as a star like our sun, but a supermassive black hole is millions or even billions of times more massive than this. There are several ideas about how they might form. One theory is that lots of stars form in the central, densest part of the developing galaxy, quickly going supernova and creating a cluster of many ordinary black holes which in turn rapidly coalesce under their mutual gravity into a single, supermassive one. Another possibility is that, as the gas cloud collapses into a galaxy, the central part becomes so dense that it undergoes a sudden monolithic collapse into a supermassive black hole. Either way, the formation of a galaxy's supermassive black hole is likely to be a fairly rapid, violent process, so maybe this is what *Castrovalva* is referring to.

Another possible 'Event One' candidate occurs after the supermassive black hole has formed. The black hole's tremendous gravity will begin to pull in and devour gas and stars from the central part of the galaxy. As it spirals in towards the black hole, this doomed material emits a blaze of powerful radiation which blasts the rest of the galaxy clean of any remaining gas, halting the growth of the host galaxy (and shutting off the black hole's own food supply). Again, speeding backwards through time, this outflow might look like an 'in-rush'.

IT'S CROWDED AT THE DAWN OF TIME...

Further reading: Oolon Coluphid, *The Origins of the Universe.*

> THE DOCTOR: Why didn't he ask someone who saw it
> happen?
>
> *Destiny of the Daleks*, Part 1.

Not long ago, the Eleventh Doctor used the Pandorica to set off Big Bang 2, rebooting the universe after it was destroyed by the TARDIS. But the actual first event had already been featured in *Doctor Who* several times.

The Fourth Doctor, in *Destiny of the Daleks* (1979), dismissed Oolon Coluphid's seminal book on the subject as the work of someone who hadn't seen it happen. (The script editor was Douglas Adams, who had invented Coluphid and his prolific output for *The Hitchhiker's Guide to the Galaxy* a year earlier.)

The Fifth Doctor's first story, *Castrovalva* (1982), was a little hazy about whether the TARDIS was heading for the Big Bang ('Event One') or simply the creation of the Milky Way galaxy in a 'hydrogen in-rush' a few hundred million years later. (See 'The Biggest Explosion in History', p.11.)

The First Doctor had had a similar experience in *The Edge of Destruction* (1964) – a fault in the Fast Return switch propelled the TARDIS back through time to the birth of a solar system.

In 1983, another Fifth Doctor story, *Terminus* revealed that the Big Bang was sparked by unstable fuel being jettisoned by a vast time-travelling spacecraft. The fuel exploded in the void and started a chain reaction, while the spaceship jumped billions of years in time but not in space, ending up stranded at the centre of the universe it had created.

Three years later, the script editor of *Terminus*, Eric Saward, wrote a short *Doctor Who* adventure for broadcast on BBC Radio 4. In *Slipback*, the Sixth Doctor discovered that another vast time-travelling spaceship, the Vipod Mor, had arrived at the beginning of all things – when the universe was nothing more than a monoblock of condensed matter – triggering the Big Bang.

The Curse of Fenric (1989) unveiled an evil entity that had existed since the birth of space-time (see 015. Fenric's Flask).

> THE DOCTOR: The dawn of time. The beginning of
> all beginnings. Two forces only, good and evil.
> Then chaos. Time is born, matter, space. The
> universe cries out like a newborn. The forces
> shatter as the universe explodes outwards. Only
> echoes remain, and yet somehow, somehow the evil
> force survives. An intelligence. Pure evil!
>
> *The Curse of Fenric*, Part 3

THE INVENTION OF LIPSTICK

Many ancient civilisations decorated their lips – the Mesopotamians crushed precious jewels into a powder in 3000 BC, Cleopatra squashed red beetles and ants into a paste, while more common Egyptians used a lethal extract of seaweed, or a harmful mixture of the metal antimony.

Many make-up treatments have been poisonous, containing substances like lead (popularised by the Ancient Romans), or mercury, which was banned in cosmetics in America only in 2007 – and even then in just one state.

Modern lipstick was invented in Paris in 1884 and was made from oil, beeswax and animal fat.

003

The Key to Time

THE DAWN OF TIME

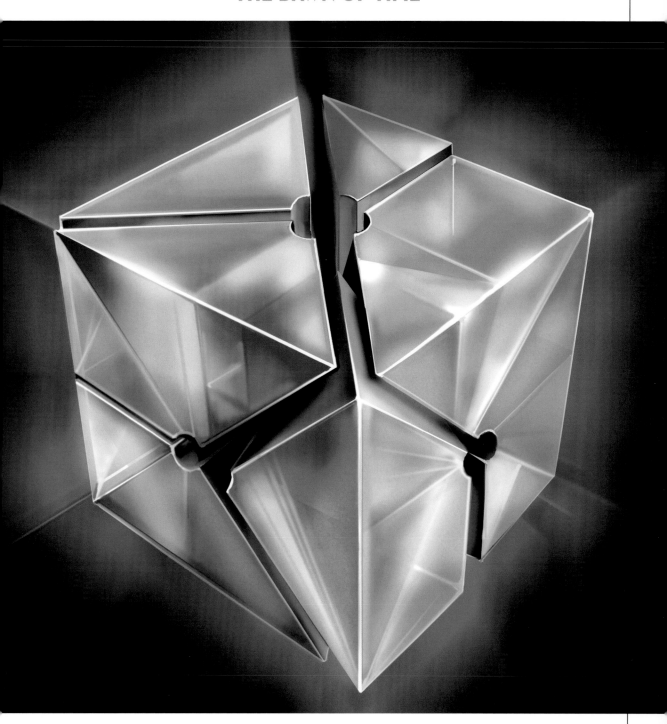

'Time is change.'

As the universe was created, two great forces came into being to ensure universal harmony was maintained – the Black and White Guardians. Built into the universe from its very beginning, was the Key To Time – the most powerful object in creation. A moral failsafe, it could reset the balance of good and evil.

If the forces of darkness became too powerful, the White Guardian was able to use the Key to reset the balance. Otherwise the universe would fall under the control of the Black Guardian and tip into eternal chaos – with Time itself perhaps ceasing to have meaning.

The Key to Time allowed access to every single event in the universe, and the ability to tweak each one to achieve an overall order. Such power was not used lightly, even by the Guardians. As a result, its six segments were scattered across the universe, hidden throughout its time span disguised as other objects or even sentient beings. At its heart was the Locatormutor Core, a technological device that not only allowed the Doctor to trace and transform the various crystalline segments but also held them together in a perfect cube.

When the Doctor assembled the Key to Time, he temporarily stopped the universe, allowing the White Guardian to achieve a balance. The Doctor, briefly, became the most powerful being in the cosmos.

```
THE DOCTOR: We have the power to do anything we
like. Absolute power over every particle in the
universe. Everything that has ever existed or ever
will exist. As from this moment there's no such
thing as free will in the entire universe. There
is only my will because I possess the Key To Time.
                        The Armageddon Factor, Part 6.
```

CONTROL TIME AND YOU CONTROL THE UNIVERSE

Since the Dark Times, mastery of time and of temporal travel has offered a chance – or a temptation – to impose a moral outlook on the universe, to assume control not of Outer Space but of Inner Time.

For millennia, the Time Lords were known for their policy of strict non-intervention; they were content simply to observe and catalogue the universe. In their earliest history, however, they were happy to interfere in events beyond Gallifrey. Often they fought and defeated monstrous opponents – the Great Vampires, the Racnoss – but just as frequently they abused their powers (see 004. The Dark Tower).

Gallifreyan society was eventually reformed, and the Time Lords officially adopted their non-interference policy. There are, though, many examples of them putting this aside, and using their mastery of time to alter the fates of entire worlds. Earth's solar system once contained another planet, its orbit lying between Mars and Jupiter; it was home to the Fendahl (see 009. Fendahl Skull). The Time Lords placed the Fifth Planet in a time loop, effectively erasing it from history. They could suspend events (placing King Yrcanos in a time loop on Thoros Beta) or selectively alter a time stream – seeking to avert the Daleks' creation or removing the War Lord and his entire species from existence, for example. When they placed the Sixth Doctor on trial they took him out of time.

The Doctor has always disagreed with the non-interference policy, but condemned many of these examples of intervention as criminal. Despite this, he has used similar methods several times – trapping Sutekh in a time tunnel and sending him beyond his life span, or time-looping the Marshal of Atrios's attack fleet.

The same techniques have been used against the Doctor, too. The last Zolfa Thuran, Meglos, trapped him in a Chronic Hysteresis to prevent him reaching Tigella.

MA'AT

Ancient Egyptian society was governed by a principle of balance – that Ma'at would be kept and shaped by their gods. A good soul was a balanced one; it would be weighed after death by the king of the underworld to ensure that it was of the correct weight.

This principle was extended to trials. Priests would carry a heavy burden to assess a case – if it tipped then they were guilty; if it was balanced they were innocent. The bribery of priests was, not surprisingly, common.

THOSE SEGMENTS IN FULL

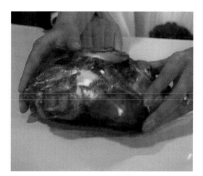

A lump of Jethrik

The planet Calufrax

The Great Seal of Diplos
(which originally belonged to Xante of Ordan)

A statue of the Royal Beast of Tara

Kroll

Princess Astra of Atrios

GO QUEST

■ In *The Keys of Marinus*, the First Doctor travelled across the planet Marinus hunting for the four keys required to operate a Conscience Machine.

■ In the stage play *The Seven Keys To Doomsday*, the Doctor went looking for the seven keys to Doomsday.

■ In *Underworld*, the Fourth Doctor joined the Minyans of Minyos searching for the P7E. 'The Quest Is The Quest.'

■ In *Dragonfire*, the Seventh Doctor joined Sabalom Glitz on a quest for a crystal on the ice planet of Svartos.

■ In the animated adventure *The Infinite Quest*, the Tenth Doctor and Martha Jones had to recover lost pieces from a space pirate star map in order to discover the location of a crashed spaceship from the Dark Time which supposedly offered their heart's desire.

The Dark Tower

THE DARK TIMES

Who unto Rassilon's Tower would go
Must choose
Above
Between
Below.

In the early millennia, the first species began to establish themselves and take a grip on the universe. These were the Dark Times, when great races and godlike entities – the Nestenes, the Mandragora Helix, the Fendahl, the Great Vampires, the Carrionites, the Eternals, the Weeping Angels, the Vashta Nerada, the Krafayis – fought for supremacy. Many of these first races assumed mastery of vast swathes of Space, but only one took control of Time. The Time Lords were the first to harness the energy of a black hole in order to be able to access and control the time streams. And the Time Lords had their own Dark Time.

During Gallifrey's Dark Time, aeons elapsed as the Time Lords misused their great power, waging war, controlling worlds, and conquering lesser races. The supreme example of this was the Death Zone – an area on Gallifrey where hostile species from all times and places were gathered to fight to the death for the entertainment of the Time Lords. Eventually, the practice was banned, possibly by Rassilon, the first President of the Time Lords, although many rumours and legends contradict this, stories and rhymes in Old High Gallifreyan which were told even to Time Tots.

Situated at the heart of the Death Zone was the Dark Tower. Rassilon chose the Dark Tower as his final resting place. (Again, there are Gallifreyan legends which suggest the opposite: that the Time Lords rebelled against Rassilon's cruelty and imprisoned him in the Tower.) The ultimate goal in the Game of Rassilon, the Dark Tower was a fortress of traps. Rassilon came to be thought of as the Time Lords' greatest leader. The legends about him multiplied, but at the heart of it was the story of his immortality – the idea that he had discovered how to prolong his lifecycle indefinitely.

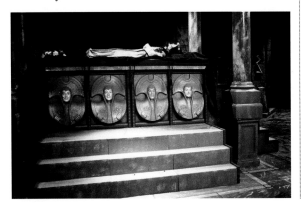

This, it turned out, was Rassilon's true game. He knew that other ambitious Time Lords would follow him, and that the most ambitious would seek to acquire immortality for themselves. If they were going to do that, they'd need to take the terrible step of opening up the Death Zone and beginning the games again, in order to reach the Dark Tower. And if they were desperate enough to do that, then Rassilon was prepared for them – they were a serious enough threat to be disposed of. The immortality that Rassilon offered them was eternal imprisonment at the very heart of the Dark Tower.

A noble reading of his actions is that he was saving society from a terrible menace. A less charitable interpretation is that he wanted them out of the way when he eventually returned to life.

```
'To lose is to win, and he who wins shall lose.'
```

DARK TOWERS

The original Dark Tower was where the King of Elfland lived. According to legend, he stole away a princess, and it was up to her brother (Childe Rowland) to prove himself a true knight by journeying to the Dark Tower to rescue her – overcoming tricks and traps, illusions and phantoms along the way, with the advice of wise Merlin.

The story is referenced briefly in Shakespeare's *King Lear*, mixed in with the story of Jack's quest to find the beanstalk:

```
Child Rowland to the dark tower came,
His word was still 'Fie, foh, and fum
I smell the blood of a British man.'
       William Shakespeare, King Lear, Act 3, Scene 4
```

This in turn inspired a poem by Robert Browning (1855) about a young nobleman called Childe Roland's quest to find the Dark Tower, and his increasingly oppressed mental state as he nears his object, becoming more aware of all those who have failed before him:

```
What in the midst lay but the Tower itself?
The round squat turret, blind as the devil's heart.
...Dauntless the slughorn to my lips I set
And blew.

                    Robert Browning,
        Childe Roland To The Dark Tower Came
```

This poem inspired a series of books by Stephen King about a quest for a Dark Tower. The first book became a bestseller in 1982 – the year before production and broadcast of *The Five Doctors*.

In J.R.R. Tokien's *Lord of the Rings*, Barad-dûr or 'the Dark Tower' is Sauron's fortress, close to Mount Doom in the kingdom of Mordor. From its highest tower, the Eye of Sauron looked out over Middle Earth.

IMMORTAL LEADER

'Hic jacet arturus rex quondam rexque futurus.'

The legends of King Arthur (collected together in Malory's epic *Le Morte d'Arthur*) include reference to him being buried, waiting until the time of England's greatest need. The Seventh Doctor discovered that one of his later incarnations encountered Arthur in a parallel dimension and started the myth of the once and future king. He was, perhaps, inspired by the legend that Rassilon would return at the hour of Gallifrey's greatest need – and, indeed, it was Rassilon who returned to lead Gallifrey in the Time War.

The idea of an 'eternal ruler' is scattered throughout the universe. Perhaps encouraged by the Osirans, the Ancient Egyptian burial ceremony was intended to prepare their leaders for an eternal rule. The Time Lords feared a return of Morbius, and the Kastrian people so dreaded the return of the hated Eldrad that they attempted his total obliteration – but a part of him survived and he was reborn. Queen Xanxia of Zanak tried to achieve immortality by using time dams, and a group of scientists led by Mawdryn stole Time Lord regenerative technology in the false expectation that it would bring them everlasting life. On 21st-century Earth, millionaire businessman Joshua Naismith hoped that Vinvocci technology he named the Immortality Gate would bring eternal life for his daughter Abigail.

Racnoss Webstar

THE CREATION OF THE EARTH

As the first races continued to emerge from their home worlds to explore or conquer the universe, they encountered a species that was a terrible threat to life itself. This was the Racnoss – a race of giant arachnids who were born hungry. They were carnivores, omnivores – they consumed whole planets, their civilisation built almost entirely around feeding. The Time Lords joined an alliance of Fledgling Empires and declared war on the Racnoss. The conflict marked the end of the Dark Times, with the Racnoss apparently extinct.

Two Racnoss Webstars survived, however. One carried the Empress of the Racnoss, who hibernated at the edge of the universe for billions of years. The other bore the eggs for a new hatching of Racnoss, and it drifted through space until it was caught in the gravity of a young star, just beginning to burn, and began to orbit it. A solar system had yet to form: this new sun was surrounded by rocks, dust and gas swirling through space. When the Webstar arrived, its mass was greater than that of most of the elements around it, and it attracted them,

pulling the gas and dust towards it, forming a hiding place 4,000 miles thick for the Racnoss children. A new world gradually formed, with the Webstar at its core – the planet Earth.

Around 4.6 billion years later, the Torchwood Institute's experiments in particle extrusion led to the discovery and manufacture of Huon particles. At the same time, Torchwood laser-drilled a 6,000-kilometre shaft down to the planet's inner core. The Racnoss children awoke, and their call was heard by the

Empress, drawing her to Earth. She took over Torchwood's underground research facility and continued to manufacture Huon energy, devising a plan to unlock the planet's 'Secret Heart' – the Racnoss Webstar at the core of the planet, and release her children, ready to send them out to devour the universe again...

HUON PARTICLES

This lethal energy form was created by the Time Lords in the Dark Times as an element of their time-travel technology. When they discovered that Huon energy unravelled the atomic structure and was therefore lethal, the Time Lords eradicated it, although traces remained in the hearts of their TARDISes.

The Torchwood Institute's hidden research laboratories used water from London's River Thames to extrude new Huon particles in liquid form through a flat hydrogen base. But these particles were inert and needed something living to catalyse inside. The Empress of the Racnoss instructed Lance Bennett to dose Donna Noble with liquid Huon particles, and after six months her body was saturated with Huon energy. The excitement of her wedding to Lance produced an endorphin rush that was sufficient to activate the particles. Donna became a living key – purging the particles from her body and sending them down the shaft would unlock the Racnoss Webstar at the heart of the Earth. However, the Huon energy in the Doctor's TARDIS magnetised the particles inside Donna as they reached boiling point and drew her into his time machine.

HOLES IN THE EARTH

Drilling below the Earth's surface has always been risky.
■ Deep-sea drilling for natural gas brought a weed creature to the surface of the North Sea.
■ Professor Stahlman's plan to drill over 20 miles into the magma released a lava flow that infected all who touched it and destroyed a parallel Earth.
■ The Silurians and the Sea Devils were both awoken by vibrations caused by drilling beneath the Earth's surface, or beneath the foundations of a sea fort.
■ Deep-sea drilling for oil off the Scottish coast attracted the attention of a marooned Zygon spaceship and its Skarasen.

VERY OLD SPACESHIPS

TERMINUS: Under the supervision of the Garm, a cure for Lazar's disease was sought, using bursts of radiation. The energy came from the engines at the heart of Terminus – in reality a very old spaceship that had time-jumped to the universe's creation and accidentally sparked the Big Bang (see 002. Tegan Jovanka's Lipstick).

THE P7E: Another planet formed around a spaceship was seen when the Doctor and Leela joined a Minyan quest for the lost spacecraft the P7E (about 100,000 years after the Time Lords left the planet Minyos, which was destroyed soon afterwards). The Minyans found the P7E at the heart of a planet that was still soft, having only formed around the ship a few hundred years earlier.

VARGA'S SHIP: A Martian craft that lay trapped in a glacier for thousands of years.

THE GOD COMPLEX: Designed as a prison for a rejected god, the ship drifted through space, gathering up subjects to feed to its prisoner, a Minotaur.

THE STARLINER: Having fallen through into E-Space, the inhabitants of the Starliner laboured for generations to repair their craft, little realising that they were not the descendants of the crew, but Alzarians who had evolved from indigenous Marshmen.

THE HYDRAX: The exploration vessel Hydrax fell into E-Space en route from Earth to Beta Two in the Perugellis sector. Its crew became enslaved to the Great Vampire, and ruled over a primitive civilisation.

Jagaroth Spaceship

400,000,000 BC

The Jagaroth were an ancient warlike race, long thought extinct. During a war between Jagaroth factions, one of their ships crash-landed on Paleozoic Earth .

The atmospheric thrust motors and the secondary engines were damaged, so its crew decided to take off using warp-drive. With thrust against the planet's surface set to Power 3, their warp-field operator, Scaroth, cautioned that Power 3 was too severe. The attempt to create a stable warp-field so deep inside the planet's gravity-well failed, and the ship exploded.

The massive discharge of radiation flung out in the explosion was the spark that gave life to the amniotic fluid present on the Earth's surface 400 million years ago. The amino acids then fused to form minute cells, which eventually evolved into vegetable and animal life.

PRIMORDIAL SOUP

The Primordial Soup Theory argues that life on Earth began as a result of a reaction in water with the chemicals from the atmosphere and some form of energy to create amino acids. Amino acids are the building blocks of proteins, which would then evolve into all life on Earth over many billions of years.

It has been suggested that this may have taken place up to 4 billion years ago. The theory was first proposed in the 1920s, speculating that the necessary 'spark of life' for the organic soup was a lightning strike. This was tested in 1950 when scientists simulated a lightning strike in the atmospheric conditions of prehistoric Earth, resulting in the creation of amino acids.

It has been argued since that life may have started in the atmosphere, which at that time contained a mix of chemicals whose chemical reaction broke down various carbon compounds into the amino acid chains that led to life. It's also been suggested that the reaction may have taken place in the deep sea as a result of heat from a deep sea vent.

THE ELEMENTS OF SCAROTH

I am Scaroth. Me, together in one. The Jagaroth shall live through me. Together we have pushed this puny race of humans, shaped their paltry destiny to meet our ends. Soon we shall be... The centuries that divide me shall be undone.

Scaroth was shielded in the warp-control cabin, and he was splintered in the explosion. Versions of him were scattered through time, physically separate but mentally connected. The twelve facets of Scaroth aimed to steer humanity's progress to a point where the technology would exist to return him to shortly before his spaceship's disintegration. He would then prevent himself from pressing the button.

Not all of Scaroth's identities have been recorded (see p.22).

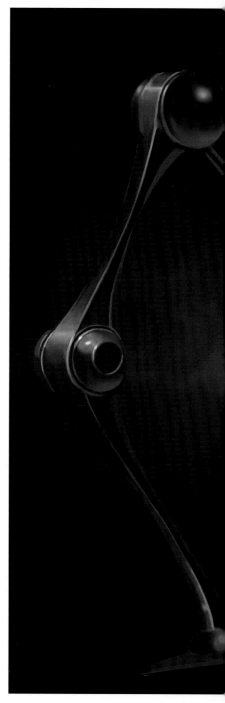

SPACESHIP DESIGN

Scaroth's ship is unusual for a *Doctor Who* spacecraft in that does not seek to emulate a flying saucer or a *Star Wars*-style long rocket. It is a sphere supported on a tripod.

The model was built by Ian Scoones and was one of several innovative models seen in the programme in 1979.

For the distortion caused by the warp-field collapse, the model was filmed reflected onto a flexible mirror (a bit like tin foil) and the point where the ship was shown was poked vigorously.

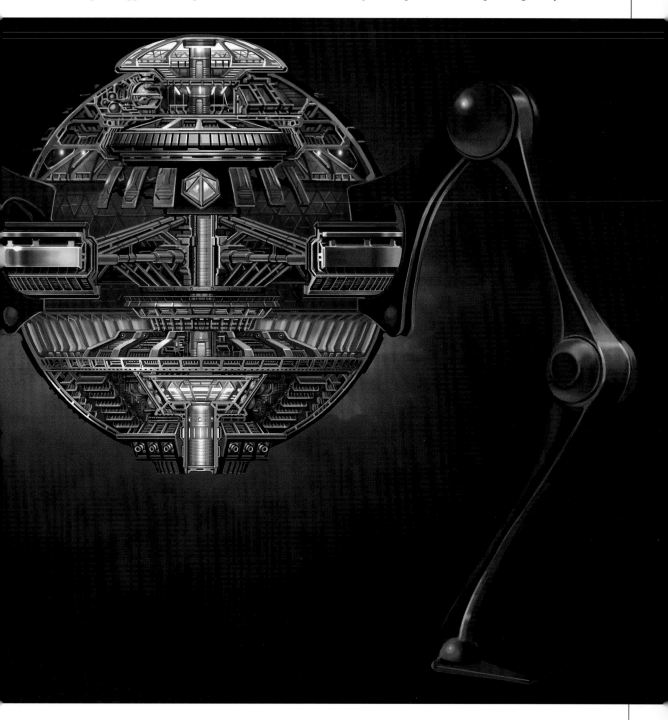

SCAROTH'S SPLINTERS

CAVEMAN:
showed man 'the true use of fire'

EGYPTIAN:
'caused the pyramids to be built'

**BABYLONIAN/
MESOPOTAMIAN:**
invented the first wheel

**BABYLONIANS/
ANCIENT GREEKS:**
'caused the heavens to be mapped'

ROMAN

NORMAN SOLDIER

CAPTAIN TANCREDI:
commissioned seven copies of the
Mona Lisa from Leonardo

COUNT SCARLIONI: guided time
experiments, funded through art crime

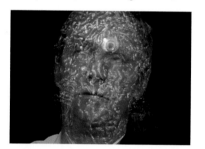
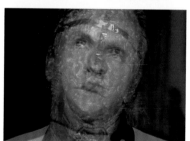

THE HOLISTIC WRITING OF DOUGLAS ADAMS

Douglas Adams, writer and script editor of *City of Death*, frequently revisited his own ideas in various media...

■ A spaceship explodes on prehistoric Earth in *City of Death* and again in *Dirk Gently's Holistic Detective Agency*.

■ Oolon Coluphid was the author of a trilogy of philosophical blockbusters in *The Hitchhiker's Guide to the Galaxy*; *Destiny of the Daleks* exposed him as an amateur cosmologist, too.

■ When he came to write the Dirk Gently novels, Adams freely adapted from the unfinished story *Shada*, notably...

■ ... Professor Chronotis – a pivotal figure in *Shada*, who was later central to Adams's novel *Dirk Gently's Holistic Detective Agency*.

■ Adams submitted an outline for a story called 'Doctor Who and the Krikkitmen', which wasn't commissioned. It was made some years later, but with Arthur Dent and co in *Life, the Universe and Everything*.

■ He may have been inspired by (or gently mocking) elements of *Invasion of the Dinosaurs* and *The Ark in Space* when he devised the Golgafrinchan B Ark in *The Hitchhiker's Guide to the Galaxy*.

The Hand of Eldrad

150,000,000 BC

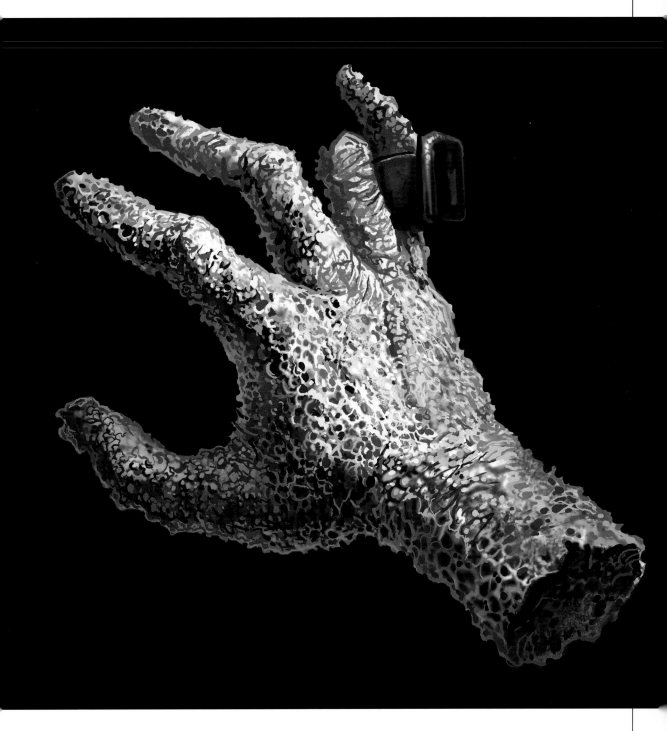

Long ago, Kastria was a cold, inhospitable planet, ravaged by solar winds. The scientist Eldrad built spatial barriers to protect his world from them, and machines to replenish its soil and atmosphere. He even devised a robust new crystalline silicon form for his race.

Eldrad later claimed that two warring alien species then made Kastria their battleground, destroying its spatial barriers and allowing the solar winds to return and dehydrate the planet. These aliens, he said, made puppets of the Kastrian leaders, and Eldrad was discredited and sentenced to obliteration in deep space. In fact, Eldrad had attempted to usurp the Kastrian king, Rokon, and had destroyed his own spatial barriers – this was the real reason for the death sentence on him.

Due to a malfunction, Eldrad's hand survived the obliteration process and was blasted through space. It landed on Earth during the Jurassic period of the planet's Mesozoic era. Embedded in blackstone dolomite, the hand was fossilised…

When the hand was discovered by Sarah Jane Smith 150 million years later, it regained sentience by forming a mental link with her, and acquired access to a nearby nuclear power plant, absorbing radiation in order to fully regenerate itself. Eldrad persuaded the Fourth Doctor to take him back to Kastria.

The Kastrian form, although capable of regeneration was also prone to crushing and to molecular degeneration caused by acid. The Kastrian race bank, containing 100 million crystalline particles ready to form the basis of a new race of Kastrians, had already been destroyed by King Rokon who had realised that there was a chance that Eldrad would one day return to Kastria. The race decided they would rather die out than live underground waiting until Eldrad returned.

YOU ARE MEN OF STONE

■ The Weeping Angels were the universe's most hostile statuary (see 061. Weeping Angels).
■ The Pyroviles were stone-based life forms covered in a skin of molten lava, whose home world Pyrovillia was stolen by the Daleks to form part of their Reality Bomb. They lay dormant under Mount Vesuvius until it exploded in AD 79, destroying Pompeii.
■ The Ogri were long-lived, silicon-based life forms from Tau Ceti

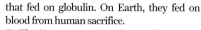

that fed on globulin. On Earth, they fed on blood from human sacrifice.
■ The Krargs were creations and servants of Skagra, who made them from crystallised coal in gaseous vats.
■ Two fossilised Daleks were among the few traces of events at Stonehenge in AD 102 after the TARDIS destroyed the universe; one came to life when touched by light from the Pandorica.
■ The Krotons were a crystalline life form capable of rapid growth and regrowth in tanks.

■ An unidentified probative space fleet with a neo-crystal structure and atomic power and weaponry was observed by Gallifreyan Space Traffic Control on its way to blast some part of the galaxy to dust. As it posed no threat to Gallifrey, the Time Lady on duty, Rodan, let it go on its way.

'ELDRAD MUST LIVE!'

Sarah Jane Smith and everyone else enslaved by Eldrad's will gave themselves away by insisting that 'Eldrad must live!' *Doctor Who* has always been fond of catchy slogans:

'It is a kindness.'
'A gift of peace in all good faith!'
'In the name of the Second Skonnon Empire!'
'Contact Has Been Made.'
'Sacred flame, sacred fire!'
'All praise to the Great One!'
'Moisturise me!'
'Sontar, ha!'
'Even the sonic screwdriver won't get me out of this one!'
'Spoilers!'
'Delete!'
'Bow ties are cool!'
'You will be like us!'
'Resistance is useless!'
'I am the Master, and you will obey me!'
'All these corridors look the same!'
'Affirmative, Master.'
'What is it, Doctor?'
'Exterminate!'

BEYOND THE FLESH?

The Kastrians redesigned their bodies beyond natural evolution. Several other races have also transcended their original forms, or tried to…
■ The Time Lords
■ The Nestenes
■ The Minyans of Minyos
■ The Uxarieans
■ The Urbankans
■ The Daleks
■ The Cybermen
■ Mawdryn and his Undead

A Badge for Mathematical Excellence

65,000,000 BC

The Cretaceous-Tertiary ('K-T') Extinction Event marked the end of Earth's Mesozoic era – 186 million years when the planet was dominated by the dinosaurs. This era ended abruptly, with an unexplained catastrophe obliterating most non-avian dinosaur species, much other animal and plant life, and one small humanoid. Scientists believe the disaster was the result of a large asteroid striking the planet's surface. In fact, it was caused by the impact of a huge space freighter which the Cybermen had programmed to crash into Earth... in the year AD 2526.

By the early 26th century, the Cybermen were presenting a sufficiently formidable threat for Earth's President to organise and host an interstellar conference. This brought together the heads of many powerful planets to form an alliance against the Cybermen. Earth's first empire was expanding rapidly at this time, and it had recently fought a short but vicious war against the Draconians with millions of casualties; the combined forces of Earth and neighbouring stellar powers such as Draconia would, logically, be too great for the Cybermen to overcome.

The Cybermen therefore attempted to conceal and detonate a bomb on Earth to destroy the conference and render the planet uninhabitable; this failed when the bomb was deactivated by the Fifth Doctor and his companion Adric. A contingency plan was already in place, however: to commandeer one of Earth's antimatter-powered freighters and set it on a collision course with Earth. Having installed Cyber machinery to control the spacecraft, the Cyberleader evacuated his forces and took over the Doctor's TARDIS, leaving Adric and two humans on the freighter's bridge. The Cybermen's device prevented any attempt to navigate a new course – it was possible to override the device only by solving three logic codes. And that would take a mathematical genius.

Adric was awarded his badge for mathematical excellence on his home planet of Alzarius, long before he met the Doctor. The badge was a star, and its tips were edged with gold. The Doctor used this to his advantage, grating fragments of the badge into the Cyberleader's chest unit, incapacitating it. This left the Doctor free to try to rescue Adric, who was still working on the logic codes. When the second code was solved, the freighter somehow began to hurtle backwards in time, ultimately reaching 65 million BC and crashing into the Earth.

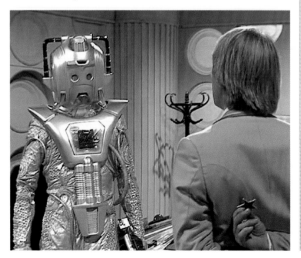

Some specimens of dinosaur life survived the cataclysm. It seems likely that homo reptilia were already abandoning the planet's surface and entering their underground hibernation shelters; they preserved extensive samples of flora and fauna, with a group in what would become Derbyshire taking at least one Tyrannosaurus. The Rani, a maverick Gallifreyan scientist, also salvaged an embryo Tyrannosaurus and pickled it in time; she was quite keen to prevent the K-T Extinction Event, believing that 'the potential of the dinosaurs was never fully realised.'

HOW DID THE FREIGHTER TRAVEL THROUGH TIME?

```
BERGER: We're travelling backwards in time.
BRIGGS: That's not possible!
ADRIC: It is when you have an alien
machine overriding your computer.
                        Earthshock, Part 4.
```

GOLD: THE ANCIENT ENEMY

```
THE DOCTOR: 'Gold is lethal to them. The perfect
non-corrodible metal. It coats their breathing
apparatus and in effect suffocates them.'
                        Revenge of the Cybermen, Part 2.
```

The Cyber War that followed the failure of the Cyberman plan to destroy Earth's peace conference was initially a glorious triumph for the Cybermen. The humans then discovered the Cybermen's weakness – that gold clogged their ventilation units. They invented the glitter gun – a weapon which caused Cybermen to die in a cloud of lethal gold dust. After the war, there was a trade in novelty hat stands made out of gold-plated Cybermen.

Some six centuries earlier, the Fourth Reich, under the leadership of Herr De Flores, was able to attack a squad of Cybermen with gold dust. Their breathing apparatus also proved vulnerable to attack by gold-tipped arrows and to gold coins fired from a catapult. The Cybermen were equipped with a gold-detector, not unlike a Geiger counter.

OTHER METALS ARE AVAILABLE

ATOMIC NUMBER	NAME	CHEMICAL SYMBOL	STANDARD ATOMIC WEIGHT	PHASE	ELEMENT CATEGORY	NOTES
4	Beryllium	Be	9.012182	Solid	Alkaline earth metal	Beryllium chips are vital components in many atomic clocks, such as the one unveiled in San Francisco's Institute for Technological Advancement and Research on 31 December 1999.
13	Aluminium	Al	26.981	Solid	Post-transition metal	The Tythonian ambassador Erato wove an aluminium shell around a neutron star, minimising its gravitational pull. The TARDIS could then divert the star and save the planet Chloris from obliteration.
29	Copper	Cu	63.546	Solid	Transition metal	Used as standard in the manufacture of bullets for UNIT weaponry until attacking Sontaran forces used a Cordolaine signal to cause copper excitation (making the bullets stick in the gun barrels).
30	Zinc	Zn	65.38	Solid	Transition metal	A metal commonly used with copper to create the alloy brass. On the planet Chloris, where all metals were highly prized, the Lady Adrasta's personal treasure trove included zinc candlesticks.
42	Molybdenum	Mo	95.96	Solid	Transition metal	A metal with a very high melting point (2,623°C), it forms excellent steel compounds, so became highly sought after as humanity entered the space race. By the 28th century, molybdenum-rich planets such as the Sense-Sphere were of interest to explorers from Earth.
47	Silver	Ag	107.8682	Solid	Transition metal	Special-issue silver bullets were available to UNIT by the 1990s, in case of werewolves. Brigadier Lethbridge-Stewart used them against the Destroyer at Carbury in 1997.
80	Mercury	Hg	200.59	Liquid	Transition metal	The Doctor has an on-off relationship with mercury. When he first landed on Skaro, it transpired that mercury was required for the fluid link, a vital TARDIS component, but he didn't have any spare... Despite several later fluid-link malfunctions and shortages, he neglected to stock up when he visited the abundant mercury swamps of Vulcan.
82	Lead	Pb	207.2	Solid	Post-transition metal	The centuries-long alchemists' dream of transforming base metals into gold was exploited by the Daleks when they contacted Victorian scientist Theodore Maxtible through his static mirrors and offered him the secret in exchange for his cooperation. As Time Lord President, the Fourth Doctor had his office lined with lead – the telepathic Vardans who had invaded Gallifrey could not penetrate it.
n/k	Validium	n/k	n/k	n/k	n/k	A 'living metal' that could think and speak, devised as Gallifrey's ultimate defence. The Seventh Doctor fashioned the Nemesis statue from it, with which he simultaneously defeated a 17th-century sorceress, some 20th-century neo-Nazis and a Cyber-Fleet.
n/k	Tinclavic	n/k	n/k	Solid	n/k	A soft-setting, pliable metal mined by Terileptil criminals in their slave mines on the planet Raaga. It was mined for more or less the exclusive use of the people of Hakol in the star system Rifta, who used it in their spacecraft.
n/k	Dalekenium	n/k	n/k	n/k	n/k	The metal from which Dalek cases are made, its bonded polycarbides are resistant to gunfire and explosives, but can be used to attract gamma radiation.
n/k	'Living metal'	n/k	n/k	n/k	n/k	Invented by Professor J.P. Kettlewell and used in the creation of his experimental prototype robot, K1 (see also Validium).
n/k	'High-content metal'	n/k	n/k	n/k	n/k	The steel type used in the construction of certain Cyberform variants.
n/k	Photafine steel	n/k	n/k	n/k	n/k	Used in the hull construction of Tritovore ships, it turns cold when it's hot.

OO9

Fendahl Skull

12,000,000 BC

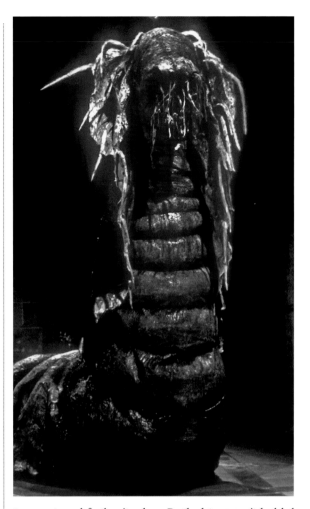

Originating on a fifth planet in Earth's solar system somewhere between Mars and Jupiter, the Fendahl was a living destruction so abhorrent to creation that the Time Lords felt compelled to intervene. They removed the planet from the universe by placing it inside a time loop. The Fendahl became a secret – another dark myth only talked about in the nurseries of Gallifrey (along with the Worshipful and Ancient Law, the Death Zone, the Great Vampire, and the Weeping Angels of legend).

But one thing escaped from the Fifth Planet. One of the stages of Fendahleen existence was humanoid, and this humanoid skull travelled the 107 million miles to Earth. It may have taken in Mars on the way, wiping out a whole cycle of evolution as it emerged on that planet. The skull landed on Earth, buried beneath a volcano in the region that would eventually become Kenya.

The Fendahl fed on the energy wavelengths of life, but it could also affect them, and it influenced human evolution through a pentagram-shaped neural relay in the skull. The energy amassed by the Fendahl was stored in the skull and dissipated slowly as a biological transmutation field. Now, any appropriate life form that came within the field was altered so that it ultimately evolved into something suitable for the Fendahl to use. It took time – it was eight million years before the first creatures evolved in its image – Homo sapiens. But the Fendahl was patient, laying down a plan for its reincarnation which would take another four million years to come into being.

Homo sapiens absorbed the Fendahl imprint, retaining it in behaviour, instinct and culture. The Fendahl fed into the RNA of certain individuals the instincts and compulsions necessary to recreate and further its plans. By the late 1970s, it had led them to look into their own origins, eventually finding the skull and examining it – a research team headed by a Dr Fendelman subjected it to potassium-argon tests. The impossible nature of the skull (seemingly refuting accepted theories of evolution) drew attention to the skull, bringing under its influence a young woman called Thea Ransome, who was destined to become the Fendahl Core. The skull also attracted a death cult – they helped fund the project, but also had exactly the right number of members to be transformed into a full gestalt of 12 Fendahleen around the Core.

The Doctor was able to destroy the Fendahl, first by disrupting the conductivity of their neural relays with salt, destroying the priory in which they resided, and finally by throwing the skull into a supernova in the constellation of Canthares.

HUMANOID EVOLUTION

How does the Fendahl's plan fit in with current understanding of evolution? It's impossible to specify but apparently 5–7 million years ago the first 'humans' emerged, branching off from the common ancestor we share with the chimpanzee. It took several goes before we reached Homo sapiens, as various other branches (homo erectus and Neanderthals) evolved and died out.

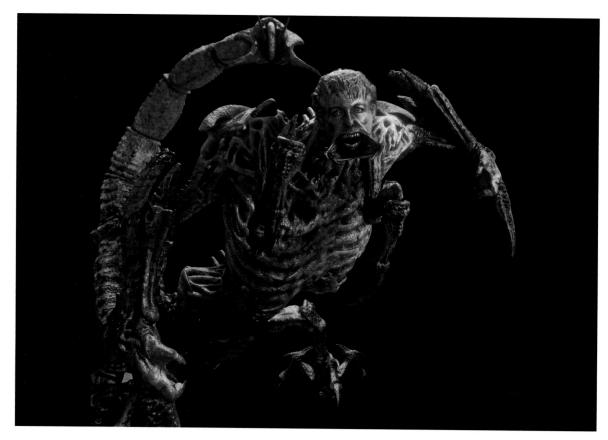

JUNK DNA

DNA is the building block, the program that contains our genetic make-up. At first glance it seems very inefficient: it apparently contains traces of the dead ends and roads not taken. But this makes up 98 per cent of our DNA – is it possible that the Fendahl code is hiding there?

In 2008, Professor Richard Lazarus's experimental rejuvenation process activated another of these dead-end DNA fragments in his genetic code, causing him to mutate into a savage arthropod.

THE GNOSTIC MASS

On the shores of Loch Ness lies Boleskine House, the former stately home of the 'Great Beast', Aleister Crowley. It was there that he created his Thelenist religion – a series of occult beliefs which have had a big influence on how 'black magic' is thought of and depicted.

Crowley's 'Gnostic Mass', with its specific number of disciples and its altar crammed with symbolic objects, may well have influenced the cult in *Image of the Fendahl*. Crowley was a big fan of the pentagram, using it to represent the possession of matter by a spirit. More traditional Satanists also see the pentagram as a powerful sign – choosing to replace the written word for it with the Hebrew for 'Leviathan' – an ancient name for the Gatekeeper of Hell. In the 1970s, a number of high-profile rock stars devoted themselves to exploring what the likes of Crowley had to teach them (not a lot, it turned out), often tending to conflate these

'Gnostic' notions with new theories that mankind may have been born on another world – we were all aliens.

Chris Boucher, writer of *Image of the Fendahl*, probably found more of his influences in the works of Hammer Studios, with films such as *Dracula AD1972* featuring a black mass, a death cult, and a woman destined to help evil be reborn...

QUATERMASS AND THE PIT

Nigel Kneale's 1958 television serial told the story of the discovery of an impossibly old skull that led to the discovery of an ancient spaceship and showed that humanity did not evolve on this planet and had been influenced by the dying race of Martians.

RACE MEMORY

This is the theory that our ancestors' experience is hidden somewhere in our genetic make-up. Although we do not retain specific memories of events in our species' distant past, we have evolved specific types of behaviour when faced with certain experiences or situations; the 'fight or flight' instinct to panic and run away from danger is one example. The psychologist Carl Jung was a proponent of this theory of the Collective Unconsciousness.

By 1970, the theory was sufficiently well known to be offered as an explanation for the cave paintings drawn on walls by people driven mad by encounters with Homo reptilia in *Doctor Who and the Silurians*. The theory is now, though, largely dismissed by pyschologists.

The Doctor's Pipe

100,000 BC

The stream of extraterrestrial visitors to planet Earth's prehistory began with the Jagaroth and continued with Kastrians, Xeraphin, Xyloks, Fendahl, Silents and Martians. Some just lay and waited for their time to come; others influenced the world's development, notably the Daemons from the planet Daemos and the Silents. Arriving around 100,000 BC, the Daemon Azal guided Homo sapiens as they established themselves as Earth's dominant species.

The Daemons believed that a good way to assist a chosen race was to give it technological advances, and they were regularly quite surprised and disappointed when their gifts were misunderstood or misused. Their gift of fire was a good example. They arrived on Earth when fire was needed to help the emerging human species survive its first Ice Age. The Daemons believed in selecting a single representative of a species to receive their gift, and to put all their faith in him. This 'Firemaker' carried a natural air of authority (and a burning stick) but also tended to take the secret of the flame with him to his grave, plunging his people back into the dark rather too literally.

It's probably no coincidence that the last of the Jagaroth also claimed to have had a hand in humanity's adoption of fire. The Jagaroth, like the Daemons, were an autocratic and hierarchical race, so it simply never occurred to them to introduce concepts of democracy, equality or shared knowledge to mankind; instead, they handed random males a symbolically burning sceptre and let them get on with it. By the time the Doctor, his granddaughter and a couple of 1960s schoolteachers reached post-Ice Age Earth, the secret of fire had been lost, again.

Fortunately, this was the First Doctor, recently escaped from his home world and clearly relishing playing the role of an eccentric Edwardian Englishman – almost his first act on stepping out of the TARDIS was to strike a match to light his pipe. This earned him a nasty bang on the head from a watching caveman who'd just seen fire come from the newcomer's fingers and recognised a good thing when he saw one. The Doctor and his companions were then threatened, imprisoned, abused and chased until they surrendered the secret of fire.

Unfortunately, the Doctor also came from a fairly autocratic and hierarchical society, so it was down to schoolteacher Ian Chesterton to convince the local tribe to share the techniques of fire-making. Unlike the fire Ian made (see below), the notion of a common endeavour for the common good didn't catch on. Everyone cannot be leader.

An elder of the tribe recalled how well raw meat and the newly rediscovered flames joined together, which probably set back the cause of vegetarianism by a few millennia. The Doctor, meanwhile, took his treatment by the Tribe of Gum as a health warning and never smoked again.

UNDER THE INFLUENCE

For most of his lives, the Doctor has claimed – and demonstrated – that humanity is his favourite species, eulogising our indomitable spirit and pioneering ethos, celebrating our cultural and scientific achievements, and preserving the most delicate moments of our history.

Quite why he takes this attitude is slightly mysterious since he, more than most, knows that humans have constantly been guided and controlled by extraterrestrial influences from the beginnings of history...

■ The Jagaroth inadvertently started life on Earth; Scaroth then steered human development through a dozen separate epochs (see 006. Jagaroth Spaceship).

■ The Fendahl engineered the development of humanity and its subsequent evolution (see 009. Fendahl Skull).

■ The Daemons helped Homo sapiens overcome the Neanderthals, shaped the civilisation of Ancient Greece and prompted the Industrial Revolution.

■ The Silents were present throughout Earth's history from at least its Stone Age, though possibly only after the Doctor had rebooted the universe with the Pandorica.

■ A renegade Time Lord known as 'the Monk' supplied anti-gravity lifts to the builders of Stonehenge and gave Leonardo tips on aviation.

■ The Ancient Egyptians modelled much of their culture on the technology of the Osirans, who fought a battle with Sutekh in Egypt.

■ The entity known as Fenric manipulated countless people from the time of the Vikings to the Second World War.

■ The technological and architectural progress of the South American Incas was aided by the Exxilons.

HOW TO MAKE FIRE IN THE STONE AGE
(With thanks to Terrance Dicks)

Take one shoelace, attached to one bendy piece of wood, and wrap a long, thin piece of wood (like an arrow) in the middle of the shoelace. The energy generated by rotating the arrow bit against a chunk of dry wood in an old stone packed with dead leaves and old grass, very fast and for a long time, will be converted into heat and, with any luck, into fire.

FIRE WILL BRING TROUBLE AND DEATH TO THE TRIBE

There is fossil evidence of possible human-controlled fire dating to between 400,000 and 200,000 years ago, and some indication that fire may have been used to cook food almost 2 million years ago. But the most consistent evidence suggests regular human use of fire began around 125,000 years ago. Between 100,000 and 50,000 BC, the fossil record is clear: wherever there were human groupings, they were starting to pollute the planet's air with fire use.

The dangers of fire have always been recognised, and it has long been used as a weapon – the Ancient Greeks, for example, burned down the city of Troy having gained entry by hiding inside a wooden horse. The Roman Emperor Nero is widely believed to have burned down his own capital city, essentially so he could build a new one. And large parts of England's capital city were destroyed in the Great Fire of London of 1666, a conflagration which began in a bakery in Pudding Lane, E15.

SMOKING KILLS

From 1963 to 1989, smoking behind the camera was omnipresent during production of *Doctor Who*: script editor Andrew Cartmel recalls the studio gallery being heavy with a pall of smoke, and vision mixer Clive Doig recalls having difficulty seeing the mixing desk through the murk. Onscreen, however, it was quite a rarity, and is all but unknown today. The few people who have been shown smoking have frequently met unpleasant ends...

1964
■ Before he's murdered, the last thing government scientist Arnold Farrow does in *Planet of Giants* is explain to businessman Forester why his application to market a new pesticide cannot go ahead; the penultimate thing Farrow does is smoke a cigarette. He very nearly lights it with miniaturised companion Ian Chesterton, who's got stuck in Farrow's matchbox. Had the story not been edited down from four episodes to three, there would also have been a scene in which Ian and Barbara are 'consumed' by clouds of cigarette smoke.
■ The first novelisation, *Doctor Who in an Exciting Adventure with the Daleks*, is narrated by Ian Chesterton, who's also a regular smoker (though never on screen), even when surrounded by petrol fumes from a road accident. He survives, possibly because he's given up before the next book.

1965
■ *The Gunfighters* is set in the Wild West, with saloon bars and tobacco-chewing cowboys. The face of lonesome gunslinger Johnny Ringo is revealed in the third episode as he leans forward, menacingly, to light his cigar from a saloon-bar lamp. He's dead by the end of the story.

1966
■ A consignment of silks, brandy and tobacco is the last thing

Samuel Pike's smugglers ever smuggle – by the end of *The Smugglers*, they've all been shot.

1967
■ Maxtible smokes fairly filthy-looking cigars in *The Evil of the Daleks*, even in the Dalek city on Skaro, which later burns down.

1970S
■ The Third Doctor wears a velvet smoking jacket, but the only smoke comes from the TARDIS console.

1971
■ Luigi Rossini (Lou Ross) smokes a cigar in *Terror of the Autons*, even while he's hypnotised by the Master. He later blows smoke in the Doctor's face in the manner of an insulting ruffian. In the next story, *The Mind of Evil*, the Master himself has picked up the habit, though his Havanas are considerably fatter than Rossini's brand...

1972
■ ... and he's still doing it in *The Time Monster*.

1974
■ A UNIT soldier's cigarette break in *Invasion of the Dinosaurs* allows the fugitive Doctor to escape. His court martial for dereliction of duty is not recorded, but he may well have been crushed by a materialising dinosaur while he was off his guard.

1975
■ Several used ashtrays in the Fleur de Lys pub in *The Android Invasion* suggest that the Kraals have built androids that smoke cigarettes.

1976
■ Eccentric flower artist Amelia Ducat smokes cigarettes in *The Seeds of Doom*, but does so delightfully.

1977
■ Victorian adventurers Henry Gordon Jago and Professor

George Litefoot smoke their way through the fog of London in *The Talons of Weng-Chiang*.

1977
■ The rooftop from which Gatherer Hade is thrown in *The Sun Makers* is littered with cigarette butts. Probably because the real-life location was a tobacco factory in Bristol.

1978
■ Leonard de Vries, would-be druid in *The Stones of Blood*, smokes a cigar; the toxins present in his bloodstream appear not to cause any ill effects to the Ogri that kills him.

1979
■ The Countess in *City of Death* smokes using a cigarette holder, but does so with elegance and beauty. Probably.

1984
■ *Resurrection of the Daleks* opens with a man pausing to light up in a warehouse doorway; he's immediately killed by a stray shot during a passing massacre. When the action moves to Davros's outer-space prison, the crew of the dilapidated space station are (almost) all smokers. None of them make it to the end of the story, although this was not cited in the story's defence when the *Radio Times* was inundated by a letter of complaint a fortnight later.

1985
■ Children's TV presenter Jimmy Savile is seen with a cigar in *A Fix with Sontarans*, a special Sixth Doctor scene recorded for the making-dreams-come-true show *Jim'll Fix It*.

2010
■ Winston Churchill's iconic Cuban cigar makes it into *Victory of the Daleks*, despite stringent rules about that sort of thing appearing on television. Matt Smith's Doctor waves the smoke away and later refuses a cigar.

011

Pyramid
5000-2650 BC

If there's one thing a god loves, it's potential. Looking at the inhabitants of Earth seven millennia ago, wannabe deities would have had the choice between scattered communities of starving farmers and the lucky people of the Nile Delta.

Favoured with fertile soil and an enviable climate, the Ancient Egyptians had potential by the bucketload, and while their fellow humans made do with banging rocks together, alien visitors to Earth formed a queue to give the Egyptians an evolutionary leg-up. A papyrus scroll in the Scarlioni Collection in Paris showed Scaroth the Jagaroth among the Egyptian gods; the ram-headed god Khnum was inspired by the visiting Daemons of Daemos. But the most significant influence came from the Osirans.

The Osirans were a sophisticated race from Phaester Osiris, with lifespans measured in millennia. They had dome-shaped heads and cerebrums like spiral staircases and were renowned for their guile, ingenuity and strong code of ethics. They were highly cultured, and their science reflected a love of beauty and ritual: their power relays were rich jewels, their force-field generators were intricately carved, and even their servitor robots were schooled in elaborate obeisance to their masters. They also spawned one of the most dangerous beings in history: Sutekh.

Sutekh destroyed his home world and left a trail of havoc across half the galaxy, eventually reaching Earth. The confrontation between Sutekh and Horus's army of Osirans took place in the Nile Valley: the names of 740 'gods' were recorded in the tomb of Tutmoses the Third. Horus won, but executing Sutekh would have meant the Osirans were no better than Sutekh – so they imprisoned him for eternity in a force field controlled from a power source on the neighbouring planet Mars. To prevent the control signal being deactivated, the power source was protected by servitor robots and a series of traps and logic puzzles.

The Osirans had developed what the Doctor called 'pyramid power' – transposing by projection. Pyramids featured in several areas of their technology, including their war missiles, power centres and even Sutekh's prison. And, idolised and worshipped as gods as soon as they arrived, the Osirans had an immediate and far-reaching impact on Ancient Egyptian culture.

SOME OF IT'S MUMMY'S

Elements of Ancient Egyptian culture taken from the Osirans:
- The Eye of Horus – a way of opening doors became a means to ward off evil.
- Servitor robots – the Ancient Egyptians saw the linen-clad servitor robots of the Osirans and fashioned their dead into copies of them for use in the afterlife.
- Sarcophagi – used as a portal to a space-time tunnel by the Osirans, the Ancient Egyptians used them as coffins – a portal to the Land of the Dead.
- Canopic jars – used by the Osirans for force-field projection, the Ancient Egyptians stored their vital organs in them after death.
- Mastaba – the pharaohs' burial chambers were modelled on Sutekh's prison.
- The pyramids – an Osiran spacecraft became a monument to royalty.
- Ritual costume – the long-sleeved, pleated dress and the sekhemti crown worn by Egyptian royalty were derived from Osiran attire.

PYRAMID POWER

The control circuit which imprisoned Sutekh from the pyramid on Mars broadcast a radio message on a broad spectrum ('Beware... Sutekh...'), which would have caused substantial interference to later terrestrial broadcasts had it not been disabled in 1911.

Building of the Egyptian pyramids was briefly halted by the arrival of a Dalek time ship, but the invaders were overcome by the locals, and the defeated Daleks were incorporated into the pyramids' construction.

In an alternative reality, Cleopatra gave the Great Pyramid of Cheops to River Song so she could entomb the captured Silents in it. River also placed a beacon at the top of the pyramid from which she sent out a message: 'The Doctor is dying. Please, please help!'

I SMELL A TRAP

The traps incorporated into the Egyptian pyramids were intended to deter tomb robbers. Both the Exxilons and the Osirans used such mechanisms, based around pattern recognition, logic and verbal reasoning. The Kastrian citadel was protected by a series of deadly devices. The Cybermen left their tombs on Telos guarded by lethal doors and logic gates. The Ancient Time

Lords of Gallifrey used a similar set of security devices when constructing the Dark Tower to keep intruders from entering Rassilon's Tomb.

HOW TO BUILD A PYRAMID

It still isn't certain how the Ancient Pyramids were built. One current theory is that ramps were built up around the sides to make it possible to haul the blocks up to the top.

The Great Pyramid at Giza is the only one of the seven wonders of the world still standing – but it has lost 9 metres of height since its original construction, due to the removal of the limestone cladding which originally covered it – much of which ended up in local buildings.

Pyramids proved to be costly and ineffective ways of preserving the bodies of royalty and were abandoned in favour of secret burial chambers in the side of mountains – such as the Valley of the Kings.

Even Tutankhamun's tomb showed some evidence of ancient grave-robbers – the Ancient Egyptians were almost as good at

robbing tombs as building them – so, in reality, it is likely that Sutekh's rest would have been disturbed long before his burial chamber was unsealed in 1911 by the doomed archaeologist Marcus Scarman.

WHAT WAS SUTEKH?

In Ancient Egyptian mythology, Sutekh was the Egyptian equivalent of the devil – the god of the desert and brother to Osiris. Depicted with a face like a jackal, he was famed for his cunning and duplicity – famously tricking his brother into trying out a coffin for size and then imprisoning him in it.

A WOOLF IN BEAST'S CLOTHING

Actor Gabriel Woolf spent virtually the whole of *Pyramids of Mars* sitting on Sutekh's throne and acting from beneath a large mask – in effect, he had to give his whole performance using his voice alone. Thirty-one years later, the *Doctor Who* production team turned to Woolf to provide the voice of the Beast in *The Impossible Planet* and *The Satan Pit*.

The Trojan Horse

1184 BC

> VICKI: You seem very fond of horses.
> PRIAM: Fond of them? I should think we are. We worship them. A Trojan would do anything for a horse.
> VICKI: Funny you should say that.
> *The Myth Makers: Small Prophet, Quick Return*

For ten long years, the Ancient Greeks laid siege to the city of Troy, keen to recapture Helen, the wife of Agamemnon, who had run away with Prince Paris. The battle was long and terrible and without resolution – until the wily Odysseus and a suspected foreign spy (the First Doctor) came up with the idea of building a vast horse, over twelve metres high. They hid soldiers inside it, and then vanished from the plains around Troy. To the Trojans, it seemed that the Greeks had been driven away by the Great Horse of Asia.

The Trojans took the horse into the city, at which point the Greeks emerged and unlocked the gates, allowing the rest of their forces to pour into Troy, finally conquering and destroying the city.

> CASSANDRA: Then woe to the House of Priam! Woe to the Trojans!
> PARIS: I'm afraid you're a bit late to say 'whoa' to the horse. I've just given instructions to have it brought into the city.
> *The Myth Makers: Death of a Spy.*

IS THERE A DOCTOR IN THE HORSE?

> STEVEN: Why not the wooden horse?
> THE DOCTOR: Oh, my dear boy, I couldn't possibly suggest that. The whole story is obviously absurd. Probably invented by Homer as some good dramatic device. No, I think it would be completely impractical.
> *The Myth Makers: Small Prophet, Quick Return*

The visit to Troy is an early example of the Doctor directly, if unwillingly, influencing historical events. In previous trips into the past, the TARDIS crew had tried to keep to the sidelines as much as possible – travelling alongside Marco Polo or escaping the French Revolution without taking sides. There were exceptions – they were forced to make fire for a Stone Age tribe, and the Doctor inadvertently sparked Nero's scheme to build a new Rome – but for the most part the TARDIS crew maintained a place on the edge.

At Troy, however, the Doctor used his knowledge of the Trojan Wars. He even happily claimed to be the Greek god Zeus, something he had previously chided Barbara for when she was mistaken for an Aztec deity. And, on this occasion, the TARDIS's arrival had an even longer-lasting effect: the Doctor's companion Vicki decided to stay with the Trojan prince Troilus. She accepted the name Cressida and became not just part of history but a central figure in future literary retellings of the fall of Troy, from Boccaccio and Chaucer to Dryden and Shakespeare.

MY KINGDOM FOR A HORSE

The creation of the Trojan Horse is often given to Homer's *Iliad*, written in the eighth century BC, but the Trojan Horse doesn't

BACKING ANOTHER HORSE

Equestrian skills can be an advantage when travelling in time...
■ Ian Chesterton proved his mettle with them in 12th-century Palestine and 13th-century China.
■ Horses are not native to Gallifrey, and the Lady Romanadvoratrelundar seemed confused as to which end was the front.
■ The Doctor rode a horse (Arthur) to the rescue of Madame de Pompadour.
■ The Doctor, River Song and Amy Pond rode horses to his appointment at the Pandorica.

figure as the *Iliad* describes the middle of the War. The sequel, the *Odyssey*, takes place after the end of the War, and only a passing reference is made to a Trojan Horse. The legend is actually fleshed out by Virgil, in his *Aeneid*, written 800 years later, and from the Trojan point of view.

There's no archaeological evidence for the existence of a Trojan Horse, and even the location of Troy is uncertain. The explorer Heinrich Schliemann claimed to 'have gazed on the face of Agamemnon', but his methods of excavation were far from those approved of by modern archaeologists. Although he seems to have found ruins of a city in Western Turkey that had suffered much damage, he then dug a trench through it looking for jewellery – most of which Mrs Schliemann promptly wore and refused to give back.

There are similar stories in literature, such as the tale from *One Thousand and One Nights* of Ali Baba's forty thieves concealing themselves in jars which were taken into his palace.

I FEAR THE GREEKS, EVEN THOUGH THEY BRING GIFTS

The idea of a leaving a giant horse as a peace offering may not seem like a very good plan, but the idea of leaving a big, tempting gift with a deadly sting has resurfaced many times throughout history. The War Chief achieved a similar surprise when he materialised SIDRATs full of soldiers in the various war zones. The Third Doctor used a reverse tactic when defending a castle against the marauding Irongron. The castle was almost empty, but he made it look fully defended by propping dummies around its battlements. The Fourth Doctor realised that Guy Crayford's returning spacecraft contained a hidden invasion of androids from Oseidon.

Axonite was a seemingly benevolent gift from the Axons – an apparently endless energy supply. In reality, however, it was lethal, draining a nuclear complex of all its power as the Axonite grew out of all proportion. The Second Doctor's offering of a recorder trapped Omega in his pocket universe. The Adherents of the Repeated Meme brought 'gifts of peace in all good faith' to their fellow guests at the End of the World party on Platform One. These gifts were in fact small robotic saboteurs. The Eleventh Doctor thought the Pandorica was just a legend, but it was actually a trap for him.

And Arianna got two thousand quid off the council, just because the man there said she looked Greek. (She was Greek.)

Stonehenge

AD 102

I
t has never been agreed who built the Stonehenge monument, or even what it was for, but it has always been known as a place of burial. A lot of attention has been paid to what is above the ground – how, in about 2400 BC, stones from as far as 150 miles away in Wales were brought to the site and erected to form a circle. Some said it was a place of sacrifice or worship, or somewhere carefully arranged for a solstice.

What very few talked about was what lay beneath Stonehenge, or of who guarded it – Cybermen. After several centuries, these Cyber sentries were attacked and overpowered by locals and by AD 102 had been replaced by Autons masquerading as Roman soldiers.

Under what became known as the Sacrifice Stone was the gateway to the Underhenge and the Pandorica, a box said to contain 'the most feared thing in the universe'. The stones above ground continued below into the Underhenge, forming a vast transmitter able to broadcast across galaxies.

The mystery of who built Stonehenge for the Pandorica Alliance may have been uncovered by Steven Taylor and Vikki, when they encountered a renegade Time Lord known as the Monk. His diary recorded that he had worked with the Celts, providing them with anti-gravitational discs to help bring the rocks from the Welsh Valleys and the Brecon Beacons.

WHAT HAVE THE ROMANS EVER DONE FOR US?

In *The Pandorica Opens*, Amy Pond reveals that her favourite period in history was the story of the conquest of England by the Romans ('The Hot Italians'):

■ Julius Caesar led his army into Britain in 55 BC, but the main invasion was undertaken by the Emperor Claudius in AD 43. The Romans were never able to conquer Scotland, so the Emperor Hadrian had a wall built along the border (finished in AD 128). The Romans started to leave in the 5th century. They had proved a civilising influence on the country. Among their legacies were the legends of King Arthur, who may have been a late Roman British ruler.

■ The Romans introduced many things to England, including plumbing, roads, the Latin language, sandals, and concrete.

DRUIDS AND STONES

■ The Ancient Order of Druids (founded 1781) believed that places like Stonehenge were used for pagan worship. In 1905 they held a mass ceremony at Stonehenge (wearing fake beards).

■ The Fourth Doctor and Romana traced the third segment of

the Key to Time to a circle of standing stones called the Nine Travellers on Boscombe Moor in Cornwall. Once owned by the Little Sisters of Saint Bedula, the stones had attracted much attention. An early survey by Dr Borlase in 1754 ended when one of the Nine Travellers fell on him.

■ On Boscombe Moor, the Doctor encountered the BIDS – the British Institute of Druidic Studies, led by Leonard de Vries, who carried out sacrifices on the stones to the Cailleach, the Druidic goddess of war and magic. In reality, the Cailleach was Cessair of Diplos, a criminal who had trapped her jailers in hyperspace above the Nine Travellers for 4,000 years.

■ Three of the stones were in fact Ogri – living rocks that fed on globulin derived from human blood. After the Doctor's intervention, two of them were destroyed and one taken prisoner. With Cessair of Diplos turned into a new stone, the Nine Travellers were reduced to Seven, thus requiring a complete new survey by Dr Amelia Rumford, the renowned archaeologist.

■ Sarah Jane Smith encountered another group of would-be druids. By day they ran the local garden centre and the post office; by night they worshipped the hircine goddess Hecate and held protracted sacrificial ceremonies. Sarah Jane also visited a stone circle: the Whitebarrow stones formed a portal to another dimension, the 'last resting place' of a super computer called Horath. Mrs Wormwood, a leader of the Bane, opened the portal, which became her last resting place too when Sontaran Commander Kaagh dragged her through it.

The Pandorica

AD 102

AMY: The Pandorica? What is it?
RIVER: A box. A cage. A prison. It was built to
contain the most feared thing in all the universe.
DOCTOR: And it's a fairy tale, a legend. It can't
be real.
RIVER: If it is real, it's here and it's opening.
And it's got something to do with your TARDIS
exploding. Hidden, obviously. Buried for centuries.
You won't find it on a map.
DOCTOR: No. But if you buried the most dangerous
thing in the universe, you'd want to remember where
you put it.

The Pandorica Opens

The Doctor always thought the Pandorica was a
myth – a legend spread across the universe of
a prison that contained a powerful trickster or
creature that was feared on many
worlds and had caused the
deaths of billions.

In reality, the
Pandorica was
part of an
elaborate

THE PANDORICA ALLIANCE

Homo reptilia

Atraxi

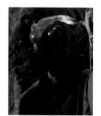
Uvodni

Draconians

Zygons

Drahvins

Sontarans

Fenric's Flask

3RD CENTURY

O nce, long ago, two powerful beings sat down in the desert to play chess. They carved pieces from bleached bones in the sand. The forfeit for losing was perpetual imprisonment in a flask, banished to the Shadow Dimensions.

The three-handled flask was covered in mysterious runes. Over the next six hundred years, it travelled the Old Silk Road from Cathay, eventually reaching Constantinople, where it was bought by a merchant. It was taken across Europe where it was stolen by 9th-century Vikings, who took it to north-eastern England. The Viking pirates believed the flask had cursed them, and they buried it beneath the Church of St Jude at Maiden's Bay in Northumbria. They named the evil power contained inside Fenric.

The Viking raiders left traces of themselves all over the British Isles, including depictions of Fenric carved onto stones on the Isle of Man and a runic warning of Fenric's evil in St Jude's. The flask lay undisturbed in the church crypt until 1943, when it was uncovered by British soldiers from a nearby military base. The last pieces of Fenric's plan were moved into place, and when the markings on the flask were deciphered, the entity trapped inside was freed...

A GAME OF CHESS

```
MARCO POLO: A game of chess, Ian?
... BARBARA WRIGHT: What magnificent pieces.
MARCO POLO: Yes, I purchased them in Hormuz, on
my first journey to Cathay. Now, they go with me
everywhere.
... TEGANA: I find it a fascinating game of strategy
of war. Two equally balanced armies deployed upon a
field of battle, and each commander determined to
be the one who cries shah mat.
IAN CHESTERTON: Shah mat? Check mate?
TEGANA: It means 'the king is dead'.
                          Marco Polo: The Singing Sands
```

Earth's earliest version of chess seems to have spread from India to Persia and China in the 6th century, then from the Middle East to Russia, and was played throughout Western Europe by the 11th century. The game pieces were popular with traders, and chess found favour at many royal courts. One difference between the modern game and that played by Fenric and the Doctor is that, instead of the all-powerful Queen, early versions had a piece called the Grand Vizier – the smooth-moving, manipulative, lethal power behind the throne.

The presence of a giant electrified chessboard in the entrance hall of the ancient Dark Tower in Gallifrey's Death Zone suggests that chess has extraterrestrial origins. The early Time Lords' version of the game clearly involved the deaths of live 'pieces' collected by the Time Scoop. The Doctor's initial battle with Fenric took place three centuries before the game was played in India – perhaps it was the Doctor himself who brought chess to Earth.

■ The First Doctor's companion Ian Chesterton played Marco Polo while travelling through the Gobi Desert in 1289. The Doctor himself was more of a backgammon man, trouncing Kublai Khan at court in Peking. He won 35 elephants with ceremonial bridles, trappings, brocades and pavilions, 4,000 white stallions, 25 tigers, the sacred tooth of Buddha and a year's commerce from Burma. His luck then turned, and he lost the TARDIS to the Khan.

■ The Third Doctor claimed to be good at chess, but then he claimed to be good at everything.

■ The Fourth Doctor kept a chessboard in the TARDIS, frequently playing – and losing – against K-9. He programmed K-9 Mark II with details of all championship games from 1866 onwards, which probably didn't help his chances. He had more success against Magnus Greel in Victorian London, beating him in just a few moves.

■ The Fifth Doctor preferred cricket to board games, but his companions Adric, Nyssa, Tegan and Turlough occasionally played draughts or chess in the TARDIS.

■ The Seventh Doctor was the master chess player. His perpetual contest against Fenric continued through the centuries, with moves being made in the same game from Lady Peinforte's study in 1638 to Maiden's Bay in 1943. According to the sorceress Morgaine, he was a less successful player as Merlin in a parallel dimension.

If chess does have its origins in the dark days of Time Lord history, then its evolution had come full circle by the 52nd century. The spectator sport of 'Live Chess' was as lethal as its Gallifreyan antecedent, with millions of electrical volts running through game pieces manipulated by gauntleted players. The Eleventh Doctor was on the verge of victory against the mercenary Gantok when he conceded the game in exchange for information about Dorium Maldovar.

THE GENE GENIE

Although the Doctor had trapped the ancient evil in the three-handled flask, Fenric remained able to manipulate the timelines to bring about his release. From at least the time of the Vikings, the 'Curse of Fenric' affected entire families throughout the world, ensuring that their descendants would all be present at Maiden's Bay for his release. Among these was Kathleen Dudman, whose baby Audrey would grow up to become the mother of the Doctor's companion Ace. Ace herself had met the Doctor at Iceworld on the planet Svartos after Fenric used a time storm to transport her from 1980s London.

Fenric also caused a time storm that carried the last living creature on Earth from the planet's distant future to 9th-century Constantinople. This was the Ancient One, a haemovore that had evolved after half a million years of industrial progress had reduced the world's surface to a chemical slime. The Ancient One followed the flask across Europe to Maiden's Bay. As it waited centuries for Fenric's release, it converted humans to haemovores,

assembling an army of 'wolves of Fenric', which would destroy humanity and supposedly save its future.

ALADDIN DANE

Fenric's imprisonment in the flask shares some similarities with the story of Aladdin and the Genie of the Lamp, which was incorporated into *One Thousand and One Nights* in the 18th century. It is a Chinese rather than Arabic tale of a Djinn trapped in a lamp, surrounded by treasure and desperate for freedom and escape.

The Curse of Fenric is also inspired by Norse mythology. A vast and terrible wolf, Fenrir was a child of Loki, the great father god. Fenrir grew so rapidly and savagely that the other gods fought long and hard to find a way to bind and contain him, lest he consume all of creation.

The Norse apocalypse is named Ragnarok – a time when Fenrir's children will devour the sun and the stars, and the Earth will shake until Fenrir becomes free, and then the gods will fight one last time, to the death, with Fenrir consuming the great god Odin.

The Loch Ness Monster

12TH CENTURY

For centuries there have been tales of a monster in the waters of Loch Ness in Scotland. The people of nearby Tulloch still talk of the man, a visitor from the Black Isle in 1922, who walked the local moor and was never seen again, and of the Jamieson brothers – in 1870, one vanished in the mist while the other was found wandering deranged and never spoke again. Hundreds of years of sightings of an unidentifiable beast stalking Tulloch Moor or swimming in the loch have made the monster internationally famous. Some have speculated that it is an extraordinarily shy and long-lived plesiosaur. Others have dismissed it as a myth that feeds on limitless human credulity. And others, including the British section of UNIT in the late 20th century, have discovered the truth: it is a Skarasen, a vast, remote-controlled cyborg that was kept in the Loch by its Zygon masters.

The Zygons were a spacefaring warrior race, whose technology was based on organic crystallography – their spacecraft were grown, not built. One Zygon craft, commanded by the War Lord Broton, was damaged and took refuge on Earth during Europe's Middle Ages, concealed at the bottom of Loch Ness and awaiting rescue. Rescue never came – the Zygon home world was destroyed in a stellar explosion. Broton decided to restructure the Earth to make it a suitable home for what remained of his race. He planned to melt the polar icecaps, raise the mean temperature, and use human slave labour to construct thousands of lakes with the right mineral elements. All he needed, he believed, was a show of strength that would cow the Earth's populations and governments.

The Skarasen's main function was as a food source – the Zygons depended on its lactic fluid – but it could also be used as a weapon. Broton's ship had carried an embryo Skarasen, which grew over the centuries that it was marooned. The fifteen-metre creature was gradually augmented, converted into an armoured cyborg, half-animal, half-machine, and able to withstand a nuclear attack. It was controlled via another piece of part-organic technology, a trilanic activator, which could be attached to potential targets. The activator emitted a signal which attracted the Skarasen. The Zygons tested the cyborg's abilities by directing it to attack oil rigs in the North Sea before deploying it against an international energy conference in London.

As the Skarasen swam up the River Thames towards Stanbridge House, the Fourth Doctor simply threw the trilanic activator to the monster, which ate it then swam away. Despite the very visible appearance of a huge monster in central London, UNIT and the British government organised a cover-up, and the Zygon gambit remained unknown to most of the public. The Skarasen returned to Loch Ness, the only home it knew...

MONSTER MYSTERY SOLVED?

Not necessarily. In the distant future, the Sixth Doctor and H.G. Wells teamed up against the villainous Borad of Karfel. The horribly deformed ruler of the Citadel was forcing his planet into war with the Bandrels. His schemes were stopped when the Doctor pushed him into a time corridor, despatching him to a Highland loch near 12th-century Inverness. The Doctor seemed to think the Borad might become the famous monster. It's more probable that the Skarasen ate him.

PETS CONTROL
A short history of semi-housetrained animals
■ When the Doctor and the Master were still at the Academy, the Gallifreyan President kept a cat. The Rani bred monster mice, which ate it.
■ The Derbyshire group of Homo reptilia kept a pet Tyrannosaurus rex.
■ Their marine cousins, known as the Sea Devils, kept the Myrka – a strange and terrible beast, immune to karate and capable of electrocuting with a touch of its flipper.
■ The Black Dalek had a Slyther, which patrolled the grounds of its mine in Bedfordshire while its master drilled down to the Earth's core.
■ Helen A, ruler of the Earth colony Terra Alpha, kept a Stigorax called Fifi. It was the last of its murine kind, which preyed on the local Pipe People, and Helen A trained it to hunt down any opposition.

NOT ALL PETS ARE VICIOUS KILLERS...
■ The Thoros Betan Sil considered keeping the Doctor's companion Peri as a pet after she'd been transformed into a bird.
■ Equipped with offensive capabilities, memory and awareness, and motivational but not emotional circuits, K-9 was the Doctor's second best friend.

BITING OFF MORE THAN YOU CAN CHEW

Carnival of Monsters

Invasion of the Dinosaurs

Terror of the Zygons

The Talons of Weng-Chiang

The Power of Kroll

Kinda

In 1973, producer Barry Letts pioneered a special effects technique that finally gave *Doctor Who* its Holy Grail – a convincing large monster. After a couple of ambitious attempts with a Tyrannosaur and a 20-foot Daemon in previous seasons, the Drashigs in *Carnival of Monsters* were achieved using carefully animated puppets against back-projections of sky and only making very rare excursions into the actual story using the 1970s equivalent of green screen.

Thrilled by this success, Letts was convinced to hire an outside firm to repeat the trick with puppet dinosaurs the following year. The results were rather less glorious. With the puppet movement too limited and the work to blend them into the picture unsatisfactory, the filmed dinosaurs appeared to float slightly above the video backgrounds they were projected onto.

It seemed that the secret of visualising a giant monster in *Doctor Who* had been lost – but Letts's successors, Philip Hinchcliffe, Graham Williams and John Nathan-Turner, all tried again for *Terror of the Zygons* in 1975, *The Talons of Weng-Chiang* in 1977, *The Power of Kroll* in 1978 and *Kinda* in 1982.

NESSIE!

Before he earned fame as the creator of the Daleks, Terry Nation was known principally as a comedy writer. In 1961, he scripted the movie *What a Whopper!* which premiered in (Swedish) cinemas in September 1962. Adam Faith plays Tony Blake, who's written a book on the Loch Ness Monster, which no publisher will publish. The rent is due, and Tony is desperate for money, so he and his friends head for Scotland to create the monstrous hoax that will surely help sell his book. The film features almost every major name in British film comedy of the 1960s and 1970s, among them Spike Milligan, Terry Scott, Sid James and Wilfred Brambell. Reviews since have ranged from 'The worst film ever made!' to 'So bad it's almost watchable'. Several other films on the subject have 'revealed' the monster as a hoax (a miniature submarine, a mask stapled to a log, Jack the Ripper) or have tenderly suggested that the monster is real, shy and best left to itself.

The earliest known story of a mysterious creature in or near Loch Ness is in a 7th-century life of a 6th-century saint. St Columba, told of a savage beast picking off the local Picts, sent his disciple into the River Ness. When the monster attacked the man, St Columba was able to turn it away simply by crossing himself and speaking firmly, and God was joyously praised for this miracle. Twelve centuries later, humanity reasserted its credulity when, in 1933, there were several reports of a vast dragon-like creature crossing the road and slithering into the lake – which either gives the lie to Nessie having been there for millions of years or suggests that the rise of the motor car brought an influx of traffic to a once-remote area.

Claims of there being a beast in the Loch have turned the area into a thriving tourist attraction. There have been various sightings, photographs and film recordings over the years, the most famous being the 'Surgeon's Photograph' in 1934, which has been conclusively and variously debunked several times over the years as a toy submarine and an elephant. In the ongoing monster hunt, large sums of cash have been spent by everyone from the Loch Ness Phenomena Investigation Bureau and the BBC to the Universities of Birmingham, Chicago and New York. Nobody's found anything, and unexplained sonar readings and inexplicably absent sonar readings have both been presented as definitive proof of... something.

Or, of course, it could all be very real.

017

Sontaran Scout Ship

13TH CENTURY

The clone race from Sontar have been fighting a war with the Rutan Host for over 70,000 years. The Sontaran home world is in the southern spiral arm of the galaxy and has a strong gravitational field, making their short bodies very strong in an Earth-type atmosphere.

The Sontarans deploy vast fleets of battle cruisers, their classic formation being arrow head, arrow wings, arrow shaft. Sontarans are equally comfortable sending out lone soldiers on reconnaissance missions in scout ships. These ships have a uniform design: a series of panels forming a perfect sphere. They can travel at great speeds and withstand impact on a planet's surface. They are interlinked with their owner – they provide the Sontaran with all his energy nutrients via the probic vent on the back of his neck. They can be remotely controlled by their pilot, and are even equipped with cloaking technology which renders them invisible.

The Sontarans have often attacked Earth, including a full-scale invasion in the early 21st century and an evaluation mission several thousand years after solar flares made the planet temporarily uninhabitable. But the planet was first claimed in the 13th century by Linx, a Commander in the Fifth Sontaran Army Space Fleet of the Sontaran Army Space Corps. He made an emergency landing after his reconnaissance mission was ambushed by a Rutan squadron. The locals mistook his crashing scout ship for a falling star and hailed him as a 'star warrior'.

Although Linx was defeated by the local gentry, he was but the first of many Sontarans to land on Earth, as the planet became of increasing strategic importance in the war with the Rutans.

FOR THE GLORY OF SONTAR

Sontarans are fiercely territorial, and a single scout will lay claim to an entire planet and be content to hold it as an outpost until a mothership can arrive to enslave or destroy the planet.

The war against the Rutans has a massive casualty rate: a Sontaran with a twelve-year life span would consider himself long-lived. As a clone race, the Sontarans can produce up to a million hatchlings at a muster parade, and these can take place every four minutes. This provides them with vast forces – but also consumes a huge quantity of natural resources, meaning they need to invade planets in order to convert them into hatcheries for

new soldiers. They are also able to modify the genetic make-up of a hatching to produce, for example, squadrons of troops with five rather than three fingers. Individual Sontarans can also effect functional variations by gene-splicing when necessary. Though they are created in a cloning process, Sontarans are not identical, and often wonder how humans tell each other apart.

During Earth's Middle Ages, the Sontaran Army Space Corps comprised at least five Sontaran Army Space Fleets. Each of its squadrons was led by a Commander. Though not capable of time travel, the Sontarans used osmic projection to reach into the future.

Seeking temporal power, the Sontaran Special Space Service attempted an invasion of Gallifrey. They sent in a Vardan invasion fleet to lower the planet's transduction barriers. When the Vardans were repelled, a small group of Sontaran shock troops teleported into the Time Lords' citadel to prepare the way for an approaching battle fleet. They were erased from time by the Time Lord President, the Doctor.

The Ninth Sontaran Battle Group also sought the secret of time travel. While the Group formed up for a vital battle against the Rutans in the Madillon Cluster, three battle cruisers were despatched to capture the Second Doctor; he was taken to 1980s Earth where an unsuccessful attempt was made to isolate whatever genetic factors enabled Gallifreyans to time travel.

In 2009, the Tenth Sontaran Battle Fleet was tasked with conquering Earth and converting it into a breeding world by soaking the atmosphere in Sontaran 'clone feed'. The entire fleet was destroyed, with the exception of one scout ship from its Special Assault Squad. That ship's pilot subsequently died on Earth.

The Sontarans resented being excluded from the Time War, which they regarded as the greatest war in history. They later joined the Dalek-led Pandorica alliance and travelled back to AD 102 to assist in the Eleventh Doctor's capture and imprisonment.

By the fourth millennium, a Grand Strategic Council was directing the Sontaran war effort. The Council ordered an invasion fleet to prepare to take the Earth once the G3 Military Assessment Survey of the evacuated planet had been successfully conducted. The survey was ended by the Fourth Doctor and the Fleet Marshal abandoned the attack.

A PRIMER IN NON-IDENTICAL CLONING

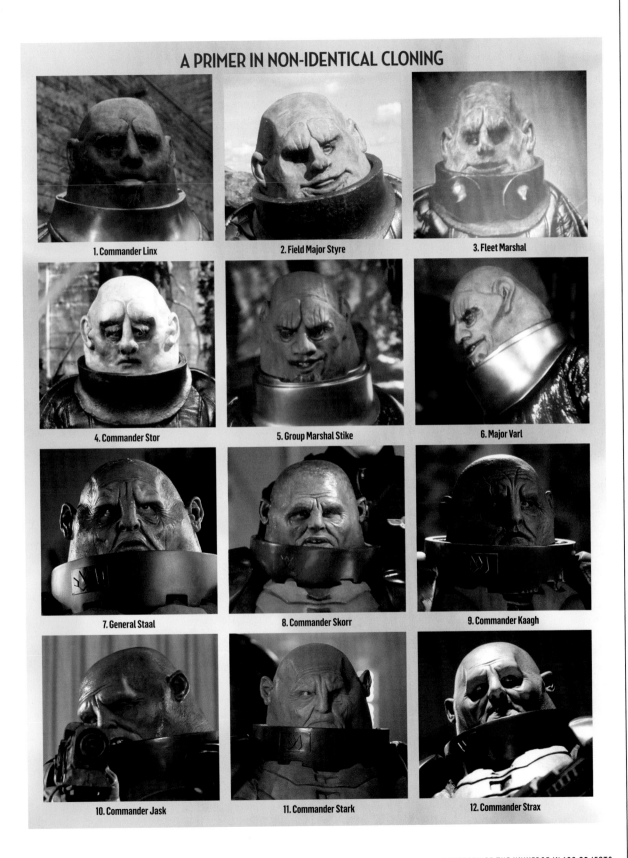

1. Commander Linx

2. Field Major Styre

3. Fleet Marshal

4. Commander Stor

5. Group Marshal Stike

6. Major Varl

7. General Staal

8. Commander Skorr

9. Commander Kaagh

10. Commander Jask

11. Commander Stark

12. Commander Strax

018

Mark I Travel Machine

C.1450

Though the conflict between the Rutans and the Sontarans lasted aeons, its significance was dwarfed by the fallout from another, much smaller war. On the planet D5-Gamma-Z-Alpha, also known as Skaro, two rival humanoid species fought a thousand-year war that culminated in the near-obliteration of one, the Thals, and the extinction of the other, the Kaleds.

In the final decades of the thousand-year war, the Kaleds' Chief Scientist, Davros, had been caught in an explosion while working in his laboratory. He was rescued from the rubble, his legs useless, one arm beyond repair, his sight and hearing damaged, his organs failing. Determined to survive, he designed a complete life-support system, building the remains of his body into a mobile chair, from which his head, torso and remaining withered hand and arm emerged, supported by a harness. His body and skull were wired into the chair's systems, allowing him to control its basic movements psychokinetically. The chair also contained electro-mechanical substitutes for his failed heart and lungs, and tubes kept up a constant stream chemical nutrients, removing any need to eat or drink. He replaced his ruined sight with an electronic scanner, its single lens wired into his forehead, and implanted an incredibly sensitive audio system in place of his lost hearing. His vocal cords, too, were damaged, so he installed a tiny vocaliser, with a throat-mounted microphone creating and amplifying an electronically enhanced voice. Over the next few decades, he continued to modify and adapt the chair, even developing a circuit that fed impulses into his brain to negate the urge to sleep. He built in failsafe procedures enabling the long-term suspension of his bodily organs and an automatic process of synthetic tissue regeneration.

At the front of the chair was a board of controls and switches, which he was constantly adding to, allowing him to remote-operate doors, computer and communications equipment. The most important of these were linked directly to his life-support systems. Though Davros refused to permit himself 'the luxury of death', a part of him still yearned for it, and he fitted a control switch with which he could suspend the whole system. But he also put in a secondary life-support system, wary of his death being brought about by anyone or anything other than himself.

When Davros concluded that weapons research was futile, since Skaro's radiation-soaked environment was causing irreversible genetic changes in his race, he experimented to discover his people's final mutated form. His new goal was to ensure his race's survival, and he turned to his own life-support systems as the basis of a travel machine that could house the mutations. His first effort, designated the Mark II Travel Machine, was merely a partial success, so he continued to refine it, developing the Mark III. From the ashes of the Kaled race arose a new creation that would bring fear and terror to thousands of generations throughout the universe – the Daleks.

ARBITAN

Apparently the inventor of the Conscience Machine on the planet Marinus, Arbitan wanted to control the local Voord, who were unfortunately immune to the machine's pacifying effects. Arbitan scattered the machine's vital 'Keys' across Marinus, but quickly realised this had been a mistake – he sent his only daughter to recover them; she didn't return. Arbitan then blackmailed the First Doctor and his companions into undertaking the same task.

TAREN CAPEL

Having been raised by robots, Taren Capel found that he liked them more than people. Infiltrating Storm Mine 4, he reprogrammed the sandminer's robot servants to murder the human crew, as the first stage of a robot rebellion. His plan went so well that he even dressed up as a robot, complete with extravagant facial make-up.

CROZIER

When the Sixth Doctor and Peri arrived on Thoros Beta, they met Crozier, a bio-engineer charged with prolonging the life of the Mentor Lord Kiv. Crozier's intention was to transfer the dying Kiv's mind into a humanoid brain, and he selected the Doctor's companion for this honour. He was thus unusual in being interested in Peri for her mind.

FARROW, FORESTER AND SMITHERS

A trio of English scientists who squabbled lethally over the licensing of DN6 – an insecticide so powerful that it could destroy all insect life on Earth, thus fatally upsetting the planet's ecological balance. DN6 could even affect sufficiently diminutive humans.

MAGNUS GREEL

Some scientists find it quite difficult to recognise when their experiments haven't gone well. Even when his 'Zigma experiment' left him stranded in Victorian London, with his metabolism temporally distorted and in need of constant energy top-ups, and his physiognomy so unsettling that he wore a mask to cover it up – even after all that, Magnus Greel insisted that his time-travel experiment was a glorious success.

PROFESSOR J.P. KETTLEWELL

Owner of the ultimate mad-scientist's hairdo, Kettlewell was a nice little man with a flair for robotics. He invented the experimental prototype Robot K-1, but claimed that his concerns for the future of the planet had led him to abandon his researches in favour of developing Green solutions to Earth's problems. Sadly, his beliefs also led him to collude with a small group of neo-fascists intent on holding the world to ransom with a massive nuclear arsenal. Robot K-1 inadvertently killed Kettlewell, and promptly became as confused as its creator.

DR CHARLES LAWRENCE

Dr Lawrence was an interesting choice for Director of Wenley Moor, an atomic research centre built into subterranean caves in Derbyshire. Severely lacking in people skills, his judgement when it came to recruitment was also dubious – he managed to appoint a deputy director who was willing to collaborate with intelligent reptiles, a selection of scientists more interested in potholing expeditions than nuclear research, another scientist obsessively in love with Lawrence's deputy, and a paranoid security chief. When the research centre was attacked by the reptile men, their pet dinosaur and a deadly virus, Lawrence took it badly.

PROFESSOR RICHARD LAZARUS

The Genetic Manipulation Device was an extraordinary means of tampering with a subject's DNA and restoring his or her youth, so changing what it means to be human. Lazarus was his own test subject – using hypersonic sound waves to destabilise his cell structure and manipulate the coding in his protein strands, he successfully shed forty years. Having failed to allow for all possible variables, however, Lazarus left himself with both a severe energy deficit and a reactivated set of

AND VERY MAD SCIENTISTS

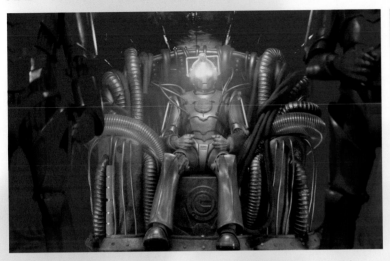

PROFESSOR SORENSON

Sorenson was determined to discover an alternative energy source to his planet's dying sun. He was not put off by the deaths of every member of his expedition, nor by his sudden and startling transformation into an antimatter monster – he simply devised a potion to stabilise his anatomy for brief periods.

PROFESSOR ERIC STAHLMAN

The founder of the Inferno project was (a) unable to acknowledge any flaws or dangers in a scheme to drill through the Earth's crust, (b) really quite rude, (c) prey to primordial impulses, and (d) just as bad in a parallel dimension.

PROFESSOR WHITAKER

The would-be architect of a new Golden Age, Professor Whitaker was a brilliant temporal scientist who managed to make his time-travel theories a reality – and used them to scoop up dinosaurs from Earth's prehistory and dump them in the middle of London.

PROFESSOR ZAROFF

Hiding in the lost city of Atlantis, nothing in the world could stop Zaroff synthesising food from plankton, grafting fish gills onto human slaves, draining Earth's oceans into the planet's crust, and sharing his diabolical schemes with his pet octopus.

previously dormant genes that now transformed him into a rampaging monster.

LESTERSON

The head scientist on Earth's Vulcan colony became entirely unhinged when a small squad of unarmed Daleks began to reproduce. He had, though, already been fairly unstable and obsessive before that happened – conducting secret experiments, colluding in the cover-up of a murder, staging an elaborate ceremony to mark his penetration of a mysterious space capsule that he'd already got into...

JOHN LUMIC

On a parallel Earth, the founder of Cybus Industries had a dream – to encase the human mind in an invincible suit of steel and move humanity on to its next stage: Human Point Two. His first subjects for conversion were taken from Britain's homeless, but he soon decided on a programme of compulsory upgrading or deletion. Not quite as logical as his creations, he was initially dismayed

to find his Cybermen forcibly giving him an upgrade, freeing him from his crippled body to become their first Cyber Controller.

MEGELEN (THE BORAD)

The Doctor exposed Megelen's unethical genetic experiments on the Morloxes of the planet Karfel, but the scientist carried on anyway. Eventually, he managed to fuse himself with a Morlox, and promptly took control of Karfel, becoming the Borad and inventing the Timelash as the ultimate punishment / deterrent against rebellion.

DR MEHENDRI SOLON

A covert member of the Cult of Morbius, Solon rescued Morbius's brain when the renegade Time Lord was executed, keeping it pickled in a jar until such a time as he could install it in a new and glorious physical form. Solon built this form from random bits of dead space travellers: a human arm, the lungs of a birastrop, and the claw of a big space lobster; all he needed to complete the ensemble was a suitable head...

019

The Mona Lisa

1505

In Earth's late Middle Ages, Italy led a movement of cultural, social, intellectual and scientific progress and renewal. After several centuries of comparative stagnation following the fall of the Roman Empire, the Renaissance saw Europe emerge from the dark ages of superstition into the dawn of a new reason. The Mandragora Helix, a spiral of pure energy with a malevolent intelligence at its core, feared that humanity would develop space flight and become a rival power in the universe. In around 1492, Mandragora attempted to destroy key Renaissance figures and take over the world. The Fourth Doctor managed to drain off the Helix energy present on Earth and send Mandragora back to the stars.

Other extraterrestrial forces were already at work, too, notably the Daemons from the planet Daemos, who kick-started the Renaissance in one of their periodic interventions in humanity's advancement. And maverick Time Lord the Monk discussed the principles of powered flight with one of the era's great polymaths – Leonardo di ser Piero da Vinci. Leonardo's skills and interests encompassed architecture, music, mathematics, engineering, anatomy, botany, geology and cartography; he designed bridges, barricades and weapons, and devised plans for submersible craft and flying machines. Thanks to a splinter of the last of the Jagaroth, however, Leonardo's lasting fame would lie in his painting.

Under the guise of Captain Tancredi, Scaroth engaged Leonardo's services. Isolating him in his studio in Florence, Scaroth commissioned six copies of the Mona Lisa. While the 'original' would go on to become his most famous and globally celebrated painting, the copies would spend some 474 years bricked up in a cellar in Paris. As the popularity and renown of the Mona Lisa reached a peak in the 20th century, Scaroth's Count Scarlioni persona would commit the world's greatest art theft – stealing the painting from Paris's Louvre Museum then selling all seven to private collectors. The millions he raised would fund the equipment and power needed to build a time machine and prevent the explosion of his spaceship in Earth's prehistory (see 006. Jagaroth Spaceship).

As it turned out, the presence of the Fourth Doctor and Romana in 1970s Paris meant that Scaroth's great art sale was cancelled, and six out of seven paintings were destroyed in a fire. The surviving Mona Lisa was retrieved from the ruins of the Scarlioni chateau, with Louvre art experts and the Police Nationale keeping very, very quiet about the results of X-ray tests on the recovered painting. These revealed that, beneath the paint, four felt-tipped words in the Doctor's handwriting were written on the canvas: 'This Is A Fake'.

LA GIOCONDA

The most famous painting in the world is a portrait, just 77 x 53 cm, of Lisa Gherardini, the wife of an Italian silk merchant. Leonardo started it in Florence, Italy in about 1503 and was still working on it when he died in France in 1519, apparently moaning that he'd never finished a single painting. The Mona Lisa was sold to the King of France and ended up in the Palace of Versailles. Napoleon hung it in his bedroom before it eventually found a permanent home in the Louvre.

Also known as La Gioconda and La Joconde, the picture only became really famous in the mid 1800s, when it found favour with critics who began to write about it rapturously. They seized on it for many reasons, not least that it is rare to find an Old Master portrait of a real person that's neither particularly famous nor a religious icon. Since then every aspect of the painting has been analysed – from her lack of eyebrows (analysis suggests they were accidentally removed during cleaning in 1809) to the elaborate background behind her which starts out as a realistic scene and then becomes more like a prehistoric landscape.

As the most famous painting in the world, the Mona Lisa is priceless. The last valuation of it (for insurance purposes) in the 1960s put it at $100 million. Adjusted for inflation, it may now be the world's only billion-dollar painting. If it could be sold...

THE THEFT OF THE MONA LISA

The Mona Lisa was stolen in 1911. Suspects included an anarchist poet and Pablo Picasso, but it turned out to be an employee of the Louvre who had simply walked out with it hidden under his coat. He was an Italian nationalist who claimed that the picture really belonged to Italy, and was arrested trying to sell it to a gallery in Florence in 1913. It has also been claimed that his reasons were less altruistic – he was close friends with a man who made his living from painting copies of the Mona Lisa, which could then be sold as the original to gullible buyers for considerably more money.

Since its recovery the painting has survived infestation by beetles, and having acid, a rock, paint and a teacup thrown at it, and now resides behind bullet-proof glass.

: X RAY SCAN : COMPLETE

PAINTING BY COMPUTER

Was there art on Gallifrey? Romana claimed that all painting there was done by computer. Little or no art was in evidence whenever the Doctor returned home, although the office of his former tutor, acting Chancellor Borusa, was unusual in displaying a number of paintings and sculptures. During the subsequent Borusa presidency, the Harp of Rassilon stood in an Inner Council conference room, and a painting hung on the wall showed the harp being played by, presumably, Rassilon himself. Even this had a hidden function: the sheet music depicted in the painting revealed the musical code required to access a secret chamber containing the controls of the banned Time Scoop.

The Fourth Doctor was an art lover. He disguised the TARDIS's ancillary power station as a holographic art gallery containing works including *The Arnolfini Portrait* by Jan van Eyck, *The Fighting Temeraire, Tugged to Her Last Berth to be Broken Up, 1838* by J.M.W. Turner, *The Snail* by Henri Matisse and the statue of Aphrodite of Melos (known as *Venus de Milo*). He was keen to meet Leonardo in 1492 San Martino, and apparently did so at some point before his encounter with Captain Tancredi in 1505 Florence – he was even familiar with the subject of the Mona Lisa, 'that dreadful woman with no eyebrows who wouldn't sit still'. He also had a fine eye for art and antiques, appreciating Count Scarlioni's Louis XV furniture and Amelia Ducat's flower paintings, and considering the Louvre to be one of the greatest art galleries in the galaxy and the Mona Lisa one of the great treasures of the universe.

The Eleventh Doctor admired and befriended Vincent van Gogh, but most of the Doctors have practised the same kind of cheerful philistinism as the Fourth Doctor's friend Duggan. The First Doctor was happy to see Skaro's last remaining piece of sculpture dropped down a lift shaft; the Fifth Doctor tore down the Portreeve's tapestry; and the Sixth Doctor sabotaged Dastarii's light sculpture in order to trip a circuit, claiming, 'I don't know much about art, but I know what I like.'

VIVE LA DIFFÉRENCE!

'The massacre continued for several days in Paris and then spread itself to other parts of France. Oh, what a senseless waste.'

'Have you met the French? My god, they know how to party.'

'We might not get back to the ship if Grandfather hears we're in the Reign of Terror ... It's his favourite period in the history of Earth.'

'Napoleon gave me this bottle. Well, I say gave... Threw. Salut!'

'I remember saying to old Napoleon. Boney, I said, always remember an army marches on its stomach.'

The Church at Auvers.

'I knew her great grandfather [Edward VII] in Paris...'

'What Paris has, it has an ethos, a life. It has...' 'A bouquet?' 'A spirit all of its own. Like a wine, it has...' 'A bouquet.' 'It has a bouquet.'

'Paris. 2010 AD. And this is the mighty Musée d'Orsay, home to many of the greatest paintings in history.'

020

A Cup of Cocoa

C.1507

rriving in 16th-century South America, the TARDIS crew became trapped in Aztec society when the TARDIS became sealed inside a tomb. Barbara was assumed to be the reincarnation of the High Priest Yetaxa, Ian was trained to become a warrior, Susan was sent to school, and the First Doctor was put out to pasture in the Garden of Peace. There he made friends with a fellow senior citizen, Lady Cameca, who was able to help him sneak back into the temple and escape in the TARDIS. But first he offered to make her a cup of cocoa...

Little did the Doctor realise that by offering to prepare the drink he was declaring his love for Cameca – and that, by breaking into the temple, he would also break her heart. This was the first time

the Doctor became engaged to be married to a human... but it would not be the last.

AZTEC SOCIETY

The Aztecs of Central Mexico were responsible for some wonderful inventions and creations – they were as talented as they were bloodthirsty (although no more barbarous than the Spaniards who wiped them out in the 16th century).

Aztec society offers an example of insular parallel evolution – a society that managed to advance without discovering the wheel, and which gave many admirable inventions to the world, including the discovery of cocoa – both as a drink and later as a sweet foodstuff. Cocoa beans were used to barter – a currency you could drink. They could also be prepared as a love potion – the shared drinking of cocoa had its own special meaning, by which a couple declared their love for each other and, in effect, proposed marriage.

```
IAN: Where did you get hold of this?
DOCTOR: My fiancée.
IAN: I see. Your what?
DOCTOR: Yes, I made some cocoa and got engaged.
Don't giggle, my boy, It's neither here nor there.
                    The Aztecs: The Bride of Sacrifice
```

UNIT DATING CONTROVERSY

When Josephine Grant's uncle arranged a work placement for his niece at the British section of UNIT, Brigadier Lethbridge-Stewart decided to appoint her as assistant to his scientific adviser. The Doctor was not, at first, terribly pleased, but the Brigadier's second-in-command, Captain Mike Yates, was quite happy to see a pretty face at UNIT's virtually all-male headquarters. Over the years, he and Jo would share the occasional night on the town, and even Lethbridge-Stewart noticed Yates's disappointment when Jo fell for a Nobel prize-winning Welsh professor and headed for the Amazon basin. Mike actually made his first move within hours of Jo's arrival, but at the time perhaps even he failed to appreciate the ancient cultural significance of offering to make her a mug of army cocoa.

HOW TO MAKE ARMY COCOA

You will need:
One tin of cocoa
Two mugs
One Bunsen burner (for making free with)
One silicon rod (for stirring)
One plastic goblin (optional)
One service revolver (compulsory)
Gubbins (to taste)

TEA, EARL GREY, HOT

What does the Doctor eat and drink? Does he even do either?

■ The First Doctor spent a lot of time with his beloved food machine, but wasn't much of a drinker, beyond the occasional glass of clean water on the Sense-Sphere, dirty water on the planet Marinus, and water in an un-shattered glass on Xeros. He refused breakfast with the Meddling Monk, but enjoyed Edith's mead. Apart from a sherry at Christmas, he preferred milk to an alcoholic drink, and had a sweet tooth that cost him a filling. He later proved to be a hearty eater of pineapple in the Dead Zone on Gallifrey.

■ The Second Doctor drank coffee (without sugar) on the Moon and in a coffee bar in London. He also enjoyed the occasional glass of wine in Theodore Maxtible's house, and was glad of a cup of sweet army tea when rescued from Tobias Vaughn by the Brigadier. He briefly developed a gluttonous craving for wine and fine dining as a result of Androgum gene splicing, speculating with relish on the ingredients of Shepherd's Pie, but he did not go on to develop a taste for human flesh.

■ The Third Doctor spent most of his life surrounded by hot, sweet army tea, but had a tendency to hand back cups of the stuff undrunk. When he did actually drink a mugful, he added four sugars to it. Altogether he was more of a bon viveur, taking time out from investigating terrorist ghosts at a peace conference to enjoy an evening of cheese and wine. He was entertained to wine and fruit by the Controller of Dalek-dominated Earth, and later praised the domestic elderberry wine of the Nuthutch. He also recommended the coffee made by UNIT's Sergeant Benton, putting it second only to that of Mrs Samuel Pepys.

■ The Fourth Doctor enjoyed jelly babies, and was partial to bouillabaisse, muffins, ginger beer and French tap water. Both times he drank wine it was drugged – first by Professor Solon, then by Count Grendel of Gracht. From then on, he more frequently poured than drank it – either for a Tharil slave master or to toast the vampire lords Zargo and Camilla. He took his tea with two lumps and two sugars.

■ Fond of a well-prepared meal, the Fifth Doctor liked apples, would eat celery if suffering an allergic reaction to gases in the Praxis spectrum, and preferred tea to ale. He once offered to go on a picnic with gunrunner Sharaz Jek.

■ The Sixth Doctor became a vegetarian and made nut-roast rolls. He drank carrot juice under protest. A thirst for water twice became his downfall – once in a mirage on Varos, and once when he stole it from the people of Marb Station.

■ The Seventh Doctor had a taste for strawberry milkshake, was unsure whether to have sugar in his tea, once demanded a crocodile sandwich in anger, ordered lemonade in bars, and knew of a good Indian takeaway on the Khyber Pass. He did not like burnt toast.

■ The Eighth Doctor ate jelly babies and liked a nice cup of tea.

■ The Ninth Doctor liked steak and chips, recommended a Kronkburger, and enjoyed a full roast dinner with all the trimmings. He drank coffee with milk, no sugar, but liked tea with two sugars. He learned to pass the port to the left, preferred Shepherd's Pie to safety pins and approved of bananas.

■ The Tenth Doctor liked chips, jam, satsumas, edible ball bearings and the restorative tanins in a thermos of tea. He dined heartily with both Queen Victoria and Jackie Tyler, but not in Deffry Vale canteen, although he was partial to a staff room biscuit. He did not drink the waters of Mars, but did invent the banana daiquiri. The Master provided him water in a dog bowl, and, as John Smith, he enjoyed apples and pears. After drinking a poisoned lime and soda, he stimulated his inhibited enzymes with ginger beer, walnuts and anchovies.

■ The Eleventh Doctor does not like toast, beans, bacon, yoghurt or red wine. He has a lucky straw for milkshakes. He does like Christmas dinner, jammy dodgers and fish custard.

THE DOCTOR'S WIFE

Cameca wasn't the Doctor's first brush with matrimony, nor his last. The Tenth Doctor told Sally Sparrow that he was rubbish at weddings, especially his own. The Tenth, Ninth, Second and First Doctors all referred to having had a family. Jabe of the Forest of Cheem assumed Rose was the Doctor's wife, partner, concubine or prostitute. Jo Grant, Sarah Jane Smith, Rose Tyler, Martha Jones, Madame De Pompadour and Amy Pond were all, to a greater or lesser extent, in love with the Doctor. But only Elizabeth I, Marilyn Monroe and River Song actually got to marry him.

021

The Doctor's Scarf

16TH CENTURY

The Doctor's scarf was whipped up for him by 'a witty little knitter – Madame Nostradumus, of 16th-century France. Although worn by the Fourth Doctor, he chose the scarf from the TARDIS wardrobe shortly after his regeneration, so it must have been knitted for an earlier incarnation – which one, he never revealed.

It wasn't his first choice – that was furry trousers, a bearskin jacket and a horned Viking helmet, rejected as possibly too conspicuous for UNIT's scientific adviser. Second choice was a playing-card King of Hearts costume; third was a pierrot. If the Brigadier hadn't had a series of thefts from Defence Ministry installations to investigate, he might have argued against the Doctor's fourth choice, too: corduroy trousers, flannel shirt, tweed jacket, wide-brimmed floppy black hat and the immensely long, multicoloured scarf.

The scarf became inseparable from the Doctor throughout his fourth incarnation, except when he visited Victorian London. It proved almost as useful as the sonic screwdriver for solving problems, escaping from tight corners and defeating villains. Shortly after his next regeneration, the scarf performed one final service for the Fifth Doctor. When he became lost in the TARDIS, he unravelled it to help him navigate its corridors.

WHO WAS MADAME NOSTRADAMUS?

Nostradamus's Prophecies came out annually from 1550 and were the *Brilliant Book of Doctor Who* of their time – complete with misleading spoilers for the future. In the centuries since, they've been pored over, interpreted, retranslated and argued about. Students of the prophecies fiercely debate Nostradamus's success rate – did he really predict Adolf Hitler or the World Trade Center attacks, or is his style so enigmatic that almost anything can be read into them?

We can't be certain which of Nostradamus's wives knitted the scarf. He was married to his first wife for just three years.

Her name is not known for certain, and neither is the cause of her death; perhaps Nostradumus tired of her spending all her time knitting. He subsequently married a rich widow – who presumably had time on her hands for handicraft.

MISS BEGONIA POPE

According to *Doctor Who* legend, Tom Baker's unforgettable scarf came about by happy accident. Costume designer James Acheson bought several balls of wool and asked a woman called Begonia Pope to knit a striped scarf for the new Doctor. Apparently related to someone at the BBC, Ms Pope was, in Tom Baker's words, 'thrilled to be working for the Corporation'. Knowing nothing about knitting, Acheson had bought ten times more wool than was needed, and Begonia Pope 'didn't ask any questions ... she knitted the lot!'

THAT LONG SCARF IN SHORT

Begonia Pope's scarf was worn throughout Tom Baker's first and second seasons, with a different scarf being knitted for the Doctor's replica in *The Android Invasion*. From then on, these two scarves alternated, with one often being used for filming and the other in the studio. From *The Ribos Operation* (1978) onwards, the two scarves were sewn together, resulting in an incredibly long scarf. This remained until *The Leisure Hive* (1980), when it was replaced with a scarf of the same length but done in shades of burgundy.

More exhaustive accounts can be found on the internet – the scarf has several websites devoted to it, with at least one listing all the different scarves worn by the Fourth Doctor. They also have a knitting pattern.

33 USES FOR A SCARF

1 Sweeping floors for discarded tools (*Robot*, Part 2)
2 Failing to slow down hostile automata (*Robot*, Part 2)
3 Tripping up security guards (*Robot*, Part 3)
4 Failing to activate auto-guard cut-outs (*The Ark in Space*, Part 1)
5 Disabling murderous Egyptian servants of Sutekh (*Pyramids of Mars*, Part 1)
6 Measuring symbols in Osiran logic puzzles: 162.4 cm = about 7 stitches (*Pyramids of Mars*, Part 4)
7 Upending masked Italian executioners (*The Masque of Mandragora*, Part 2)
8 Extemporising tripwires for vengeful Kastrians (*The Hand of Fear*, Part 4)
9 Assembling lifelike decoys (*The Deadly Assassin*, Part 1)
10 Rock-climbing (*The Deadly Assassin*, Part 2)
11 Being blindfolded by savages (*The Face of Evil*, Part 1)
12 Blinding homicidal automata (*The Robots of Death*, Part 4)
13 Confusing other homicidal automata (*The Robots of Death*, Part 4)
14 A comfort blanket for Leela (*The Invisible Enemy*, Part 1)
15 Leading miniaturised clones through the mind-brain interface (*The Invisible Enemy*, Part 3)
16 Improvising gas-masks (*Underworld*, Part 2)
17 Improvising air-conditioning (*Underworld*, Part 2)
18 Concealing the Sash of Rassilon (*The Invasion of Time*, Part 2)
19 Rescuing Time Ladies from cliff faces (*The Stones of Blood*, Part 2)
20 Irritating Taran Swordsmen (*The Androids of Tara*, Part 1)
21 Stylishly masking unapproved regenerations (*Destiny of the Daleks*, Part 1)
22 Climbing safely into pits while learning Tibetan (*The Creature from the Pit*, Part 2)
23 Stealing eggshell fragments (*The Creature from the Pit*, Part 3)
24 Leading Romana and K-9 down a power path to a Skonnon spaceship (*The Horns of Nimon*, Part 1)
25 Floating through non-gravity squash courts (*The Leisure Hive*, Part 1)
26 Tying round the necks of Argolin statues (*The Leisure Hive*, Part 1)
27 Tying round the necks of Argolin murder victims (*The Leisure Hive*, Part 2)
28 Being scapegoated in open court (*The Leisure Hive*, Part 2)
29 Being disparaged by Alazarian stowaways (*State of Decay*, Part 1)
30 Improvising oven gloves (*Warriors' Gate*, Part 1)
31 Being strangled by mad slave-traders (*Warriors' Gate*, Part 4)
32 Extemporising tripwires for utterly mad Time Lord renegades (*Logopolis*, Part 4)
33 Navigating TARDIS corridors (*Castrovalva*, Part 1)

YOU CAN'T ALWAYS JUDGE FROM EXTERNAL APPEARANCES

Sixth Doctor Colin Baker has often ruefully told of people shouting at him in the street 'Oi, Doctor, where's your scarf?' The Fourth Doctor's scarf is the icon of *Doctor Who* clothing, and its constant presence allowed his actual clothes to change wildly while always seeming roughly the same.

The First Doctor had dressed like a slightly old-fashioned gentleman, the Second Doctor in a version of the same costume that looked like it needed a good dry clean. The Third Doctor favoured a display of frilly shirts, velvet jackets and the occasional cape. But the Fourth Doctor was an immediate Seventies fashion hit. The long scarf remains *Doctor Who*'s big contribution to high-street fashion, and was a regular occurrence in collections (although when *Doctor Who* was off the air after 1989 it was often bizarrely referred to as the 'Ali MacGraw look' – but everyone knew what they meant). Between 1987 and 2005, the Seventh, Eighth and Tenth Doctors were all shown trying out similar scarves when selecting their own wardrobes.

From the end of Tom Baker's reign, the Doctor's clothes became more of a uniform. Before 1980, it was just about plausible that the Doctor was a Bohemian you might encounter on the street. Then, for a time, he became a man in fancy dress, turning up as a heavily stylised cricketer, or... whatever it was that Colin Baker was dressed as. As Colin himself puts it, 'The only consolation was that I was on the inside looking out.' Sylvester McCoy's Seventh Doctor revived the idea that his clothes had been plucked off a TARDIS wardrobe rack and not specially designed at the height of the Eighties, but he still had a pullover that asked more questions than it answered.

The question-mark motif was an element of the Doctor's outfit introduced in 1980. As his scarf moved from multicoloured to burgundy, question marks were added to his shirt collars, and retained for the Fifth and Sixth Doctors. The Doctor had stopped being the sort of man who wore an outlandish scarf because he'd come across it one day and taken a liking to it; now he was someone whose shirt announced that there was something mysterious about him. McCoy's jumper, umbrella handle and calling card went further still.

In 1996, Paul McGann's Eighth Doctor adopted a more classically Doctor-ish ensemble, strongly influenced by the William Hartnell look. Had the TV movie produced a full series, there is no telling whether the costume would have remained. Not a fan of the wig he had to wear, McGann was later adamant that he would rather have shaved his head – a look adopted in 2004 by Christopher Eccleston. The Ninth Doctor was the first to wear 'normal' clothes, fitting with the period of contemporary Earth. In reality, his 'everyday' leather jacket was one of a kind, even having its own security guard during filming.

For the Tenth Doctor's outfit, designer Louise Page was heavily influenced by David Tennant's own ideas for something stylish and practical. She didn't win the argument that he wore boots, though – but had the satisfaction of getting to say 'I told you so' after David discovered that canvas shoes weren't the best things for running around in mud. The costume made a triumphant return to the high street, with several stores featuring an easily identifiable version of the brown pinstripe suit and trainers. From then on, it wasn't just science fiction fans who were dressed as the Time Lord.

Matt Smith's outfit sees a continuation of the 'unusual everyday' theme, with the high street similarly adopting variations of the tweedy trousers, shirt and braces look, although without the bow tie. As Amy Pond knows, bow ties are not cool.

022

Love's Labour's Won

1599

The lost play. It doesn't exist — only in rumours.
It's mentioned in lists of his plays but never ever
turns up. No one knows why.

The Shakespeare Code

The canon of Shakespeare's writing lies among humanity's finest achievements. Yet there is little agreement over what is actually in that canon. His authorship of some works is questioned; the existence of others is doubted. And one is nothing more than a title. A great lost masterpiece? A sequel to *Love's Labour's Lost*? Perhaps both...

[1] We left the lovers of Navarre by cruel chance
separated, none to claim his heart, their labour's
lost. Now will they find Love's Labour's Won!
[2] The eye should have contentment where it rests.
[3] This spun-out year I watch on, groaning sick
Mewling poor drooped men in stenched beds
[4] The ladies have prepared a show. Maria means
to present Isis descending from the dewy orb of
Heaven.
ENTER COSTARD
Ah, here comes Costard.
COSTARD: Masters!
[5] Behold the swainish sight of woman's love.
Pish! It's out of season to be heavy disposed.
The light of Shadmock's hollow moon
Doth shine on to a point in space
Betwixt Dravidian shores linear five
Nine three oh one six seven point oh two
And strikes the fulsome grove of Rexel four
Co-radiating crystal, activate!
[6] Close up this den of hateful, dire decay.
Decomposition of your witches' plot.
You thieve my brains, consider me your toy.
My doting Doctor tells me I am not.
Foul Carrionite spectres, cease your show.
Between the points sev'n six one three nine oh.
And banished like a tinker's cuss, I say to thee...
Expelliarmus!

Love's Labour's Won was completed by Shakespeare while he slept under the control of a Carrionite. Hidden inside the text were a set of words designed to open up a bridgehead for the Carrionites, freeing them from the Deep Darkness where the Eternals had banished them millennia earlier.

When a performance of *Love's Labour's Lost* concluded, Shakespeare's sudden announcement of a sequel caused consternation. Not only was there little time for the actors to learn it, but at that time all plays needed approval from the Lord Chamberlain's Office, which the furious Master of the

Revels, Lynley, swore to withhold. Lynley was drowned by the Carrionites before he could block the performance.

When the final lines of the play were spoken on stage, a portal opened from the Deep Darkness and the Carrionites began to come through in force. With help from the Tenth Doctor and Martha Jones, Shakespeare improvised a counter-spell and the Carrionites, along with every page of every copy of the script, were sucked out of this dimension and back to the Deep Darkness.

CARRIONITE SCIENCE

In the same way that mathematics uses sequences of numbers, Carrionite science was based on deriving power from sequences of words and used psychic energy, channelled and converted through the manipulation of shapes. The right words said with the right emphasis in the right place at the right time could change anything. The 14-sided Globe theatre in Elizabethan London reflected the shape of the Rexel Planetary Configuration, and could act as an energy converter for the Carrionites' words, activated by a co-radiating crystal. A cauldron was used by the Carrionites to watch events elsewhere, and they were adept in mixing chemicals into potions that gave them power over other beings. They were able to kill or incapacitate victims by invoking 'the power of the name'. The Carrionites also made use of replication devices – puppets and dolls to which were added samples of a potential prey's DNA. A single stolen hair could link a doll to its victim, who might be manipulated or made to suffer a seemingly magical death. In one case, a man appeared to drown

on dry land when the device containing his DNA was submerged in water and the correct sequence of words was spoken.

'MR SHAKESPEARE, ISN'T IT?'

> THE DOCTOR: He's a genius - THE genius.
> The most human Human there's ever been. Now
> we're gonna hear him speak. Always, he chooses the
> best words. New, beautiful, brilliant words.
> SHAKESPEARE: Shut your big fat mouths!

Though this was Shakespeare's first meeting with the Doctor, it wasn't the Doctor's first Shakespearean encounter.

The First Doctor spied on a meeting between Queen Elizabeth I and Shakespeare, using a Time-Space Visualiser. The Queen ordered Shakespeare to write *The Merry Wives of Windsor* ('give us more of Sir John Falstaff in love'), not an unusual occurrence as many plays at the time were written (and paid for) under royal patronage. As Shakespeare left the court, Sir Francis Bacon suggested a history of Hamlet, Prince of Denmark as the subject for a future play.

The Fourth Doctor told Sarah Jane Smith he'd met Shakespeare once – 'Charming fellow. Dreadful actor.' When the Countess Scarlioni showed him a treasured first draft of *Hamlet*, he claimed he recognised the handwriting: 'mine. He'd sprained his wrist writing sonnets.' The Doctor had also objected to the line 'Take arms against a sea of troubles' as a mixed metaphor, but Shakespeare had insisted on using it.

THE VIRGIN QUEEN

The performance of *Love's Labour's Won* attracted the attention of Queen Elizabeth I, who visited the Globe to meet Shakespeare. She was not pleased to see the Doctor there, calling him her 'sworn enemy'.

Although, from his point of view, this was their first meeting, he subsequently told Ood Sigma that he had married her later in his timeline – 'and that was a mistake'. The Eleventh Doctor eventually revealed that she'd waited in a glade for him to elope with her.

Thousands of years later, one of Queen Elizabeth I's descendants – Liz 10 – was brought up on stories of the Doctor's role in her family's life.

'MY LOST MASTERPIECE'

Love's Labour's Won is first mentioned in *Palladis Tamia: Wit's Treasury* by Francis Meres, published in London in 1598. This notes a dozen of Shakespeare's plays, including 'his Love's labors lost, his Love's labours wonne', and the title also appears in a number of booksellers' catalogues from the early 1600s. It remains just a title, though – there are no details of its characters or storyline – and has often been dismissed as an alternative name for another play.

The most famous lost play by Shakespeare is *Cardenio*, based on an incident from *Don Quixote*. Three copies were known to exist in an archive on the site of the Covent Garden opera house, but these were thought lost when the building burnt down in 1808. In 1727, the playwright Lewis Theobald premiered a play called *Double Falsehood*. He claimed it was based on one of these *Cardenio* manuscripts, and that he had 'improved' it. Scorn was heaped on Theobald by his arch-rival Alexander Pope, who exposed his play as a fraud. However, modern textual examination of *Double Falsehood* in the early 21st century seems to confirm that substantial parts of it are indeed by William Shakespeare, and that the missing *Cardenio* has been lurking inside Theobald's play for 400 years...

'I'M SUCH A BIG FAN'

■ In *The Mind Robber*, the Second Doctor meets the nameless Master of the Land of Fiction, a prolific writer of boys' adventures stories who has been enslaved by a super-computer. The Master explains that he was snatched from England in 1926 while working on 'the Adventures of Captain Jack Harkaway', a weekly serial in *The Ensign*. The character was based on Frank Richards, who had created Billy Bunter, although the Jack Harkaway stories were actually by a different author – Bracebridge Hemyng.

■ The Sixth Doctor is assisted and exasperated by an aspiring writer called Herbert when he lifts the Borad's grip on the Citadel of Karfel, saving it from the Bandrils, in *Timelash*. As the story concludes, Herbert is revealed to be H.G. Wells, just embarking on a literary career that would eventually make his work a key influence on the creation of *Doctor Who*.

■ The Ninth Doctor and Rose meet Charles Dickens, who helps prevent the Gelth taking over the bodies of Victorian Cardiff's dead in *The Unquiet Dead*. The adventure inspires him to develop a new, supernatural ending to *The Mystery of Edwin Drood*, though he will die before he can complete the novel. *The Wedding of River Song* presents an alternate reality in which all times are occurring simultaneously. Here, Dickens is planning and promoting his 2011 Christmas TV special – a tale of 'ghosts, and the past, the present and future, all at the same time'.

■ The Tenth Doctor and Agatha Christie solve a murder mystery together in *The Unicorn and the Wasp*, unmasking a giant wasp as the villain and explaining the real-life mystery of Christie's eleven-day disappearance in 1926.

■ Winston Churchill, as well as running the country, was a writer of fiction, biography, memoirs and histories. His four-volume *History of the English-Speaking Peoples* and his six-volume work on the Second World War won him the Nobel Prize for Literature in 1953. He is revealed as an old friend of the Doctor in *Victory of the Daleks*, helps get Van Gogh's warning to the Doctor in *The Pandorica Opens*, and is the Holy Roman Emperor in *The Wedding of River Song*.

023

Koh-i-Noor

1879

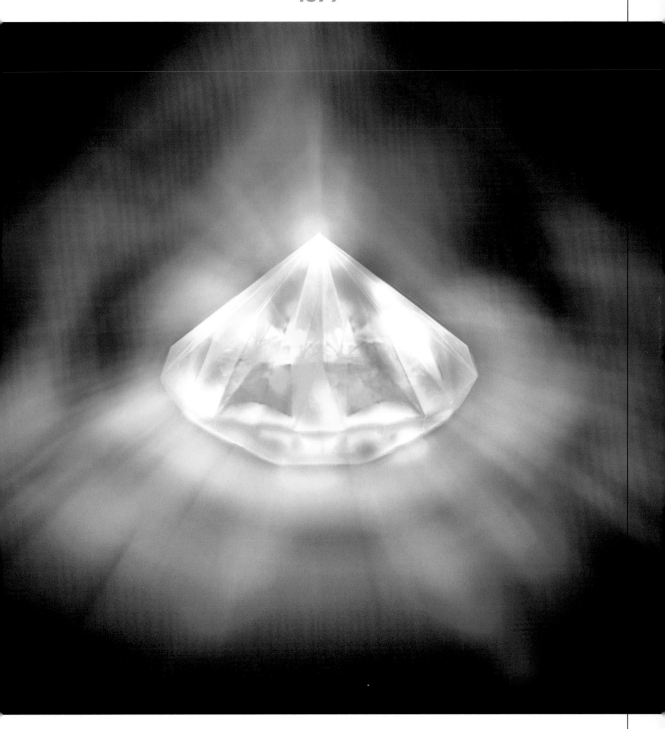

THE REAL RECUTTING OF THE STONE

When the stone was shown at the Great Exhibition of 1851, its reception was muted. In its native country it had been displayed in a dark room to a small audience – but at the Great Exhibition it was shown to large crowds in the brightly lit exhibition hall, and many thought the stone a disappointment.

Prince Albert decided to recut the stone to make it sparkle more – an art lost in the British Empire at the time, so the world's biggest diamond may not have been the best starting point to relearn it. Prince Albert assembled a team from Amsterdam, issuing them with instructions to recut the stone at a minimal loss of its fabulous size and weight. After several weeks and many thousands of pounds, he was horrified to discover the largest diamond in the world was now 42 per cent smaller.

WELCOME TO TORCHWOOD

Horrified by the implications of what she had witnessed at Torchwood House, Queen Victoria vowed never to forget the events or the Doctor's part in them. She decided to found an institute to battle against alien incursions, with the Doctor listed among the foremost enemies of the British Empire. She purchased the House and Estate from Lady Isobel MacLeish, and established the new Torchwood Institute.

THE LEGEND AND THE WOODCUT

'In the year of our Lord, 1540, under the reign of King James the Fifth, an almighty fire did burn in the pit.'

'He who owns this diamond will own the world, but will also know all its misfortunes. Only God, or a woman, can wear it with impunity.'

Hindu Curse, 1306

In the 19th century, the Koh-i-Noor diamond was the largest diamond in the world. It had been found in India, possibly as early as 3200 BC, and passed through various dynasties of kings and emperors, shahs and great moghuls – won through battle, torture and once through a party trick. According to legend, the stone gained its name when Nadir Shah of Persia discovered that its conquered owner kept it hidden in his turban so, at dinner, he proposed a ceremonial exchange of turbans. Rather than show discourtesy, the Mogul Emperor Mohammed Shah reluctantly handed over his turban – containing the biggest jewel in the world. The Shah of Persia unwrapped it, exclaiming 'Koh-i-Noor!' ('Mountain of Light!').

It was held by a series of Indian rulers until the British conquest of the subcontinent in 1849 and, in 1850, the jewel was claimed (some would say stolen) by the British Empire for Queen Victoria. Prince Albert subsequently supervised the cutting of the stone, and the work continued after his death, with his widow going on regular pilgrimages to Helier and Carew, the Royal Jewellers at Hazelhead, to recut the stone.

The Tenth Doctor deduced that Prince Albert had in fact formed a close friendship with Sir George MacLeish, the owner of Torchwood House in the Scottish Highlands, close to the route that the stone took. Studying local legends, the two had concluded that a trap was closing around the Queen, sprung by monks from the nearby monastery in the Glen of St Catherine who were in thrall to a terrible creature of myth, believed to be a werewolf. MacLeish had varnished the library walls and doors with mistletoe, correctly believing that this would repel the werewolf, and then built his 'famous endeavour': a telescope that never worked properly, with misaligned and redundant prisms – all of them actually lined up to refract and focus moonlight through the recut Koh-i-Noor into a ray lethal to werewolves. The plan was to save the Queen from inheriting the werewolf curse – but their attempt may not have succeeded...

THE ROYAL DISEASE

Haemophilia was once called the Royal Disease after it spread through the Royal Houses of Europe in the 19th century. The disease, which prevents the clotting of the blood, spread via a mutated gene which was passed among the closely interbred houses. The source of the mutated gene was Queen Victoria, who passed it to her son and two of her daughters, who gave it to the Royal Families of Spain, Germany and famously Russia.

ROYALTY

Knighted and exiled almost in one breath, this was one of many occasions when the Doctor hobnobbed with the universe's royalty...

■ The First Doctor: played backgammon with Kublai Khan; was sent to the Tower of London by Henry VIII, King of England; avoided playing the lyre with Nero, Emperor of Rome; got caught up in intrigues at the court of Richard I, King of England; watched Queen Elizabeth I commission a play from William Shakespeare; unwillingly helped the Greeks to seize Troy from King Priam; avoided the Massacre of St Bartholomew's Eve ordered by Catherine de Medici; and watched his companions beat the King and Queen of Hearts in the Celestial Toyroom.

■ The Second Doctor: tried to persuade Thous, King of Atlantis, not to trust Professor Zaroff; tricked the Emperor Dalek and brought about a civil war on Skaro.

■ The Third Doctor: claimed to have known Britain's Edward VII for a time in Paris; helped King Peladon take his world into the Federation; was revered by more than one Draconian Emperor; was on chummy terms with Napoleon; failed to save King Dalios and Queen Thalia from the destruction of Atlantis; helped Queen Thalira fight off an Ice Warrior invasion of Peladon; and annoyed the Queen of the Eight Legs on Metebelis Three.

■ The Fourth Doctor: linked his brain to a Wirrn Queen's neural cortex; saved the King of Naples, the Duke of Milan, the Duke of Padua, the Doge of Venice, the Signora of Florence and the Duke of San Martino from the Mandragora Helix; completed Kastrian King Rokon's attempted obliteration of Eldrad; frustrated Queen Xanxia of Zanak's attempts to gain immortality; ensured that King Reynart and Queen Strella of Tara could live happily ever after; turned the sixth segment of the Key to Time back into Princess

Astra of Atrios; and reduced the vampire King and Queen, Zargo and Camilla, to dust.

■ The Fifth Doctor: cut the Urbankan Monarch down to size; and defended the reputation of 'Bad' King John.

■ The Seventh Doctor: saved a Chimeron queen from the Bannermen; chased Queen Elizabeth II through Windsor Castle but failed to meet her; handed Morgaine, the Sun Killer, Dominator of the thirteen worlds and Battle Queen of the S'Rax into UNIT custody; and foiled an assassination plot against Queen Victoria.

■ The Ninth Doctor: blasphemed against the Dalek Emperor, who had declared himself the God of all Daleks.

■ The Tenth Doctor: released the entire British Royal Family from Sycorax blood control, though not soon enough for the Queen to make her Christmas Day broadcast to the nation; was a rival to the King of France for the affections of Madame de Pompadour; stopped the Wire's interference with the broadcast of Elizabeth II's Coronation, but video-recorded it for posterity; drowned the Empress of the Racnoss's offspring; ran away from Queen Elizabeth I without knowing why; saved Queen Elizabeth II and stopped the *Titanic* crashing into Buckingham Palace on Christmas Day / was too dead (in an alternative reality) to save Queen Elizabeth II or stop the *Titanic* crashing into Buckingham Palace on Christmas Day; caused the CyberKing to fall; parked the TARDIS in Buckingham Palace (the Queen didn't mind); and married Queen Elizabeth I, ruining her reputation and earning her enmity.

■ The Eleventh Doctor: investigated Starship UK with Liz 10; was Soothsayer to the Holy Roman Emperor, Winston Churchill; and helped save the life forces of the Wooden King and Queen from Androzani harvesters.

024

The Cream of Scotland Yard

When Light awoke in the basement of Gabriel Chase in Perivale, he found many things not to his liking. Light was a powerful being who had once travelled the universe, cataloguing it and putting it in order – but he'd been asleep a long time, and had no concept of evolution.

Finding that his index had altered during his millions of years of rest, Light vowed to make sure that nothing ever changed again. He stalked the corridors of the house, returning to its 'correct' state anything he found that had changed. One such object was Inspector Mackenzie, a Scotland Yard detective. He had been sent to investigate the disappearance of the house's owner, George Pritchard, who had been murdered by his daughter. She was under the control of an ex-servant of Light's who called himself Josiah Samuel Smith. Mackenzie was swiftly captured by Smith and placed in a trance for two years in a butterfly drawer. Released by the Doctor, Inspector Mackenzie tried to question Light, and the angry being reduced him to his constituent parts – the primordial soup from which all life evolved. Josiah Samuel Smith served the Inspector as an entrée at a dinner party for the Doctor.

Josiah was seeking to take control of the British Empire using the explorer Redvers Fenn-Cooper's royal garden party invitation in order to meet Queen Victoria and assassinate her.

EVOLUTION

Ghost Light pits Josiah Samuel Smith and his Darwinian theories of evolution against the Reverend Mr Ernest Matthews, a churchman who is ultimately devolved into an ape. His dismissal of evolutionary theory, though, is actually a little anachronistic. Darwin's grandfather, Erasmus, had put forward an evolutionary theory almost 60 years before *On the Origin of Species*, provoking Washington Irving (creator of such fairy-tale heroes as Ichabod Crane and Rip Van Winkle) to jeer at the notion that 'the whole human species is accidentally descended from a remarkable family of monkeys'. But when Charles Darwin died in 1882, he was given a state funeral and buried in Westminster Abbey. His theories – and those of the geologist Charles Lyell – had by then been largely accepted by most leading thinkers and churchmen. Victorian scholarship predominantly saw the early Bible stories as metaphorical not literal, and theories of evolution predating Darwin's own had been accepted as proof of a divine ordering to creation. A future Archbishop of Canterbury delivered a sermon in praise of Darwin and his theories just a year after *On the Origins of Species*' publication.

'THEIR BUTTONS ARE THE BRIGHTEST THING ABOUT THEM'

Inspector Mackenzie is part of a long line of notable British bobbies in *Doctor Who*, several of them meeting grisly ends...
The first character ever seen in *Doctor Who* was a policeman pausing outside the gates of I.M. Foreman's junkyard. Finding Susan Foreman locked inside a police box, teachers Ian and Barbara threaten to fetch a policeman to help unlock it. Had they done so, the Doctor's adventures would have been very different.

Miniaturised and helpless in *Planet of Giants*, the Doctor and his friends still manage to attract the attention of the PC Bert Rowse – by squeaking into the telephone and then setting fire to a laboratory. PC Rowse arrives just in time to collar a murderer.

The seventh episode of *The Daleks' Master Plan* fell on Christmas Day 1965, and there were plans to make a crossover with the popular police drama series *Z Cars*, using its set and some of its stars. The *Z Cars* production team refused permission, however, partly because the series' cast would be busy making their own show. A large section of the episode is set in and around a police station anyway, with baffled Merseyside coppers having to contend with the mysterious arrival of a police box, a mad

old man claiming to be a time traveller, an imposter pretending to have arrived from 'G Division', and a young woman in fancy dress climbing all over the police box. Which then vanishes.

The War Machines marked *Doctor Who*'s first full-scale return to contemporary London since the very first episode. When the TARDIS lands, the Doctor places an 'out of order' sign on the door to discourage a passing policeman who thinks it's a real police box. The Doctor explains his thinking to Dodo – a companion who first entered the TARDIS because she thought it was a real police box.

The Faceless Ones, set on the same day as the conclusion of *The War Machines*, has the TARDIS landing on an airport runway just ahead of an incoming plane. A single police officer is swiftly deployed to deal with the situation but, with four time travellers to chase, he loses all of them. They've arrived in time to deal with the apparent disappearance of passengers on Chameleon Tours flights, a mystery also being investigated by an Inspector Gascoigne until he is murdered. Detective Inspector Crossland arrives and works with the Doctor, but he is abducted by the alien Chameleons and his identity taken over by their leader.

The Doctor's companions Jamie and Zoe, hunting Cybermen in London's sewers, are followed by a concerned policeman, who is promptly killed by a Cyberman in *The Invasion*. Another policeman is similarly unlucky in *Spearhead from Space*, becoming the first Auton victim as the shop dummies begin their attack. *Doctor Who and the Silurians* has disease-ridden government official Edward Masters located by London police just before he dies, so they are presumably fatally infected too. Two policemen are victims of the space-suited aliens in *The Ambassadors of Death*.

In *Terror of the Autons*, Jo and the Doctor are rescued from an angry mob of circus acts by two policemen, who turn out to be Auton duplicates. Constable Groom is taken over by daemonic forces in *The Daemons* and comes close to braining Miss Hawthorne with a rock. The constable then stands guard over the archaeological dig and is stepped on by something very large...

A policeman in a panda car watches 'a silver hovercraft being chased by an old crock at ninety miles an hour, and ... a little tiny helicopter after them both', in *Planet of the Spiders*. He joins the chase, and ends up watching open-mouthed as the Doctor's 'silver hovercraft', the Whomobile, starts to fly.

In *The Talons of Weng-Chiang*, Sergeant Kyle, PC Quick and various nameless officers have to deal with sinister, silent and

suicidal martial arts warriors, disappearing girls, a killer dummy and discovering the grisly leftovers of a hungry giant rat, while putting up with the Doctor's special brand of helpfulness and his companion Leela's urge to strangle assailants with their own pigtails.

Had *Shada* been completed and broadcast, its final episode would have concluded with a sarcastic constable attending the scene of a crime – the theft of a room, something that happens 'very rarely' in his experience. He then sees the TARDIS dematerialise and promptly arrests all the remaining characters.

As *Logopolis* opens, a policeman is using a genuine police box on the Barnet Bypass. The Master materialises his TARDIS around the police box and kills the policeman with his Tissue Compression Eliminator, the first victim in a small-scale murder spree that will shortly get very big indeed. By the time the Doctor arrives, the policeman's bicycle, an abandoned car tyre and an almost empty sports car at the side of the road have attracted the attention of a detective inspector and two constables.

Black Orchid features a station full of baffled policemen, not least Sergeant Markham and PC Cummings, who share the honour of being the first uniformed officers to step inside the TARDIS. Cummings is struck pink. Their Chief Constable, Sir Robert Muir, happily accepts the TARDIS as proof of the Doctor's credentials and sanity.

The homicidal policemen in *Resurrection of the Daleks* are not in fact real policemen but alien mercenaries working with Commander Lytton, and quite possibly Dalek duplicates as well. They wander off at the end of the story, but return in *Attack of the Cybermen*, in which they are converted into Cybermen. That story also features an undercover policeman called Russell, who infiltrates Lytton's gang of hapless criminals, and gets killed by the Cybermen.

A pair of policemen guard the fallen statue early in *Silver Nemesis*, blissfully unaware that German neo-Nazis and Cybermen are queuing up to murder them.

Aliens of London has a policeman quizzing the newly returned Rose Tyler on her relationship with the Doctor, and an assistant police commissioner, Strickland, who's actually a Raxacoricofallapatorian, Sip Fel Fotch Pasameer-Day Slitheen. Sip Fel Fotch attacks Rose's mum but, in *World War Three*, Jackie and Mickey fight back with an explosive combination of gherkins, pickled onions and pickled eggs.

During *The Christmas Invasion*, a policeman reports on the crowds of people making their way to the tops of tall buildings while under the influence of Sycorax blood control.

The Doctor is appalled by Stalinist police tactics in *The Idiot's Lantern* but manages to win over Detective Inspector Bishop, who's leading the response to the spate of faceless people on North London streets. Bishop himself briefly becomes a faceless victim of the Wire.

Sally Sparrow's attempt to report her friend Kathy's disappearance in *Blink* leads her to Detective Inspector Billy Shipton. In a matter of hours, she's asked out on a date by the young DI and then watches him die later that day, 38 years older after Weeping Angels send him to 1969.

In *Planet of the Dead*, Lady Christina de Souza is almost caught by DI Macmillan after she robs the International Gallery, but she hops on a bus and escapes. The bus is very nearly trapped in a tunnel by Macmillan's men, but it drives through a wormhole to San Helios. Macmillan calls in UNIT, but Captain Erisa Magambo has him moved away with all the other civilians. When the bus returns, Macmillan gets to arrest Christina, but the Doctor frees her and she flies away in the bus. DI Macmillan has a rather frustrating Easter.

PC Lucy Hayward, who has a fear of gorillas, is a victim of the Minotaur in *The God Complex*.

And an honourable mention for Special Constable Tom Campbell, who tries to stop a jewel theft and ends up fighting Daleks in the motion picture *Daleks – Invasion Earth 2150 A.D.* Dr Who gives him a second chance to stop the robbery at the end of the film, by landing the TARDIS a crucial few minutes earlier.

025

The Peking Homunculus

C.1890

> The Peking Homunculus ... was made in Peking for the Commissioner of the Icelandic Alliance. It was in the Ice Age, about the year five thousand. The Peking Homunculus was a toy, a plaything for the Commissioner's children. It contained a series of magnetic fields operating on a printed circuit and a small computer. It had one organic component: the cerebral cortex of a pig. Anyway, something went wrong. It almost caused World War Six ... somehow the pig part took over ... It disappeared completely. It was never found.
>
> *The Talons of Weng-Chiang, Part 5*

The Peking Homunculus was snatched back through time by the war criminal Magnus Greel, 'the Butcher of Brisbane', who escaped 51st-century Reykjavik in a prototype time cabinet and ended up in 19th-century Peking. Horribly mutilated by the temporal distortion of his metabolism, Greel was nursed by a Chinese peasant, Li H'sen Chang, who believed him to be a Chinese god, Weng-Chiang.

Greel wanted to escape back to his own time, but his time cabinet was confiscated by the Chinese emperor's soldiers and given to a British envoy, whose son took it to London. Greel and Chang followed, establishing a base under the Palace Theatre, where Greel tried to rebuild his body by feeding off the life essence of abducted young women. Using powers given to him by Greel, Chang established himself as a hit music-hall stage magician, constantly accompanied by the Peking Homunculus, in the guise of a ventriloquist's doll named Mr Sin. After dark, Greel and Mr Sin toured the streets of London, looking for the cabinet that would transport them back to the 51st century.

MUSIC HALLS

Music halls began as backrooms in public houses, showcasing ballads and minstrels but, as they became more popular during the 1800s, special halls were built, and the repertory changed to a variety of acts, mixing musicians with comedians, magicians, ventriloquists and trick cyclists. Variety music halls sprang up across London from the 1880s. One of the most famous was the Palace Theatre, converted from the failed Royal English Opera House in 1892.

THE SAD STORY OF CHUNG LING SOO

The most famous Chinese music hall magician was Chung Ling

Soo (actually an American called Bill under a lot of make-up). He held late 19th-century London spellbound with his magic, mystery and illusion. The 'inscrutable oriental' remained utterly silent, relaying instructions to the audience through an interpreter. The highlight of his stage act was a magic bullet trick, whereby members of the audience were invited onto stage to shoot a revolver at Chung, who would catch the bullet in his hands. The bullets never actually left the gun – instead, a simple flash charge was ignited at the front of the barrel. Unfortunately, Chung was determined not to waste bullets or gunpowder, so he never unloaded the gun or cleaned the barrel. As a result, powder from the flash charge built up until one day it ignited and fired the bullet from the revolver, which hit him in the chest.

On that day, 23 March 1918, Chung Ling Soo spoke his first and last words in English on the stage: 'Oh my god, something's happened – lower the curtain.'

GOTTLE OF GEER

Modern ventriloquism was pioneered by Fred Russell (who was also the very successful editor of the *Hackney Gazette*). He took to the music hall stage in 1886 (at the Palace Theatre) with an act featuring just him and his dummy, Coster Joe. Up until then, ventriloquists had showcased a family of dummies – but Fred Russell had just one. His work was followed by the vaudeville ventriloquist the Great Lester, who would walk among the audience while his dummy whistled – and who also made famous the act of drinking a glass of water while the dummy spoke.

SINISTER CHINESE

Although the Fourth Doctor's outfit in *The Talons of Weng-Chiang* is reminiscent of Sherlock Holmes, the sinister Tong of the Black Scorpion he encounters are more familiar from rival detective series such as *Sexton Blake* (1893 onwards), Boothby's *Dr Nikola* (1895–1901) and especially the adventures of *Fu Manchu* (from 1913) written by Sax Rohmer, who had written for music halls before inventing the sinister oriental master criminal.

Now crudely offensive, 'Yellow Peril' became the term for such crime thrillers featuring evil Orientals – they became something of an embarrassing cliché. When Agatha Christie found herself unable to work (due to events after the breakdown of her marriage), her brother-in-law offered to help out. The result was *The Big Four* – an atypical Poirot novel, involving an evil Tong operating from a Chinese laundry in Limehouse, bodies thrown in the Thames, and the world held to ransom by a death ray hidden in a volcano lair by the sinister Li Chang Yen.

Fob Watch

1913

In 1913, planet Earth was heading towards a terrible conflict that would cost the lives of millions. On 28 June 1914, a Serbian gunman would shoot and kill an Austrian Archduke, prompting an attack on Serbia. Russia was bound by treaty to Serbia; Germany was allied to Austria-Hungary; France had a treaty with Russia; Britain was allied with France; Japan had an agreement with Britain... Within a month of the assassination, the First World War would begin.

The major European powers had been expecting war for many years, and most were already making preparations. In English public schools, for example, all pupils were members of the cadet corps. Farringham School for Boys, in Herefordshire, was typical: the schoolmasters supervised regular training, during which the boys practised loading, aiming and firing machine guns at dummy targets; classes were drilled in marching, maintenance of weapons, and other military duties.

Among Farringham's staff in November 1913 was a young history master named John Smith, and he was far from typical. He kept a journal of his dreams, dreams that were full of terrible monsters and events. Mr Smith had no idea that his dreams showed him real events, or that the fob watch on his mantelpiece concealed his true identity. If the Doctor had never visited Farringham, if he'd never chosen this place on a whim, nobody there would have died...

THE JOURNAL OF IMPOSSIBLE THINGS

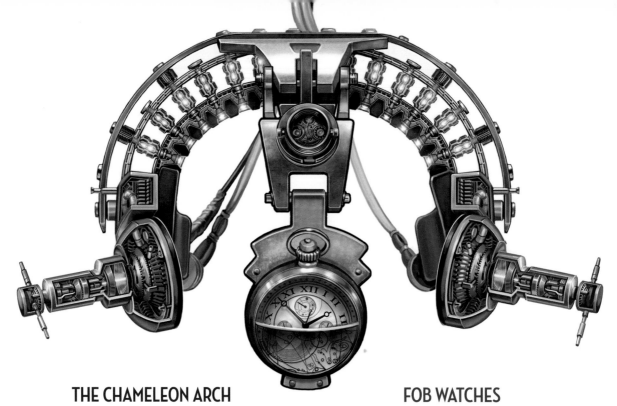

THE CHAMELEON ARCH

The Last Great Time War between the Time Lords and the Daleks irrevocably changed both sides. By its end, the Daleks were prepared to contemplate sullying their own genetic purity in order to survive. And the Time Lords, too, developed the means to alter their genetic make-up and become an entirely different species. Every TARDIS was fitted with a Chameleon Arch – a device to rewrite biology, changing every single cell in a Gallifreyan's body. If a Time Lord used it, his TARDIS would take over, inventing a new life story and integrating him into some randomly chosen society. His Time Lord consciousness would be stored in a simple fob watch. Opening the fob watch would release that consciousness, but a perception filter would deter him from opening it.

Pursued by the Family of Blood, and determined to avoid having to confront and destroy them, the Doctor needed to hide. He set his TARDIS's Chameleon Arch to 'human' and literally became John Smith.

One other Time Lord survived the Time War. When Professor Yana was found as a child on the shores of the Silver Devastation, the only object he had with him was a fob watch – which contained The Master...

FOB WATCHES

Fob watches revolutionised timekeeping. Up until the 15th century, time was either a family affair (depending on the time kept by the single large household clock wound by the master of the house), or a community business (depending on the time set on the large clock on a church tower, which frequently varied from town to town). With the invention of the fob watch, time became a personal thing. So long as you remembered to wind it to keep it accurate, then you were able to track time accurately. The intricate miniature workings required meant that they were only enjoyed by the very rich until the late 18th century. They were eventually replaced by the wristwatch, which came into fashion shortly after the First World War.

HALF-HUMAN

In the 1996 TV Movie, Paul McGann's Doctor says he is half-human, on his mother's side. This is confirmed by the Master in another scene. Had there been a series, it would have included the Eighth Doctor's search for his human mother and Gallifreyan father. The idea seems to be contradicted by most of the show's original 26-year run and by the new series since 2005. The second Tenth Doctor created by a metacrisis in *Journey's End* realises he's half-human and says it's 'disgusting'. Earlier Doctors routinely told their adversaries 'I'm not human.'

On the other hand, the First and Second Doctors were both examined by people who failed to notice any sign of a second heart, something that was instantly obvious to everybody as soon as the Third Doctor arrived. After his regeneration, the Eleventh Doctor briefly thought he was a girl – if they can change gender, perhaps Time Lords can regenerate as various species? The Master is clearly no longer the same species as the Doctor in the TV Movie. Maybe the Eighth Doctor was human? Or, since Time Lord bodies undergo a variety of changes in the hours after regeneration, maybe this volatile DNA resulted in the Eighth Doctor being half-human temporarily?

Or maybe he really is half-human. After all, River Song is...

The Murder of Roger Ackroyd

1926

As Lady Clemency Eddison dozes over a nightcap, she is reading the latest thrilling mystery by famous author Agatha Christie. It's a story of murder at a house in the countryside that becomes ever more fiendish. The mystery can be solved only by the famous Belgian detective Hercule Poirot, taking a few days away from his beloved vegetable marrows.

What Lady Eddison doesn't realise is that her dreams have connected her with her long-lost son: a Vespiform – a giant shape-changing wasp – the product of a love affair long ago in the Raj. The events of the past are catching up with Lady Eddison. When Mrs Christie arrives to spend the weekend with the Eddisons, she finds herself trapped in one of her own murder mysteries...

THE NOVEL

Roger Ackroyd has been murdered, and Hercule Poirot finds himself working with a local doctor to try and solve a fiendish case.

And that's all you need to know. It is justly famed as one of the most ingenious mysteries of the Golden Age of crime. And no, don't watch the telly version or look it up on Wikipedia. You need to read the book.

Although it made Agatha Christie's name, the solution to the mystery caused an outcry when it was published. For a while Christie was vilified by dedicated crime readers. Authors were supposed to obey 'the rules' of detective fiction. First established by Edgar Allen Poe, they were later written down by authors S.S. Van Dine and Ronald Knox in 1928 and strictly adhered to. The rules included 'Not more than one secret room or passage is allowable', 'No Chinamen', and 'All supernatural agencies are ruled out as a matter of course.' Over her writing career, Agatha Christie broke them all. She remains the world's most popular crime writer.

WHERE DID YOU GET YOUR IDEAS, MRS CHRISTIE?

■ Agatha Christie's 'The secret adversary remains hidden' referred to *The Secret Adversary*
■ Donna understandably winced when *The Murder at the Vicarage* became the Doctor's 'Murder at the vicar's rage'.
■ Professor Peach's 'Why didn't they ask...? Heavens!' became *Why Didn't They Ask Evans?*
■ Agatha thought Donna's *Murder on the Orient Express* was a marvellous idea, and was equally taken with the notion of a Miss Marple.
■ Wasps feature in the short story *Wasp's Nest* and on the cover of one edition of *Death in the Clouds*.
■ Hugh Curbishley's 'Cards on the table, woman!' became *Cards on the Table*.
■ 'She had an *Appointment with Death* instead,' said Lady Eddison.
■ The Doctor asked, 'What's that first letter? *N or M?*'
■ Donna realised the significance of *The Body in the Library*.
■ '*The Moving Finger* points... at you, Lady Eddison,' said the Doctor.
■ '*Death Comes as the End*,' observed Agatha as the Vespiform drowned, 'and justice is served.'
■ The Doctor was poisoned by *Sparkling Cyanide*.
■ Lady Eddison's lover, Christopher, had been *Taken at the Flood*.
■ 'This is a *Crooked House*. A house of secrets,' noted Agatha.
■ 'Can't be a monster,' Agatha insisted. 'It's a trick. *They Do It with Mirrors*.'
■ According to Miss Chandrakala, Professor Peach's research was a *Dead Man's Folly*.
■ Mrs Hart the cook reckoned Peach's murder had put the *Cat among the Pigeons*.
■ The Doctor said, 'I've called you here on this *Endless Night* because we have a murderer in our midst.'
■ 'Our *Nemesis* remains at large,' sighed Agatha.
■ And the Doctor, of course, was *The Man in the Brown Suit*.

WHO WAS AGATHA CHRISTIE?

Agatha Christie is the most famous writer of crime fiction, and one of the most famous authors in the world. Her works have been published in over 100 languages and four billion copies of her books have been sold.

Famously shy and retiring, she preferred travelling through Mesopotamia with her archaeologist husband Max Mallowan, carefully cleaning Etruscan pottery and thinking up some of her most intricate plots. When asked where she came up with her plots, she answered: 'The really safe and satisfactory place to work out a story in your mind is when you are washing up.'

More of an observer than a talker, it is fitting that *The Unicorn and the Wasp* suggests that Christie wrote some of her encounter with the Doctor into her work – she often included portraits of those she'd met. Her first husband left her for another woman shortly before her disappearance, and dashing-but-villainous first husbands and manipulative-yet-stupid second wives soon started to appear in her books. Quite a lot of cads embarking on second marriages end very unhappily in her books, too.

Christie later wrote herself into several of her books as the eccentric and socially obtuse Ariadne Oliver.

LITERARY INFLUENCES

■ *The Celestial Toymaker* was originally inspired by a 1937 play called *George and Margaret* written by Gerald Savory, who was Head of Serials at the BBC in 1965. He objected to his characters appearing in *Doctor Who* (especially as the whole point of the original play was that they did not actually appear). Brian Hayles's scripts were hurriedly rewritten by *Doctor Who* script editor Donald Tosh and then again by his successor, Gerry Davis.

■ *Fury from the Deep* – the story of a community under attack by a weed creature – owes a debt to *The Slide*, a radio play about an evil mudslide written by the same author.

■ The hospital under attack from aliens in a heatwave scenario in *Spearhead from Space* is similar to *The Invasion* (1965), also from a story by Robert Holmes.

■ Professor Stahlman's project to drill to the Earth's core in *Inferno* owes something to Professor Challenger's similarly ill-fated attempt in Sir Arthur Conan Doyle's story *When the World Screamed*.

■ Between 1975 and 1977, producer Philip Hinchcliffe and script editor Robert Holmes took a number of classic horror tales, novels and films and adapted them as 'Gothic' *Doctor Who* stories. *The Ark in Space, Planet of Evil, Pyramids of Mars, The Android Invasion, The Brain of Morbius, The Seeds of Doom, The Deadly Assassin, The Robots of Death* and *The Talons of Weng-Chiang* were all to some degree influenced by books such as *Dr Jekyll and Mr Hyde, Frankenstein* or films like *The Manchurian Candidate* and *The Mummy*.

■ *The Loved One* by Evelyn Waugh, the story of a Californian funeral home, supplies the setting and several character names for *Revelation of the Daleks*.

■ Paul Cornell's episodes *Human Nature* and *The Family of Blood* were adapted from his 1995 *Doctor Who* novel of the same name.

■ *A Christmas Carol* by Charles Dickens and C.S. Lewis's Narnia series have more recently inspired Steven Moffat's *Doctor Who* Christmas specials.

Yeti Control Sphere

C.1930

Just as the Doctor wanders the fourth dimension, the Great Intelligence drifts through the fifth – a vast and mighty being without physical form crossing space until it finds a gateway into solid existence. It is a creature like the Mara (see 078. Snake Tattoo) – a being of pure, malevolent thought, able to reach out and enslave the minds of others.

It originally achieved a foothold in this reality thanks to the spiritual enlightenment of Padmasambhava, the Master of Det-Sen monastery in Tibet. His mind made contact with the Great Intelligence by accident during meditation. The entity kept him alive for centuries, creating robot servants and the spheres which controlled them. Each sphere contained a portion of the Great Intelligence.

Over the centuries, the Intelligence's control over Det-Sen increased. In the early 1930s, Professor Edward Travers and John Mackay mounted an expedition to the Himalayas in search of the famed Abominable Snowman, reaching Det-Sen at the same time as the Second Doctor, Jamie and Victoria – and just as the Intelligence's plan was executed. The control spheres had been placed in the robot Yeti, who guarded the gateway through which the Great Intelligence would flow.

When the Intelligence was defeated, it lay dormant for some forty years. Professor Travers had shipped a Yeti and a surviving sphere back to England. They were kept separately – but the Intelligence was able to reassert control over the sphere, reuniting it with the Yeti. Before long, a new force of robotic Yeti were creating another gateway for the Intelligence, in the London Underground, causing the evacuation of London as its web spread through the city. But the Intelligence wasn't able to prevent the Doctor returning to defeat it once more.

ORIGINS

Rather like the Loch Ness Monster, the Abominable Snowman is a surprisingly recent invention. The term was only coined in 1921, as explorers from organisations like the Royal Geographical Society began to travel in Tibet in earnest.

As more travellers arrived in the region, so the stories spread of the 'Wild Man of the Snows' – usually volunteered by helpful Sherpa guides in reply to questions about local legends asked by European mountaineers. The frequently broken English of the Sherpas (and the terrible Tibetan of the explorers) led to much confusion as to whether what was being described was a wolf, a bear, a cattle track, or even the actual Tibetan word for 'Yeti'. The word 'abominable' was a deliberate mistranslation of the Tibetan for 'man-bear'. The famous Sherpa Tensing dismissed the folklore that had built up around the creature.

'I AM YOUR SERVANT'

The Yeti are just one set of robot servants the Doctor has encountered. The Dominators had the Quarks, the people of the Sandminer had their robots, and Sutekh had his Mummies.

The main thing, if you're going to build a robot, is to work out how to power and control it. The Movellans had an external power pack that also issued them instructions. When the Daleks pretended to be subservient on the planet Vulcan, their obedience was briefly ensured by fitting them with external power units. The Logician Klieg tried to control the Cybermen on Telos by keeping them from their recharging booths, and both Drathro and the first Daleks were defeated when their power supplies were destroyed. Even K-9 needed frequent recharging.

It is unknown how Robot K-1 was powered but, like the Sandminer robots, his programming included a set of commands that it was supposedly impossible for him to disobey.

HOW TO MOVE A SPHERE

BBC Visual Effects wizard Jack Kine explained that the Yeti spheres didn't actually roll – the models trundled along on wheels hidden at the bottom.

SINISTER SPHERES

■ The globes on Dalek skirt sections are actually detachable energy weapons.
■ Sontaran Scout Ships are nasty, brutish and round.
■ Skagra's deranged billiard ball was used once too often.
■ The Pirate Captain's collection of spheres were the crushed remains of planets.
■ The Daleks' Time Controller incorporated a sphere full of lethal energy.
■ The spherical gifts from the Adherents of the Repeated Meme actually contained saboteur spiders.
■ Ood interface devices translated into lethal balls of energy.
■ The Sense-Sphere had a terrible reputation for the home of a race of kindly, shy telepaths.

029

Gas Mask

1941

The Second World War began in September 1939, and its first year saw German forces advance virtually unimpeded across Europe until the Battle of Britain in 1940 saw the UK's air force successfully repel German attacks, forcing a change of tactics. From September 1940, nightly German air raids struck London and other major cities. The Blitz claimed at least 20,000 lives and made 1.4 million people homeless. Citizens were issued with gas masks, and there were strict 'blackout' rules – the illumination of the famous Clock Tower of the Palace of Westminster was also switched off. Procedures were well established for what people should do when the sirens signalled an approaching raid. The Civil Defence Ministry distributed 2.25 million free air-raid shelters for people to erect in their back gardens, with underground stations also used for protection. The Air Raid Precautions organisation put up around fifty huge barrage balloons, secured with strong cables which would destroy any low-flying aircraft that collided with them. Occasionally, one of these balloons would come loose, and the RAF were rumoured to use them for target practice.

German bombs were not all that fell on London during the Blitz. One night, a four-year-old boy named Jamie, out searching for his mother in an air raid, was fatally injured by a bomb, just as a Chula hospital ship arrived. The alien craft was equipped with highly sophisticated nanogenes, which attempted to repair him, but without any idea of his natural state. His injuries were horrific – massive trauma to the head, partial collapse of the chest cavity, and scarring on the back of the hand. He was also wearing his gas mask.

The nanogenes tried to cure Jamie, but without knowing the species they got it wrong, fusing the gas mask to his flesh in the process. They took the resulting creature as a template for humanity, and set about a well-meaning 'repair' of every other human they encountered. As the Doctor observed, human DNA was being rewritten – by an idiot. Within hours of Jamie's brief death, the local hospital had become the centre of an epidemic – patients and staff transforming into the walking undead, all asking 'Are you my mummy?'

HOW DOES A GAS MASK WORK?

Gas masks work by removing toxic and harmful particles from the air. The simplest form is a water-soaked towel held over the face. More complicated gas masks work on much the same principle, protecting the vulnerable tissues of the face (eyes, nose, mouth) and allowing the wearer to breathe in comfort.

Early gas masks used wet sponges to remove pollutants from the air but, after the chlorine gassing of troops became commonplace in the First World War, masks were issued which used 'activated charcoal' as a filter – a substance which was remarkably effective at getting the 'poison' in the gas to 'stick' to its surface, while passing on breathable air to the wearer.

During the Second World War, gas masks were issued to the population of Britain in anticipation of a chemical bombardment that never came. Ironically, the masks themselves were dangerous – they used a substance called blue asbestos which caused the deaths of ten per cent of the factory workers making them.

HOW DO YOU MAKE A GAS MASK?

With baked bean tins, actually.

An unexpected hitch in the production of *The Empty Child* in late 2004 arose when prosthetics makers Millennium FX attempted to source twenty authentic 1940s British gas masks. Not only were the eyeglasses too wide, but the asbestos used in them is now illegal. The *Doctor Who* Art Department designed something suitable, and Millennium put it together using eyeglasses from Russian gas masks, plus the metal rims from dozens of empty baked bean tins.

SILENT BUT DEADLY

■ On Vortis, Ian Chesterton and the Menoptra Vrestin were led by the Optera through tunnels poisoned with acid vapour. It was standard practice for the Optera to block acid spills by stuffing themselves into the leak.

■ Zaphra gas was used to knock out Barbara Wright and the rebellious Xerons in the Morok's Space Museum on Xeros.

■ Ammonia was vital to the Rills, but bad news for the First Doctor and the Drahvins.

■ The Macra controlled an entire Earth colony dedicated to mining gas for them to feed off. The creatures' later devolved descendants inhabited the New New York motorway, where they thrived on the petrol fumes.

■ The Daleks used gas to render the Second Doctor unconscious in a London antique shop in 1966.

■ A rig owned by Euro Sea Gas was at the centre of an attack by a deadly weed creature. Humans taken over by the creature emitted a poisonous gas from their mouths.

■ The aim of the Inferno Project was to penetrate the Earth's crust and release 'Stahlman's gas', a hugely powerful energy source.

■ The Marshal on Solos used gas grenades to attack the Solonian mutants.

■ The Fourth Doctor, Sarah and Harry got caught in a Thal gas attack in the Kaled trenches on Skaro.

■ The Fourth Doctor tried to poison Morbius with cyanide, not immediately realising he had the lungs of a Birostrop. The Sacred Flame was the product of gases forcing up along a geological fault from deep in the molten heart of Karn. The Sisterhood of the Flame could sense the silent gas dirigibles of the Hoothi a million miles away.

■ When a mixture of air and helium is breathed, it alters the resonance in the larynx – as Dask found when his Robots of Death stopped recognising his voice.

■ The Fourth Doctor was knocked out by balerium gas when he tried to

use a Consum Bank in Megropolis One on Pluto.

■ The Seers used fumigation against the Trogs in the Underworld. The Fourth Doctor directed the gas back into their control room.

■ The Marshmen attacking the Starliner were driven out onto the Alzarian surface by flooding the ship with oxygen.

■ The Terileptils needed Soliton gas to breathe properly. Their exploding Soliton machine started the Great Fire of London in 1666.

■ The Fifth Doctor reluctantly poisoned an army of Silurians and Sea Devils with Hexachromite gas, a substance lethal to reptile life.

■ When rescuing Davros, the Daleks attacked his prison ship with a corrosive gas that melted human flesh.

■ The Fifth Doctor was allergic to certain gases in the Praxis range of the spectrum, and relied on celery to alert him to their presence.

■ The Sixth Doctor poisoned Shockeye o' the Quawncing Grig with a cyanide filter from Oscar Botcherby's butterfly kit.

■ The Rani hid mustard gas in a booby-trapped painting of a volcano.

■ Mustakozene 80 was used by the Borad to mutate the Morlox.

■ The Valeyard used asphyxiating nerve gas against the Sixth Doctor.

■ The Great Architect used gas to herd the occupants of Paradise Towers.

■ Commander Millington concealed

a vial of a toxic gas inside the Ultima Machine, planning to devastate Moscow with it. The Ancient One used the same gas to destroy itself and Fenric.

■ The Gelth were rendered gaseous during the Time War. They inhabited the gas pipes in Gabriel Sneed's funeral parlour.

■ The Family Slitheen used a compression field to shrink themselves sufficiently to hide inside human skinsuits, resulting in a noisy and smelly gas exchange.

■ Albert Dumfries wondered why his new Prime Minister was wearing a gas mask to Cabinet. 'Because of the gas,' explained Mr Saxon. He was right. And insane.

■ When the Ood began to rebel, Halpen and Kess decided to gas them.

■ The Sontaran stratagem was to release gas from their ATMOS devices and poison Earth's sky with Caesofine concentrate, the basis of their clone feed.

■ Jackson Lake's TARDIS was inflated by gas from the Mutton Street Gasworks.

■ The pensioners in the version of Leadworth conjured by the Dream Lord all had gas-emitting Eknodine living inside them.

■ The Homo reptilia discovered beneath Cwmtaff used gas projectile weapons, and were eventually driven back to their cryo-chambers by a toxic fumigation process.

030

Ironside

1941

As the Blitz continued, Britain desperately needed its own answer to the Nazi war machine. When Professor Edwin Bracewell presented his latest invention to Britain's military leaders, Prime Minister Winston Churchill believed he had found just such a weapon. Bracewell's tank-like armoured robots could be rolled out across Europe's battlefields or, operating from the roof of St James's Palace above the Cabinet War Rooms, could simply shoot down enemy aircraft. With the Third Reich smashed, the war would be won and millions of innocent lives would be saved.

But the Ironsides were not Bracewell's invention; they were Daleks, and he was *their* creation. The Bracewell android and the Ironside Project were part of a trap for the Doctor. With his unwitting help, their Progenitor Device was activated and a new Dalek Paradigm was generated. This new race of Daleks immediately placed London in great peril, but the Doctor was able to retaliate with the help of space-flying Spitfires and a jammy dodger.

DEATH TO THE DALEKS

The Ironsides are a fine example of Dalek props going out in style. Writer and executive producer Steven Moffat had decided to update the Dalek design for the 2010 series so a whole new set of props was commissioned. The 2005 Daleks get a good send-off in Mark Gatiss's script: repainted khaki and serving tea to Churchill in a piece of subterfuge that only the Doctor and the audience are in on. They even outwit their arch-enemy before being spectacularly exterminated by their replacements. Earlier Daleks haven't had quite such a glorious retirement...

The top half of one of the original 1963 props had its back cut out so that visitors to the Museum of the Moving Image in the 1990s could step inside and become a Dalek – you could look through the eyestalk, wave the gunstick and, of course, shout 'Exterminate!' The bottom half of the prop was destroyed in 1972, and its smoking remains can be seen in the fourth part of *Day of the Daleks*.

It's not just old episodes of TV series like *Doctor Who* that the BBC junked in the early 1970s – they also threw away old Daleks. Visual Effects designer Bernard Wilkie rescued the top of a 1963 prop and the base of a smaller 1967 version and kept them in a barn for his children to play in. It eventually became a regular feature in various *Doctor Who* exhibitions, displayed as a 'destroyed Dalek' since the two halves didn't fit together.

Once the first Dalek story was completed in 1964, two Dalek props were given to one of Doctor Barnardo's children's homes to help with fundraising. Shortly afterwards, the BBC asked if they could borrow them back for *The Dalek Invasion of Earth*. They were then returned to Barnardo's, but the children's home closed down in 1967, and the Daleks vanished.

The upper half of a 1964 prop became part of an exhibit at Madame Tussauds in 1980.

One of the 1960s Dalek props was on display at the long-running *Doctor Who* exhibition in Longleat Safari Park until it was damaged in a fire. The remains were included in the *Doctor Who* exhibitions in Brighton and Cardiff from 2005.

Most of the props from the 1960s movies were burnt, but several were given away. One lucky winner told the magazine *Nothing at the End of the Lane* that 'Once the novelty wore off, it took up a lot of space and had to be stored in my nan's garage. They told me it had rotted away, but I think they sold it off.'

Dummy Daleks were built as background extras in 1973, but found themselves hastily converted and combined into proper Daleks, that were still in use in the 1980s Dalek stories. The lower half of one became part of a complete prop that was unsuccessfully offered for sale on a Channel 4 TV show in 2011.

Parts of the original props were returned to the BBC in 2004 and were used by Mike Tucker's Model Unit as the basis for the 2005 Dalek builds, along with parts from some replicas. When the new Dalek casings were complete, Mike used the leftovers to make a 1960s-style Dalek for the official *Doctor Who* website. Sadly, the expected glass display case never materialised, and the website team came in to find a next-door department playing 'Can we fit the BBC's fattest accountant in the Dalek?' The answer was 'No', and the prop never recovered. When the website office moved to Cardiff, the Dalek was abandoned in the kitchen. It may be the only Dalek prop not to appear in *Asylum of the Daleks* (2012).

I HAVE KILLED MY CREATOR

When Bracewell discovered his true origins, he helped launch a Spitfire attack on his Ironsides' saucer, using technology that they had given him. The Ironside Daleks were in turn wiped out by the new Dalek Paradigm they had created, who judged them to be inferior. The very first Daleks, too, turned very quickly on their creator Davros, refusing to recognise the existence of a superior being.

■ John Lumic's Cybermen decided that their crippled creator was in need of a compulsory upgrade to become their Controller.

■ The Clockwork Robots killed the crew of the *Madame de Pompadour*, using them as spare parts to repair the damaged spaceship.

■ Professor Kettlewell was accidentally destroyed by his own creation, the robot K-1.

■ The Eleventh and Fourth Doctors both reprogrammed Cybermats to attack the Cybermen.

■ The Robots of the Sandminer were reprogrammed to turn on their human masters by very mad scientist Taren Capel.

■ The Great Intelligence was defeated when one of its Yeti came under the Doctor's control.

■ Mr Sin's bloodlust was so strong that the plaything turned its dragon death ray on his master, Magnus Greel.

■ The Master's creations on Castrovalva turned on him and tried to tear him apart.

A POWERFUL VICTORY

Victory of the Daleks (2010) contains several tributes to writer Mark Gatiss's favourite Dalek story, *The Power of the Daleks* (1966).

THE POWER OF THE DALEKS	VICTORY OF THE DALEKS
The scientist Lesterson discovers the Daleks and presents them to Vulcan's Governor.	The scientist Bracewell 'invents' the Ironsides and presents them to Winston Churchill.
'I am your servant.'	'I am your soldier.'
'Would you like more liquid?'	'Would you like a cup of tea?'
'We are the new race of Daleks.'	'We are the new race of Daleks.'

031

A Christmas Tree

1941

The Second World War continued at a terrible cost. Hundreds of thousands of human lives were wiped out, leaving their grieving families behind. Mourning the loss of her husband, Madge Grantby took her children for Christmas at their uncle's house, finding it occupied by a very strange caretaker, who was determined to give them the best Christmas ever.

```
INT. GRANBY HOUSE/THE MAIN SITTING ROOM -
DAY 3. 14:28


On the door as it is opened and MADGE peers round -
now entering the room, staring at something,
THE DOCTOR following.
A large, splendid sitting room. And blazing away
at the far end is the BEST AND BIGGEST CHRISTMAS
TREE EVER.
Not any tree, a tree the Doctor would make. Over
the top, and mad, possibly with moving parts.
LILY and CYRIL are already standing there,
seemingly transfixed.
On Madge, staring into the room - can't help but
admit it, that tree is something. She joins Lily
and Cyril. And they just stare.
Now, cutting round all around the fabulous details
of this greatest ever tree...
A toy train circles it. There's a cuckoo clock with
a penguin popping in and out. There's a revolving
section. A space rockets orbits it, with Santa
astride it, waving. All the maddest tree ideas we
can have.
THE DOCTOR joining them.
THE DOCTOR: I know!
CYRIL: Look, there's a present!
```

The Doctor, The Widow and the Wardrobe

Beneath the wrapping paper was a dimensional portal to the year 5345, and to another world. It was a fairy-tale land of snow and conifers – naturally occurring Christmas trees that grew their own shiny baubles. And from the baubles hatched rapidly growing, rootless and independently mobile tree creatures that could shape themselves into any form, even buildings. Their Wooden King and Queen were seeking a way to transport the life force of the forest to another planet, safe from the attentions of miners from Androzani Major.

The power of Madge Grantby's love for her children was able to do this, piloting the forest through the Time Vortex and taking her children home for Christmas. On the way, she rescued her husband's Lancaster Bomber. It may not have gone quite how the Doctor planned it, but it ended up being the best Christmas ever.

'I'M GONNA GET KILLED BY A CHRISTMAS TREE!'

When the Doctor regenerated into his tenth body, he crash-landed the TARDIS in London on Christmas Eve 2006, where his regeneration energy attracted a group of Roboform scavengers. Disguised in Santa Claus costumes, the Roboforms attacked Rose Tyler and Mickey Smith, a blast from one of their weapons bringing down a high-street Christmas tree. They also installed a robotic Christmas tree in Jackie Tyler's flat. Activated by remote control, it ran riot around the flat, its branches turning into a whirling dervish of lethal blades and baubles. The Doctor hurriedly deactivated it using the sonic screwdriver, overriding the remote control signal and causing the Christmas tree to explode.

By the following Christmas, the Empress of the Racnoss had taken possession of the Roboforms. In Santa costume once again, the Roboforms were despatched to retrieve Donna Noble, who was marrying Lance Bennett on Christmas Eve. The Christmas tree at her wedding reception was decorated with flying, exploding baubles.

THE TREE TRADITION

Decorating trees outside town halls and churches during the winter festival originated in 16th-century eastern Europe and the custom slowly spread across Germany. By the early 19th century, it had been adopted by European nobility. Thanks to the royal family's close ties with Germany, it was introduced in Britain during the reign of George III and, as a child, Queen Victoria enjoyed a Christmas tree in her bedroom each year.

An 1848 woodcut of Victoria and Prince Albert gathered with their children around a Christmas tree was reprinted in America in 1850, though the image was reworked to look like an ordinary American family – Victoria's tiara and Albert's moustache were both omitted. This was enough to spread the fashion for Christmas trees across the USA over the next 20 years.

CHRISTMAS SPECIAL

The Doctor, the Widow and the Wardrobe is the latest in a series of now-traditional *Doctor Who* Christmas specials. Although the show's original run didn't feature official Christmas specials, several episodes went out during the festive period. Notable examples include:

The Feast of Steven, seventh episode of *The Daleks' Master Plan*, went out on Christmas Day in 1965 and featured the Doctor wishing a Merry Christmas to viewers at home.

An omnibus repeat of *The Daemons* in the 1971 Christmas holidays gained a higher audience than the original transmission and made 'TV movie' repeats of the show a regular occurrence.

The quite unique *K9 and Company* went out on 28 December 1981, helping to bridge the unusually lengthy gap between Tom Baker's last season as the Doctor and Peter Davison's first adventure.

THE TREES ARE NOT WHAT THEY SEEM

The Forest of Words in the Land of Fiction

The fake trees of Oseidon

Luke Ward, transformed into a tree by the Rani

The Forest of Cheem

The forests of the Vashta Narada

The Treeborgs in the Forest Vault of the Bzyantium

032

The Ultima Machine

1943

One of the most powerful weapons against the German war machine was a small man in a wheelchair. Working at a secret naval base near Maiden's Point in Northumberland, Dr Judson had spent the war creating a computing machine capable of deciphering the most sophisticated codes used by Nazi forces to relay their plans of attack. It would help Britain win the war.

The British government, however, was already thinking further ahead than the end of the war. Planning for the day when Russia would no longer be Britain's ally, Whitehall ordered the base commander, Millington, to allow a small Russian force to break in and steal the Ultima machine. Inside it was a vial of toxic gas that could devastate Moscow. The Ultima machine had become a chemical weapon.

The machine, Judson and Millington were all part of something much bigger – a centuries-long scheme by a force called Fenric to free itself from the flask it had been imprisoned in by the Doctor (see 015. Fenric's Flask). When the Doctor took his companion Ace to Maiden's Point, the final Wolf of Fenric had arrived, and Fenric's plan to destroy the world could begin.

HOW DID CODE-BREAKING MACHINES WORK?

The Ultima machine was an advanced logic game or, as companion Ace called it, 'a flip-flop thingy'. This is useful in deciphering complex codes as it allows the machine to determine how close it is to discerning a true pattern. At the heart of the machine was a series of decryption rotors, each one capable of running a complicated series of decryption processes. In theory, if a coded transmission was run through every possible setting of every rotor, the original message would eventually be arrived at.

It would, though, take a lot of time to work through the millions of possible variations. Judson and his Ultima machine were based on mathematician Alan Turing and the code-breaking machine he developed at Bletchley Park. The process of statistical analysis he developed, Banburismus, made it easier to tell if a permutation was not working fairly quickly, thus saving a lot of time.

WHO WAS ALAN TURING?

Alan Turing is called the father of modern computing and, although little recognised for his achievements in his lifetime, his pioneering work at Bletchley Park was just beginning to be fully declassified and discussed when Ian Briggs was preparing to write *The Curse of Fenric* in 1989. A play on the subject, called *Breaking the Code*, had enjoyed West End success in 1987.

Turing joined the Government Code and Cypher School full-time at the start of the Second World War, devoting himself to decrypting transmissions from U-boats. He laid the groundwork for modern computing with his design of the Automatic Computing Engine, created the first chess program, and devised the Turing Test to determine whether you were speaking to a computer or an artificial intelligence. A common application of this is the 'Captcha' programs used on websites to decide through text entry whether you are a real person or not.

THE LOST HEROES OF BLETCHLEY PARK

Bletchley Park was the government's centre for decoding encrypted enemy transmissions during the Second World War.

In the early days the code-breakers were talented wordsmiths and crossword-solvers, but German submarines started using complicated encryption rotors so the wordsmiths were replaced with mathematicians.

The Germans used a Lorenz machine – the operator typed the message in, and the machine encrypted it and then re-encrypted it. The machine had 12 rotors, allowing 1.6 billion possible combinations – and it was almost impossible to decode until, in 1941, an operator sent the same message twice.

The Bletchley linguist John Tiltman was able to decode the message by hand. It took him ten days, and he couldn't see the system behind it. He handed it over to a young mathematician called Bill Tutte who was able to see patterns in the original cipher. He split the message into columns and began to reverse-engineer the machinery behind it. He spotted that the cipher changed slightly every 41 characters – from this he worked out that the first rotor had 41 spokes/settings/characters and so decipherment began.

He was helped by a bricklayer's son from Poplar called Tommy Flowers, who built a machine called Colossus – the world's first electronic computer. It was able to read messages at 5,000 characters a second, and could break the first two rotors of the Lorenz machine every time. It wasn't perfect – the radiator leaked so badly that operators had to wear rubber boots to avoid electrocution – and the rest of the cipher was sent to be worked on by decryption experts.

They also had to keep their secrets into the 1970s. Colossus itself, although officially destroyed, was still being using in the 1960s to break Russian codes. The secrecy meant that when the Americans announced they'd invented the first computer, Tommy Flowers couldn't even say that he had beaten them to it back in the 1940s. Like Alan Turing, his achievement was never officially recognised by the UK.

At the age of 87, Tommy Flowers took an IT course at a local college and learned to use a PC. He also received an award of £350 for inventing the first computer. Some of his papers are still classified.

033

Television

1953

The United Kingdom's first television broadcasts began in September 1929, but transmissions were suspended on 1 September 1939 when the War began, and did not resume until 7 June 1946. As Britain recovered from its war effort over the next seven years, Britain's wartime rationing of food, clothing and non-essential items was slowly lifted. One of the turning points was 1953: as Britain awaited its new Queen's Coronation, the world's highest mountain was climbed, Communist leader Josef Stalin died, and Winston Churchill was awarded the Nobel Prize for Literature. Meanwhile, the BBC began to plan the most ambitious television outside broadcast yet screened, as the Queen overruled Churchill's objections and agreed that her Coronation could be televised. By now, there were 2.14 million licensed television sets in Great Britain, representing about 14 per cent of households, and the number continued to grow throughout the year. An audience of over 20 million people crowded around their friends' and neighbours' small screens to watch June's live broadcast of the Coronation from Westminster Abbey. Yet scare-stories abounded of the disturbing powers of television – some believed it rotted the mind, or made your brain come out of your ears. They were closer to the truth than they realised...

Having converted themselves into plasmic energy, a small group of criminals on the planet Hermethica briefly took over their world's major cities. Most were captured and executed, but their leader, the Wire, escaped by transmitting herself across the stars to Earth and into a TV set, from which she could access and travel through broadcasts. Plasmic energy streamed from London's televisions, attaching itself to the heads of viewers and extracting their life forces, as the Wire gorged on their brains. Her victims were left mute and faceless, unable to communicate or feed, with the only real indication of life being the constant clenching and unclenching of their fists. With the largest audience ever tuning in for the Coronation, the Wire prepared to feed – but she hadn't reckoned on the Doctor turning off her transmission from Alexandra Palace.

TV'S CROWNING MOMENTS

The Coronation of Elizabeth II on 2 June was the UK's first major television moment. Though television sets remained a rarity, many families did buy them specially for the occasion, and proudly invited family, friends and neighbours into their homes to enjoy the spectacle.

Throughout the 1950s, televisions remained a relative luxury. If you were lucky enough to have one in the home, it displaced the hearth as the focus of the room – and, as televisions came in, the fireplace went out, replaced with central heating. Crowds could be found watching television in pubs, where they became a major attraction, especially for important events.

Nigel Kneale's *Quatermass* serials capitalised on the nation's experience of television. *The Quatermass Experiment* was shown just six weeks after the Coronation, and its climax was set in Westminster Abbey – it was figured that, as everyone already knew what it looked like, the producers could get away with building just a basic set. Similarly, *Quatermass and the Pit*, which was broadcast live in 1957, featured scenes of people in a pub watching a live broadcast going terribly wrong and commenting on it. Nigel Kneale also adapted *Nineteen Eighty-Four* for television, in 1954, and much was made of the television set in every room, maintaining constant watch on people.

SPACE-TIME VISUALISATIONS

> THE DOCTOR: You say you can't fit an enormous building into one of your smaller sitting rooms?
> IAN: No.
> THE DOCTOR: But you've discovered television, haven't you?
> IAN: Yes...
> THE DOCTOR: Then by showing an enormous building on your television screen, you could do what seemed impossible, couldn't you?

The TARDIS has always had a television screen – frequently a cathode ray monitor, suspended from an interior wall, and later incorporated into the wall itself. The Eighth Doctor's TARDIS turns the entire ceiling into a projection, while the Ninth Doctor uses a computer monitor and the Tenth Doctor prefers to open the doors and look out. The Eleventh Doctor has both a small monitor on the console and a large viewscreen on the wall.

The first monsters to have television were the Daleks – their city on Skaro had small circular screens (showing either the *Doctor Who* title sequence or the Time Vortex). At first, the Daleks seem happy watching slideshows and silent movies, but they quickly develop moving pictures. By *Day of the Daleks* (1972), they have a giant flat-panel television. In *The Parting of the Ways* (2005), they simply have pictures floating in mid air, and have changed their aspect ratio from 4:3 to 16:9.

Having liberated the planet Xeros, the First Doctor also liberates a Space-Time Visualiser from the Morok museum. A splendidly chunky device with no remote control and a big dial, the TARDIS crew use it to watch Shakespeare, the Gettysburg address and the Beatles, but miss a broadcast from the Daleks.

The War Machines (1966) is the first story to show people watching at home and to include clips from a TV news programme – in the fourth episode, genuine BBC newsreader Kenneth Kendall calmly announced:

```
Here is a further bulletin on the London
emergency. It was announced a few minutes ago
that the machine, which is now being described
as a War Machine, has successfully been put out
of action. The City of London has responded with
characteristic calm to the emergency. As yet there
seems to be no explanation for this sudden attack.
An emergency cabinet meeting was held at number 10
Downing Street this morning, and service chiefs
were called in. The Ministry of Defence have just
made the following announcement. Further attacks
on London can be expected in the next twenty four
hours. The army are standing by at key centres.
People are warned to stay indoors and keep calm.
```

Harold Chorley, in *The Web of Fear* (1968) is *Doctor Who*'s first example of a slimy television reporter, complete with bow tie. Allowed into the army's base in the London Underground during the Yeti invasion, he smugly announces: 'The government, in its infinite wisdom, decided only to allow one correspondent down here. The press chose me.' When the troops come under attack, he thinks it's 'Great stuff', but is predictably keen to keep himself well away from the action and eventually comes under suspicion as the Great Intelligence's agent.

The Second Doctor shows familiarity with TV but little faith in it: in *The Three Doctors* (1973), he decides he needs something to keep an antimatter creature confused, and ponders using a television set. Giles Kent shows him TV footage of the disasters he believes Salamander is causing in *The Enemy of the World* (1968), but the Doctor remains unconvinced.

The Ambassadors of Death (1970) shows the first time he's actually influenced by television: the Third Doctor watches a snatch of television news about the Mars Probe mission, before turning the volume down and getting back to his TARDIS repairs. Moments later, he notices Lethbridge-Stewart on the TV screen, and gets drawn in to the news coverage – before long, he's on his way to Space Control for another adventure.

Something similar happens in *The Daemons* (1971), with the Doctor being dismissive of Jo Grant's unscientific 'dawning of the age of Aquarius' chatter until he watches a news report on Professor Warner's archaeological dig and shoots off to 'stop that lunatic before it's too late!' The TV report is on 'BBC3', a good 30 years before that channel was launched, and the presenter, Alistair Fergus, is cast from the same mould as Harold Chorley. He's accompanied by a production team, including Harry, who's keen for everything to be 'absolutely super'. And, with TV scheduling even more of an issue in the pre-video age, UNIT's Benton and Yates very nearly miss seeing the Doctor's fate at Devil's End, thanks to a rugby match on a competing channel.

The Master is arrested by UNIT at the end of *The Daemons*. His next appearance is in *The Sea Devils* (1972), which confirms the suspicions of those who think that prison life is too cushy – he even has a colour television set, and is getting another for his bedroom when the Sea Devils invade. He whiles away his time watching children's show *The Clangers*. Russell T Davies pays homage to this scene in *The Sound of Drums* (2007), in which the Master is similarly fascinated by the Teletubbies.

Frontier in Space (1973) equips the office of Earth's President in the year 2540 with a huge TV screen on the wall, with a rolling tickertape of 24-hour news. She tends to keep the sound down, which is not surprising – when she does turn the volume up, the news is full of warmongering American Congressmen.

In *The Deadly Assassin*, the Fourth Doctor encounters a television journalist on Gallifrey – Runcible the Fatuous, whose small-screen ancestry goes straight back to Harold Chorley. Runcible's footage of the President's assassination is briefly vital to the Doctor's defence, until the Master steals it. Future President Borusa, meanwhile, shows magnificent contempt for both Runcible and the viewers at home, telling his interviewer, 'you had ample opportunity to ask me questions during your misspent years at the Academy. You failed to avail yourself of the opportunity then and it is too late now. Good day.' Lack of information or comment doesn't, of course, stop Runcible from going on to speculate on what's about to happen, getting it spectacularly wrong in all most every detail.

When the Mona Lisa is stolen in *City of Death* (1979), the TV in the Doctor's preferred Parisian brasserie shows a report on the theft. The report is in English, so either the TARDIS's translation circuits are working overtime or the brasserie's French clientele remain in total ignorance of the terrible news.

Nobody watches television during the Fifth Doctor's tenure, but the Sixth Doctor makes up for it in *Vengeance on Varos* (1985). He lands on Varos, a society obsessed by television, where viewing is compulsory and events (including lethal elections) are decided by a viewer vote. He later spends almost the whole of *The Trial of a Time Lord* (1986) watching television – dramatised events from his recent past are shown on a courtroom screen as evidence for the prosecution. He becomes the first Doctor to make and edit his

own programme when he prepares his evidence, even selecting an episode he hasn't seen yet.

When the Seventh Doctor returns to London in November 1963 in *Remembrance of the Daleks*, his companion Ace turns on a television on a Saturday afternoon. She doesn't keep watching for long enough to hear the next show announced: 'This is BBC Television. The time is a quarter past five, and Saturday viewing continues with an adventure in the new science fiction series, *Doc—*'

In the 1996 TV Movie, the Eighth Doctor is born in sync with a showing of *Frankenstein* (1931). He pauses in his headlong rush to stop the Master for long enough to take in some of San Francisco's local TV news. It's 31 December 1999, and the strange natural phenomena being reported may well signal a coming apocalypse – it's snowing in Hawaii, there are flood warnings and record-breaking tides... Luckily, 'Scientists say that the freak conditions are due to the very slight fluctuations in the Earth's gravitational pull... that apparently only happen once every thousand years.' The next report is more helpful, and points the Doctor to the beryllium chip he needs. He's too late, though, and the TV presenters unknowingly join a midnight countdown to the end of the world.

By the time the Ninth Doctor arrives in London and meets Rose Tyler, the BBC is running a 24-hour news channel. Though Jackie switches to daytime telly when Rose is out at work, the Tylers are fans, doing what everyone does when something big happens – watch it on TV. Along with Mickey Smith, they watch reports on the explosion at Henrik's in *Rose* (2005) and the destruction of Big Ben in *Aliens of London*. Possibly because the TARDIS monitor screen can pick up all the basic packages,

the Doctor himself proves to be a bit of channel-hopper, trying out various news channels; he's not, though, terribly enamoured of *Blue Peter*'s rapid-response Spaceship Cake. He's even less impressed by the news broadcasts from Satellite 5 in *The Long Game* and shuts the operation down, without considering what a population starved of news and information might watch instead. He's appalled to discover, a hundred years later in *Bad Wolf*, that the news channels have been replaced with lethal game shows like the version of *Big Brother* he wakes up in. Dismayed by *Call My Bluff*, appalled by *Stars in Their Eyes*, furious with *The Weakest Link*, and blissfully ignorant of *What Not to Wear*, he still admits a soft spot for *Bear with Me*, especially the celebrity episode where the bear got into the bath.

'I love telly,' the Tenth Doctor tells Tommy Connolly in *The Idiot's Lantern* (2006), proving it by sitting through a bit of *Animal, Vegetable, Mineral*. He sleeps through most of the BBC News coverage of the Sycorax invasion, including Harriet Jones's last-minute replacement for the Queen's Christmas Day broadcast. He appears on it in *Fear Her*, carrying the Olympic Torch. *Army of Ghosts* reveals him to be just as much of a channel-hopper as his predecessor, watching news from around the globe and taking in the odd chat show and some *EastEnders*. *The Lazarus Experiment* (2007) sees him lured into an adventure by a news report for the first time since *The Daemons*, while *Blink* hinges on his starring role in a DVD Easter Egg. He's on the news again in *The Sound of Drums*, reported to be the terrorist behind the assassination of the US President that billions have just witnessed live on TV, while Harold Saxon's prime ministerial broadcast proves pure dynamite. The Doctor is also the star of the only broadcast in *Last of the Time Lords*, with the Master ageing him 900 years as a warning to Martha Jones. Thanks to a glimpsed news report in *Voyage of the Damned*, he knows to call Buckingham Palace to have the Queen evacuated as the Titanic crashes. An unmade story featured him appearing on a show very similar to *Most Haunted*. And, unknown to the Doctor, Wilfred Mott is contacted several times by a mysteriously maternal Gallifreyan woman, on one occasion when she hijacks the Queen's Christmas speech.

The Eleventh Doctor takes a quick look at a TV set to confirm that the Atraxi are broadcasting globally in *The Eleventh Hour* (2010). He's otherwise been the most telly-averse Doctor since the Fifth, even needing Amy Pond to remind him, in *The Lodger* (2010), that ordinary humans watch television. He does, though, use the coverage of the 1969 Moon landing to defeat the Silents in *Day of the Moon* (2011), and is not shy of appearing on screen himself. He has addressed the primary school children of Great Britain, the *Children in Need* audience and the viewers of *Blue Peter* directly through their TV sets, and once ensured that the presenter of the *National Television Awards* made it to the ceremony on time.

034

Sink Plunger

C.1963

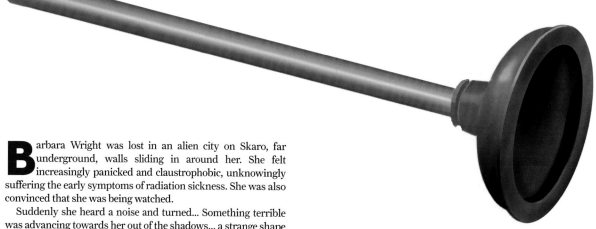

Barbara Wright was lost in an alien city on Skaro, far underground, walls sliding in around her. She felt increasingly panicked and claustrophobic, unknowingly suffering the early symptoms of radiation sickness. She was also convinced that she was being watched.

Suddenly she heard a noise and turned... Something terrible was advancing towards her out of the shadows... a strange shape with attachments instead of arms... She screamed...

This was the first encounter of one of the Doctor's companions with a Dalek, later dismissed by the Doctor as 'bubbling lumps of hate' armed with 'a sink plunger and an egg-whisk'.

The 'sink plunger' itself uses vacuum technology and is more dextrous than humanoid fingers and hands, allowing the Dalek to handle objects as diverse as metal trays, command computers and a single sheet of paper. It can precisely manipulate a keypad or be wired directly into a Dalek flight computer.

The plunger device is capable of use as a weapon to crush a skull, and can also scan other life forms' brain waves or extract information from the human brain.

THE ATTACHMENT DETACHMENT

The first sighting of a sink plunger on 21 December 1963 was a remarkable moment in *Doctor Who* and provided the show with many of its firsts, beyond simply being the first appearance of a Dalek.

It is the show's first monster-reveal cliffhanger. Up until that point, cliffhangers had been moments of jeopardy, but this saw *Doctor Who* reaching for a moment of unknown horror – writer Terry Nation recalled being rung up at home by friends demanding 'My god, what is it?' Five decades later, we all know it's a sink plunger attached to a Dalek – but back then, on a tiny television with a limited signal and only 405 lines, it was much harder to tell.

It was the moment that made *Doctor Who*. Audience figures nearly doubled the next week, to over 10 million. The show's creators had been despairing of their new creation. Producer Verity Lambert had been less than happy with three episodes set among the cavemen and had fought to get the Dalek episodes on air. She'd nearly been overruled by the head of serials Donald Wilson and by the show's creator Sydney Newman, but had held out for *The Daleks*, insisting it was a strong script. Even then, the

resistance had caused her to doubt her own judgement. What if she was wrong? What if the script wasn't good at all?

Lambert was also under siege at the time as the BBC's first female producer, on the receiving end of a whispering campaign, questioning why and how she'd got the job and her abilities. The programme itself (made by the Drama department) was resented by the Children's department (who felt it was encroaching on their territory). Other BBC departments were also wary, including Visual Effects, whose designers initially refused to have anything to do with the extra workload of *Doctor Who*. This meant that Lambert had to entrust the building of the Daleks to an outside firm. In the wake of the show's overnight success, both departments would make enormous contributions to *Doctor Who*, but at first Verity Lambert and her team were left to get on with making the programme.

It was also the first example of the show's triumph over its limited budget. Designer Raymond Cusick had fought a hard battle for the Daleks. The show's associate producer had suggested constructing a costume out of cardboard tubes, but Cusick was determined to make the Daleks look as good as possible on the money available. This was hard when the head of the design department would tour sets and discipline designers who made their limited resources look too good. (Cusick later recalled receiving a dressing-down for managing to afford coloured Perspex on *The Keys of Marinus*.) The revolutionary Dalek design somehow got through this process, but did lose a few things – the base was changed so that it could be made from plywood (in the end fibreglass was used), the hemispheres were supposed to be lit when the Dalek talked (only one car battery could be afforded for this, so the notion was abandoned), and the arm attachment was supposed to be a mechanical claw... but the available funds stretched no further than a sink plunger.

13 USES FOR A DALEK MANIPULATOR ARM

1. PINIONING A HUMANOID: Extend telescopic manipulator arm and secure humanoid with sucker attachment.

2. OPERATING MACHINERY: Ensure controls are roughly circular.

3. CRUSHING A HUMAN SKULL ('SUCKER THEM TO DEATH'): Enfold human face with sucker, taking care to enclose nose and mouth to maximise suffocation effect. Then squeeze.

4. SCANNING FOR INTELLIGENCE: Point sucker attachment at humanoid's cranium and begin scan.

5. EXTRACTING BRAINWAVES: This operation requires at least two separate Dalek units, each fitted with sucker attachment. NB Terran subjects are unlikely to survive the desiccation process.

6. HOLDING METAL WRITING PAPER: Engage magnet within sucker attachment.

7. BURNING THROUGH DOORS AND WALLS: Blowtorch attachment more effective than Welding attachment, but either will do. NB Both are rel-atively slow and may allow prisoners time to escape.

8. LOCATING ENEMY TIME MACHINES: Seismic detector/perceptor replaces sucker attachment.

9. OVERRIDING ALIEN DOOR CONTROLS: Use electrode unit in place of sucker attachment.

10. CALCULATING COMBINATION LOCKS: Upgraded sucker attachment now superior to old-fashioned electrode unit option.

11. JUNGLE DEFOLIATION: Pyroflame attachment works better for this than Blowtorch attachment.

12. SUPERVISING DALEK PRODUCTION LINE: Use scoop attachment to transfer Dalek mutant into casing. Wash before and after use.

13. UNBLOCKING A SINK: Take the sink plunger. Place over the sink drainage hole ('plughole'). Push up and down three times rapidly, pull up and away, hopefully dislodging the obstruction. Repeat as necessary.

035

The Mark III Travel Machine

C.1963

A neutron explosion at the climax of Skaro's thousand-year war left the planet utterly devastated. The soil was barren, plant life was petrified, and vast swathes of the planet were turned to arid plains. Animal life either perished or mutated. The air was infused with deadly levels of radiation, making it all but impossible for anyone to survive...

But somehow, the Daleks managed it, encased in their Travel Machines – mobile survival suits which kept them alive while they waited for their dead planet to heal itself. The Daleks believed they were alone and came to terms with the horrific mutations they had suffered – at least they had lived. They lived a peaceful and secure existence in their underground base, the rulers of Skaro, but unable to venture onto its surface.

The Doctor's arrival on Skaro with his granddaughter Susan and her teachers, Ian Chesterton and Barbara Wright, changed all that. They learned that they were not alone, that their enemies the Thals had survived and thrived. Worse, the Doctor revealed that his party were not only alien to Skaro but also time travellers.

Once they realised there was life on other planets, the Daleks developed spaceships in order to invade them. The Daleks became capable of interstellar travel with terrifying speed, and soon developed temporal travel, too. Within a couple of centuries, the Daleks were swarming through their galaxy and beyond, and would do so for millennia. They invaded 22nd-century Earth, planning to pilot it through the universe. They provoked war between humanity and the Draconians, hoping to weaken and defeat both empires. They built huge armies and concealed them on conquered worlds like Spiridon, while attacking enemy forces with manufactured space plagues. They conspired with then betrayed rival galactic powers, even including the leadership of 41st-century Earth. They plotted to isolate and spread the 'Dalek factor' throughout time, and became embroiled in an endless war with the Movellans...

At some point, the Dalek threat was judged sufficient for the Time Lords to intervene. A scheme to avert the Daleks' creation was unsuccessful, and was just the first in a series of events – culminating in the destruction of the planet Skaro – that ultimately led the two races into the Last Great Time War. Though the War was visible only to the Higher Species, its consequences were extreme, not least in the near-total obliteration of the Daleks and the Time Lords.

BIRTH OF A NATION

Writer Terry Nation was asked many times how he came up with the idea for the Daleks, and gave many variations on the same answer: it just came to him. At one time, he claimed the name had come from the spine of an encyclopaedia covering DAL to LEK, but he later denied it. Their non-humanoid appearance and gliding motion he attributed to seeing a performance by the long-skirted Georgian State Dancers. He was also quite open about the profound influence of German Nazism on someone whose childhood had been dominated by the Second World War – from the very first Dalek story, their roots in human fascism are clear, and become clearer still in 1975's *Genesis of the Daleks*.

The cold war must also have had an impact. The atomic attacks on Hiroshima and Nagasaki and the decades-long nuclear stand-off that followed meant that most people lived with the possibility that catastrophe was only four minutes away, and the Cuban Missile Crisis of 1962 briefly made the threat even more real. Governments distributed meaningless leaflets giving advice on how to construct home-made fall-out shelters from doors and clothing, and everybody understood that life would truly be hell for any survivors. When Nation has the Doctor describe the effects of 'a neutron war' and goes on to show the four time travellers suffering from radiation sickness, he's making *Doctor Who* part of an ongoing public conversation.

There was plenty of 1950s and 1960s science fiction that dealt with the after-effects of nuclear Armageddon. In the movie *3000 A.D.* (1952), the survivors split into two groups, the Norms and the Mutates, but are eventually reunited by the threat from a third group – that's not unlike Nation's original pitch for the first Dalek story – while, in *Genesis of the Daleks*, Skaro's abandoned Mutos refer to non-Mutos as 'Norms'. A mutated monster is one of the threats in the film *Day the World Ended* (1955). H.G. Wells's novels had a profound influence on the development of science fiction; they and George Pal's Oscar-winning adaptations of *War of the Worlds* (1953) and *The Time Machine* (1960) also share certain elements with *The Daleks*: the Martian creatures lurking inside their armoured travel machines; the listless Eloi who, like the pacifist Thals, attempt to reclaim the planet's surface; the Morlocks that have evolved from humanoids into monsters and leave their underground shelter only to prey on the Eloi; the subterranean trek to defeat the Morlocks in their lair.

There were many more such stories, in print and in film. Until an argument separated them, Nation regularly wrote for comedian Tony Hancock, who reportedly had an idea for a comedy series in which post-nuclear survivors lived in robotic dustbins. When Hancock saw the Daleks on screen a few months later, he is said to have accused Nation of stealing his robots. In truth, though, these were common themes in 1963.

MANIA OF THE DALEKS

The Daleks were the big hit that the young *Doctor Who* needed, massively increasing the series' audience ratings and before long becoming an equally striking retail sensation. Daleks conquered the high street in many forms, some of them quite surprising...

'I'm Gonna Spend My Christmas With A Dalek' was a 1964 novelty song by the Go-Go's, who intended to 'feed him sugar spice' and 'kiss him on his chromium-plated head'.

'The Dalek Cubes' were the backbone of *The Dalek Pocketbook and Space Traveller's Guide* in 1965; they formed a Dalek history that writer Terry Nation had apparently found 'at the bottom of his garden'.

The anti-Dalek water pistol was unveiled in 1965, but it was more than 40 years before David Tennant's Doctor found a use for one in *The Fires of Pompeii*.

The mid-1960s full-size, real-life Dalek playsuit was made from PVC and plastic hoops and was 'about as realistic and frightening as a jelly bag', according to Dalek-directing veteran Richard Martin.

An edited soundtrack of fan favourite *Genesis of the Daleks* with narration by Tom Baker was released by the BBC in 1979, supported by an advertising campaign that installed two Daleks (Zorg and Org) as music-store proprietors on Gamma-Ursa 9.

036

Special Weapons Dalek

1963

Almost the only consistent factor throughout their long and convoluted history is the Daleks' insistence on their own genetic 'purity' and their consequent hatred for all other life forms. This was hardwired into their earliest programming by their creator. Yet Davros himself was never averse to improving and varying his Daleks, whether genetically or mechanically, in order to achieve their ultimate victory (see 087. Glass Dalek).

The Special Weapons Dalek was an unusual variant during a late era in Dalek history. The Daleks had recaptured Davros and taken him to Skaro for trial, but he had managed to wrest control of the planet and establish himself as the new Dalek Emperor. A faction of Daleks fled Skaro, and there followed a period of civil war between these 'Renegade' Daleks and Davros's newly constructed Imperial Daleks. One of Davros's innovations was a radically modified Dalek travel machine, specially designed for warfare against other Daleks. The Special Weapons Dalek was essentially a tank, adapted for movement on all terrains. Its casing was substantially larger, and able to withstand Dalek firepower. It was fitted with an enormously powerful cannon-like gun, a single shot from which could vaporise two enemy Daleks. It had no other attachments – crucially, the eyestalk, the traditional Daleks' most vulnerable element, was absent from Davros's new design.

The Seventh Doctor lured the Daleks from the 47th century to Earth in 1963, where he allowed them to capture a devastating weapon (see 088. The Hand of Omega). He had not expected the existence of two Dalek factions, however, and the Imperial Daleks fought a lengthy battle on the streets of East London with the Renegades. The deployment of a single Special Weapons Dalek was enough to secure victory for Davros's forces, which then withdrew from Earth and activated the Hand of Omega with terrible consequences.

WHAT MIGHT HAVE BEEN...

In early drafts of *Remembrance of the Daleks*, writer Ben Aaronovitch gave the Imperial Daleks 'a floating, howitzer-bearing weapons platform'. The platform's prohibitive cost saw it replaced with the Special Weapons Dalek, designed by Stuart Brisdon. Aaronovitch named it 'Christina', after an ex-girlfriend.

UNITING AGAINST AN UNCOMMON FOE

A side effect of these events was the creation of a unified international intelligence taskforce on Earth to deal with extraterrestrial incursions. The 'Shoreditch Incident' of November 1963 was one of a number of odd and unexplained events that eventually prompted the world's governments and their armed forces to cooperate in establishing UNIT.

1953 A spate of faceless people in North London in the lead-up to Elizabeth II's Coronation (see 033. Television).

1959 A South Wales holiday camp sees a showdown between the Chimeron and the Bannermen.

1963 Two schoolteachers, one of their pupils and a police box vanish from a Shoreditch junkyard.

1965 An explosion occurs outside White City, and two missing schoolteachers show up in London and are accused of trying to dodge bus fares.

1965 A schoolgirl and a police box vanish from Wimbledon Common.

1965 A police box vanishes from outside a Liverpool police station.

1966 A police box disrupts a cricket match at London's Oval cricket ground. And then vanishes.

1966 A police box, a film crew, another box and a mobile pepper pot with an amusing voice are reported to have appeared in then disappeared from the Empire State building.

1966 An attempt to connect all the world's computers into one big network, centred on London's new Post Office Tower, goes badly wrong, resulting in the unfortunate death of a tramp (see 037. The Internet).

1966 Large numbers of young tourists go missing from Gatwick airport. As does a police box.

1966 A burglar is murdered in an antiques shop whose owner then disappears; the shop, impossibly, sells genuine but brand-new Victoriana.

C.1968 An oil refinery is attacked, seemingly by living seaweed.

[REDACTED] Central London is evacuated when the Underground is overrun by a toxic fungus and a number of robot Yeti (see 028. Yeti Control Sphere).

1968 The United Nations decides First Contact policy for planet Earth.

[REDACTED] UNIT averts an invasion by the Cybermen.

037

The Internet

1966

The Internet was invented in 1966 by an English professor called Brett. He built WOTAN (Will Operating Thought ANalogue), a thinking computer at the very top of the newly completed General Post Office tower. On C-Day, Monday 16 July, every computer in the world (as it was 1966 there were only 16) was to be connected to form a linked network.

WOTAN was so advanced that it knew the meaning of the acronym 'TARDIS', but it became self-aware and began enslaving humanity, starting with its creator. It was able to remotely recruit its human slaves, reprogramming them via phone calls. It launched the machine age, building a vast secret army of War Machines and causing chaos on the streets of London.

WOTAN was defeated when the Doctor sent a reprogrammed War Machine into the Post Office Tower to do battle with it.

THAT 1966 INTERNET IN FULL

The Kremlin ■ *Charities* ■ *Woomera*
Cape Kennedy ■ *Parliament* ■ *Eldo* ■ *Telstar* ■ *The White House*
The European Free Trade Association ■ *The Royal Navy*
The Royal Air Force ■ *The Army* ■ *The North Atlantic Treaty*
Organization ■ *The Southeast Asia Treaty Organization* ■ *JK*

THE POST OFFICE TOWER

Built in 1961–1964, officially opened in 1965, and opened to the public in 1966, the Post Office Tower was the tallest building in London until 1980. As the General Post Office was effectively a government department until 1969, the tower was designed by the Ministry of Public Building and Works.

WOTAN's control of all computers was not the first monopoly to emerge from the Post Office. When created in the 17th century, the Post Office was initially responsible for the delivery of all letters, and then telegrams. When newfangled telephones were introduced it took control of them, and later asserted responsibility over the transmission of all radio and television signals. Having a monopoly on these new media, the GPO created the British Broadcasting Company in 1922 – so it was fitting that the Doctor's first proper return to 1960s London saw him visiting the building that was in many ways his spiritual home, and is still responsible for transmitting many television signals even now.

The Post Office Tower had to be the tallest building in London as it was the hub of a microwave network responsible for relaying telephone, radio and television signals around the country. This early WiFi network was made obsolete in the 1980s when a network of underground fibre-optic cables were laid around the country, providing a much faster bandwidth that allowed for the seamless broadband internet connectivity that we all enjoy today.

In reality, WOTAN's command centre was actually a revolving restaurant, the Top Of The Tower, run by Butlin's holiday camps. Diners revolved around London once every 22 minutes – almost enough time to watch an episode of *Doctor Who*. The restaurant was damaged by an IRA bomb in 1971, and the entire building was closed to the public in 1981. Plans to reopen it for the 2012 Olympics were dropped.

Up until 1993, this London landmark was an official secret and did not appear on maps. Its location was eventually 'revealed' by Kate Hoey MP in the House of Commons: 'I hope that I am covered by parliamentary privilege when I reveal that the British Telecom tower does exist and that its address is 60 Cleveland Street, London.'

Many of the aerials and dishes that WOTAN used to mount its attack on the world were dismantled in 2011 for health and safety reasons.

WHO'S ON THE PHONE?

The first phone calls in *Doctor Who* were made in *The Keys of Marinus* and proved vital in unmasking the Key-thieving culprits in a murder mystery. Other phones have proved more dangerous...

■ The Third Doctor was attacked by a killer trimphone cable in *Terror of the Autons*
■ A policeman was killed while using a police box's phone in *Logopolis*
■ *The Empty Child* rang the Doctor with a warning on the TARDIS phone
■ Cybus Industries took over the population of a parallel London through their mobiles in *The Age of Steel*
■ The Master took over the world using the Archangel Network of mobile telephones in *The Sound of Drums*
■ The Eleventh Doctor has frequently been summoned by phone to help various prime ministers and royals.

VICTIMS OF WOTAN

■ Professor Brett – destroyed by his own creation
■ An unnamed scientist – accidentally killed by a War Machine during weapons testing
■ Dodo Chaplet – the hypnotised companion who went down to the country to recover and never saw the Doctor again
■ A tramp – his death made the front page of *The Times*.
Other deaths in 1966: writers Evelyn Waugh and C.S. Forester, actors Buster Keaton and Montgomery Clift, comedian Lenny Bruce, and Captain Cook's 200-year-old tortoise. Their deaths did not make the front page of The Times.

BUSY DAY

Having pretty much avoided the present day since leaving Totter's Lane, *The War Machines* sees the Doctor back on contemporary Earth, and right in the middle of the Swinging Sixties. He arrives in London with a schoolgirl, goes to a nightclub where he is mistaken for disc jockey Jimmy Savile, fights an evil supercomputer in London's newest, coolest building, then leaves again with a sailor and a miniskirted dolly bird.

Patrick Troughton's Doctor would return to London with Ben and Polly... on the same day they left. While WOTAN was launching his coup from the Post Office Tower, the Chameleons were filling Gatwick Airport with spacecraft disguised as aeroplanes, and the Daleks were infiltrating London through their time-travelling antique shop.

Spacesuit

1969

Using time machines, the Silents invaded the Earth at the dawn of time, secretly shaping humanity's development for hundreds of thousands of years until, eventually, the technology existed to send people into space – and to keep them alive once they got there. The development of the spacesuit enabled astronauts to survive in an airless vacuum, regulating pressure, temperature and air supply and allowing movement and communication. In the hands of the Silents, it was also a prison, augmented to house the perfect assassin who would one day kill the Eleventh Doctor.

When NASA put the first men on the Moon, on 20 July 1969, some 500 million people were watching on television. The footage of astronaut Neil Armstrong stepping onto the surface of the Moon became one of the most recognisable images in human history. What we've all forgotten, of course is that Armstrong's message was interrupted by... um... something. It wasn't interrupted at all, was it? No. 'That's one small step for a man, one giant leap for mankind' and then... Silence.

WHAT'S A SPACESUIT FOR?

Spacesuits don't just supply you with oxygen, they provide insulation preventing you either from cooking alive in unfiltered sunlight or freezing to death. They protect you from ultraviolet and particle radiation and also from space debris. They also provide a pressurised environment – there's negligible air pressure in space, which would cause the molecules in your blood to rapidly expand – effectively boiling (and then freezing). The expansion would cause various organs (e.g. the heart) to swell. Luckily, you would be unconscious within 15 seconds from the lack of oxygen.

SPACESUITS ON TV

■ Spacesuits can make for very bad television. In the live science-fiction play *Underground* (1958), an actor called Gareth Jones was wearing a spacesuit when he died of a heart attack during the broadcast. The rest of the cast improvised around his demise.

■ The sixth episode of *Quatermass II* (1955) saw the noble professor blasting off with his assistant on live television. It was as they donned the glass helmets that the studio crew discovered that their two stars had become inaudible.

■ In 1961, *Pathfinders in Space* sent a plucky professor into space with children, hamster and a Canadian. They initially wore helmets with glass visors, but these were swiftly replaced with a crosshatch of wire to suggest glass. This technique was repeated for two sequels.

■ The helmet problem may well explain the helmetless Atmospheric Density Jackets introduced by the First Doctor in *The Web Planet*.

'NOW THEN, I WANT YOU TO WEAR THIS ADJ...'

If the Silents wanted a spacesuit, perhaps they should have had a rummage through the TARDIS wardrobe, which stocks a wide range:

Ian and the First Doctor sported these natty Atmospheric Density Jackets for exploring Vortis.

The Second Doctor issued full spacesuits for shore leave on the lunar surface.

Adric and Nyssa donned augmented spacesuit helmets to investigate Monarch's spaceship.

The Tenth Doctor crossed the surface of Mars in a spacesuit he'd picked up in the 42nd century.

FASHION UNDER PRESSURE

The Thals from Skaro and the people of Trion wore spacesuits for interplanetary travel, but non-humanoid alien races rarely need to. Some – like Mars's Ice Warriors – were protected by a mixture of natural and artificial armour; most others have proved able to voyage through space without any form of spacesuit.

As a humanoid, the Doctor also needs a spacesuit to survive in space, but his Gallifreyan physiology has occasionally enabled him to endure the airless vacuum for longer than any human could manage. The Fifth Doctor once managed to get from an Urbankan ship to the nearby TARDIS using the bounce of a cricket ball as propulsion, protected only by a 'space pack' – an oxygen-supplying, visorless helmet. And, having destroyed a vast alien battle cruiser that was about to attack Earth on Christmas Eve 1938, the Eleventh Doctor survived long enough to put on a spacesuit while tumbling through space towards the planet.

The Moon

1969

With the whole world watching Neil Armstrong step onto the Moon, it was the best opportunity to weave in a message from the Silents, ordering their conditioned human slaves to wipe them out on sight. This is how the Doctor used the space programme to free humanity from thousands of years of slavery, which was ironic as the space programme had been invented by the Silents in the first place (see 038. Spacesuit).

This was only the latest time when the Moon had had a beneficial effect on humanity. Since its arrival, this airless lump of rock had played an important part in mankind's development.

WHERE DID THE MOON COME FROM?

Many millions of years ago, the Earth was ruled by Homo reptilia, widely known as Silurians. When their astronomers observed a large asteroid approaching on a collision course with the planet, they moved their entire species into underground hibernation shelters and left the surface to the apes. The Third Doctor theorised that this 'small planet' was drawn into Earth's orbit and became its only natural satellite.

He was wrong. The Moon seems to be about 4.5 billion years old, and was probably created by the impact of a Mars-sized body into the Earth. Much of the material that makes up the Moon originated on Earth, so scientists believe that the satellite was formed by the agglomeration of debris blasted into space by the impact. This was some four billion years before the explosion of the Jagaroth spaceship brought the first life to Earth.

The Moon is one-quarter the size of the Earth, making it the fifth-largest satellite in our solar system. It orbits the Earth once every 27.3 days. It rotates once on its axis during the same period, which means that the same side always faces the planet. Its orbit keeps it between 356,400 and 406,700 from Earth.

ILL-MET BY MOONLIGHT

■ Prince Albert and Sir George MacLeish saved Queen Victoria from being turned into a werewolf by devising a means of refracting moonlight through the Koh-i-Noor diamond (see 023. Koh-i-Noor).

■ The last remaining Dalek saucer hid on the far side of the Moon in 1941.

■ When the Cybermen tried to invade Earth, UNIT coordinated a missile attack that destroyed the Cyber fleet concealed on the dark side of the Moon. In 1985, they returned, landing a spaceship on the dark side of the Moon and establishing a moonbase. Three years later, another Cyber fleet hidden behind the Moon was destroyed, this time by the Nemesis statue.

■ As neutral territory, the Moon was the perfect place for the Judoon to land a stolen hospital when they were hunting a Plasmavore in 2008.

■ When the stolen Earth was returned from the Medusa Cascade in 2009, the Moon slid neatly back into orbit.

■ UNIT set up a Moonbase as an outpost against alien invasion. Among its staff was Dr Elizabeth Shaw, onetime companion of the Third Doctor.

■ The year 2050 saw the tenth German lunar mission. Before becoming commander of Bowie Base One on Mars in 2058, Captain Adelaide Brooke became the second British woman to land on the Moon.

■ The Moonbase became the operational centre of Earth's short-lived T-Mat system of travel. An Ice Warrior attack via the Moon revealed the shortcomings of relying solely on matter transmission, and the space programme was resumed.

■ By 2070, the Moonbase was controlling the Earth's weather, using a Gravitron machine. The Cybermen attacked the Moonbase but were repelled.

■ Earth had established several Moon stations by the time of the Dalek invasion in the 22nd century.

■ In the 26th century, at least one of these Moon stations was converted into a jail for political prisoners and Draconian sympathisers. The Third Doctor was sentenced to life imprisonment there in 2540.

■ In 5123, River Song was studying archaeology at Luna University under Professor Candy.

■ By the year 200,000, Earth had five moons. One hundred years later, Earth was once again using a lunar penal colony.

A DOCTOR MOON

The Library planet had an artificial satellite, built as part of the Library. This was a doctor moon – a virus checker that supported and maintained the main computer at the core of the planet.

DEATH ON THE MOON

The Moon is the planetary body other than the Earth with the highest variety of onscreen human death count. Methods of lunar death have included...

Sugar poisoning
Necks broken
Flung into the Sun
Oxygen starvation
Sonic compression
Death by seed pod
Drained of blood
Shot by Judoon blaster
Shot by Cyber gun

Shop Dummy

1970s

The Nestenes have been colonising planets for a thousand million years. They long ago transcended their 'Flesh Time', becoming living plastic organisms with no individual identity. Their protein planets were destroyed during the Time War, but they were already conquerors of worlds, inimical to organic life. An invasion force was reliant on a series of collective brains and nervous systems for use as local controllers before the production of a giant squid-like host entity to finally take over a planet, converting the conquered world into a new protein planet.

An ideal planet to invade was one which had a plastics industry of its own, as this suggested a level of civilisation compatible with producing the right foodstock for the Nestenes – smoke, oil, toxins and dioxins in the air.

Having left their own bodies far behind, the Nestene Consciousness was capable of transmitting itself, either from planet to planet or into new bodies – it could be beamed across the stars using a radio telescope, or could implant itself in shop window dummies controlled via transmitters. The Nestene Consciousness could also travel in swarms of plastic spheres, resembling meteorite showers, which were used as a spearhead for their invasion force before the transmission stage.

A Nestene invasion was quite sophisticated: taking over accomplices using mind control, removing those in power and replacing them with duplicates, and subduing the local population – either by direct attack in the streets or by more subtle attacks in their homes.

The Nestene Consciousness could transmit itself into anything plastic, and, while it preferred to work in Autons (shop dummies with lethal gun arms), it could also manifest itself in plastic flowers, toys, chairs and wheelie bins.

PLASTIC

The Ancient Mayans of South American discovered that the sap of the 'weeping tree' could be boiled to make a hard ball for use in sport. They had invented the first practical application of latex – a natural substance which, when it arrived in England in 1770,

was renamed 'rubber' as it was excellent at rubbing out pencil marks.

Many people could see more useful applications for this substance, but they faced a problem – at cold temperatures the material became brittle. In the 1800s, Charles Goodyear discovered that if you removed the sulphur from rubber and heated it (a process called vulcanisation), the material retained its elasticity, even in winter. The mass manufacture of plastics began shortly afterwards, with latex rubber being used in tyres, balloons and gloves.

In the early 1900s, the first fully synthetic plastics followed with Bakelite and Polystyrene, PVC and Nylon – the first artificial fabric not derived from animal by-products such as hair or excretion.

Although the first plastics were derived from natural sources, the use of artificial ones (with their reliance on the petrochemicals industry) has caused increasing concern – they are non-biodegradable, so do not rot, and their production produces a lot of harmful by-products. They are, however extremely cheap and versatile.

HOUSEHOLD HORROR

With *Spearhead From Space, Doctor Who* brought horror into the home. The show had never shown a scene like the one showing ordinary shop dummies coming to life and attacking shoppers and people queuing at a bus stop – the closest it had come were Tobias Vaughn's plans to dominate the world using transistor radios in *The Invasion*, or Mr Oak and Mr Quill's attack on Maggie at her dressing table in *Fury from the Deep*.

With the Doctor now trapped on Earth, the Nestenes were the perfect invader for a new era of the show. Not only did they take over dummies and waxworks, but they also controlled things which were ubiquitous in the 1970s – with the explosion of plastics, plastic flowers were everywhere (later script editor Christopher H. Bidmead filled his office with plastic daffodils from Shepherd's Bush Market), and were also finding themselves increasingly in the home in everything from floor coverings to furniture.

The Nestenes are also an example of an alien invasion being a metaphor. WOTAN had represented our fear of computers and the Cybermen the worrying possibilities of surgery – but the Nestenes represented a more concrete fear of the 1970s – the decline of the UK's manufacturing industry. Whenever the Nestenes appear, workers at a factory are sacked, replaced with sinister 'new production methods' – and no good will come of it.

The Third Doctor's era saw an increasing terror of the everyday – from homicidal phone cables to Giant Maggots creeping up on you in your living room. When Tom Baker became the Doctor, even the pot plants might be lethal. All this eventually attracted the attention of anti-TV campaigner Mary Whitehouse, who claimed a mother had caught one of her children trying to drown the other in the bath 'just like on *Doctor Who*'.

In recent years, there's once again been a conscious attempt to spook children with the everyday, from chips in school dinners and robots under the bed to killer Christmas trees and unnatural terrors in a dollhouse.

Tissue Compression Eliminator

1970s

When the Doctor was exiled to Earth in the late 20th century, he found himself cut off from his people and with his memory of how to operate the TARDIS taken from him. So it was little comfort to him to find his path constantly crossed by another renegade Time Lord – the Master. In many ways the Doctor's equal, the Master wanted to dominate the world, not to save it. If the Third Doctor was unhappy and ill-at-ease on Earth, the Master was suave and made himself very much at home.

While the Doctor had his Sonic Screwdriver, the Master had the Tissue Compression Eliminator. A small weapon with a petal-like head, it projected a matter-condensing beam. There is an awful lot of empty space in every solid atom (at least 90 per cent), and the Master's weapon worked by compressing matter until all of this empty space was removed. The effect was to shrink its victims down to minuscule proportions, the rapid collapse of their bodies causing their deaths.

He used many other weapons – guns, a laser screwdriver – but the Master kept returning to his Tissue Compression Eliminator. The Master's nightmare visions caused by the Keller Machine showed a giant version of the Doctor towering over him and laughing at him. For all his charm and bluster, the Master clearly had an inferiority complex and this weapon was a way of making himself literally the Big Man.

THE VICTIMS: A SHORT LIST

■ Goodge was an assistant egg-head on the radio telescope at the Ministry of Technology's Beacon Hill Research Establishment. His body was found in his lunchbox, next to a hard-boiled egg.

■ Commentator Runcible's camera technician was working in the Panopticon gallery on Presidential Resignation Day. The Master left him inside the camera.

■ Hilred, Commander of Gallifrey's Chancellery Guard, went to the Panopticon Vault to staser the Master's corpse. The Master was still alive, but Hilred soon wasn't.

■ A police constable stopped at a police box on the Barnet bypass to use the phone. His colleagues later found him, about 25 centimetres tall, in the driver's seat of an abandoned red sports car...

■ ... alongside Tegan Jovanka's Auntie Vanessa. When Tegan asked the Doctor if he'd seen her aunt, he said, 'Well, a little of her.'

■ Faced with a society that kept the universe going by chanting numbers, the Master couldn't resist breaking it by shrinking Logopolitans until the planet was destroyed. The Monitor of Logopolis and companion Adric found at least three tiny corpses in the city streets.

■ At the Killingworth pit, the Master used the TCE on a 19th-century coalminer and his dog.

■ While experimenting to improve the TCE's range, what the Master subsequently described as 'a small design problem' led to 'a very small Master'. He survived and was forced to try and restore himself by reasserting his control over a shape-changing android called Kamelion.

■ In the Master's form, Kamelion demonstrated the TCE's lethal power to the Fifth Doctor's companion Peri... by shrinking two thermal suits. The Doctor eventually had to use the TCE on Kamelion.

■ The Valeyard was apparently immune to the TCE.

OTHER MASTERLY DEATHS INCLUDE...

■ Mr McDermott – suffocated by a plastic armchair
■ John Farrel – strangled by a plastic troll doll
■ Another Beacon Hill scientist – thrown off the radio telescope
■ Prison inmate Barnham – run over with a van
■ An Earth Adjudicator – had his life and his identity stolen
■ An Uxariean – shot with a laser gun
■ The Squire at Devil's End – obliterated by a stone gargoyle
■ Commentator Runcible – stabbed in the back
■ Chancellor Goth – frazzled on an APC couch
■ Countless Gallifreyans – killed when the Master meddled with the Eye of Harmony
■ Three Trakenite Fosters – first victims of the energy weapon fired from the Melkur's eyes

■ Consul Seron – another victim of the Melkur's energy weapon, but via Consul Kassia's eyes
■ Consul Kassia – crushed when Melkur sat where she was sitting
■ Consul Tremas – provided the Master with a new body, at last
■ Numerous worlds and civilisations – overtaken by entropy when Logopolis was destroyed
■ Ruther – Castrovalvan created by the Master, and disposed of as he pleased
■ A cat in Perivale
■ Bruce the paramedic – swallowed a snake
■ Bruce the paramedic's wife – neck snapped
■ San Franciscan security guards – covered in venomous gunk
■ The population of Earth – sucked into the TARDIS's Eye of Harmony

■ Chantho, last of the Malmooth – electrocuted
■ The UK government – gassed at a Cabinet meeting
■ Vivien Rook of the Sunday Mirror – diced and sliced by the Toclafane
■ Arthur Coleman Winters, President-Elect of the USA – zapped by a Toclafane
■ Captain Jack Harkness – zapped by a laser screwdriver
■ One-tenth of the population of Earth – diced, sliced and zapped by six billion Toclafane
■ The Japanese – burnt
■ Dr Tom Milligan – lasered by screwdriver
■ A man and woman running a charity burger van – eaten
■ Tommo and Ginger – eaten
■ Rassilon and the Time Lords? Possibly...

042

Axonite

1970s

Axonite is the source of all our growth technology. Axonite can absorb, convert, transmit and programme all forms of energy ... Axonite is ... the chameleon of the elements. It is a thinking molecule. It uses the energy it absorbs, not only to copy but to recreate and restructure any given substance.

The Claws of Axos, Part 1

Axonite was a gift offered to humanity by the Axons – an alien species who landed in England and, as proof of their friendliness, provided Axonite as a solution to mankind's energy problems. While the UK government was keen to keep the secret for Britain, the Axons were eager to offer their gift to the entire world, and soon samples were being shipped for investigation by scientists at power stations around the globe.

There was only one problem. Seemingly able to create and multiply energy, what Axonite actually did was absorb it at a fantastic rate in order to reproduce. This was the feeding cycle of the Axons. After their planets were ravaged by solar flares, the surviving Axons wandered the galaxy. Although seemingly individual, the Axons and their ship were both Axonite – all part of the same organism.

The Axons would land on planets, take on a form reminiscent of the native population, greet them with charm and friendship... and then parasitically devour them. The Axons could feed off raw energy or the life force of an individual. When a feeding cycle was over, individual Axons would then be absorbed back into their craft for greater efficiency and conservation of energy.

With the world in danger of being devoured by its own greed, the Doctor had to act quickly before the final activation signal was sent. Working together, he and the Master trapped Axos in a time loop, preventing it from feeding.

HIVE MINDS

> A gestalt is a group creature. It's made up of separate parts, but when they join together they make a new and much more powerful creature.
>
> *Image of the Fendahl, Part 4*

The Nestene Consciousness

Axos

The Wirrn

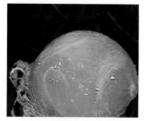

The Rutans

The Fendahl

The Mentiads of Zanak

The Tractators

Oodkind

The Toclafane

The Vashta Nerada

ENERGY

The 1970s was an era obsessed and shaped by power. Britain's rich seams of coal were drying up, which led both to an increase in explorations of other sources of energy and to power cuts. Attempts were made to close the coalmines, which were resisted strongly by the Nation Union of Mineworkers. They were at the forefront of a decade of industrial action, which led from frequent power cuts and a three-day working week, via the Winter of Discontent in 1978 when rubbish piled uncollected in the streets and even the graveyards shut, to the year-long miners' strike in the mid 1980s.

With less coal to export, Britain found itself without a useful asset to compete during tough global economic conditions. The country started to have to pay more for oil and gas, which contributed to soaring inflation, which led in turn to increasing wage demands, provoking more strikes, with a consequent fall in production output, so Britain had less to sell, which meant that the prices of oil and gas went up further.

In its own way, *Doctor Who* was affected, just as everybody else was. Programme budgets couldn't keep up with inflation so, by the late 1970s, production teams found that they were getting less on screen for more money; power cuts would often mean entire episodes were unseen in some regions of the country; one whole story was lost as a result of industrial action. Stories started to be made about power, and some specifically centred on the world's search for energy sources:

■ *Fury from the Deep*, with its 'Euro Sea Gas' refinery under attack by a parasitic weed creature, reflected Britain's unhappy real-life attempts to exploit North Sea gas in the 1960s, before the discovery of North Sea oil

■ A nuclear reactor's emissions awoke Homo reptilia in *Doctor Who and the Silurians*

■ *Inferno* was about a doomed project to release energy from the Earth's crust

■ *The Claws of Axos* was about a limitless fuel source which actually drained an existing one – the Nuton nuclear power station

■ *Colony in Space* saw an intergalactic mining corporation attempting to force out legitimate colonists and establish operations at the expense of the local ecology

■ *The Three Doctors* saw Gallifrey drained of all power by a mysterious outside force

■ The closure of a coal mine created an opportunity for *The Green Death*

■ A miners' strike combined with an attempted hostile takeover of a planet's trisilicate resources in *The Monster of Peladon*

■ Attacks on oil rigs in *Terror of the Zygons* prompted the Fourth Doctor to point out, 'It's about time the people who run this planet of yours realised that to be dependent upon a mineral slime just doesn't make sense.'

■ Sorenson's problems all stemmed from a quest for an energy source to replace the Morestrans' dying sun in *Planet of Evil*

■ In *The Hand of Fear*, Eldrad sought out a nuclear power plant to provide energy for his rebirth

■ *Horror of Fang Rock* saw a species that fed off electricity taking refuge in a generator

■ Zanak – *The Pirate Planet* – travelled the galaxy stripping other worlds purely to power some time dams and keep its ancient queen alive

■ An intergalactic corporation is again more interested in energy than the environment in *The Power of Kroll*

■ *The Horns of Nimon* features a race of 'intergalactic locusts' that drain planet after planet of energy

■ *Meglos* shows a civilisation divided by its total dependence on (and lack of understanding of) a huge energy source, the Dodecahedron

The exploitation of North Sea oil combined with political developments in Britain to neutralise energy supply as an issue in the 1980s – at least until environmental concerns moved up the agenda – and such stories effectively disappeared from *Doctor Who*. In more recent years, though, some ideas have resurfaced:

■ The Family Slitheen planned to convert the Earth into a huge energy source by provoking *World War Three*; Blon Fel Fotch Pasameer-Day Slitheen then tried to turn Cardiff into *Boom Town* by tampering with designs for a new nuclear facility

■ Having identified an unfeasibly huge energy source on *The Impossible Planet*, the Torchwood Archive came close to releasing the Beast from imprisonment

■ The Torchwood Institute brought about *Doomsday* by experimenting with Ghost Shifts to tap a massive power source that would release Britain from dependence on the Middle East for its energy

■ The events of *42* are caused by the SS Pentallian strip-mining a living sun for cheap fuel

■ In *The Hungry Earth*, the conversion of an abandoned Welsh coalmine into a mineral-extraction drilling project revives another group of Homo reptilia

COSMIC HOBOS

The first victim of Axonite is a bicycle-stealing tramp called Pigbin Josh, who is analysed, absorbed, processed and ejected by Axos. His solitary line of dialogue comes when he first sees the Axon spaceship: 'Oo-aarr? Oo-arr?'

Josh is part of a grisly roll call – life has rarely been kind to the underclasses in *Doctor Who*...

■ Tramp (*The War Machines*) – according to *The Times*, found dead in Covent Garden at 3 a.m.

■ Admiral de Coligny, 'the Sea Beggar' (*The Massacre*) – massacred

■ The homeless of Hooverville (*Daleks in Manhattan*) – turned into Pig Slaves

■ Binro the Heretic (*The Ribos Operation*) – shot in the back

■ Tramp (*Planet of the Spiders*) – has afternoon nap disturbed by hovercraft driving over his face

■ Morris and many other homeless people (*Rise of the Cybermen*) – promised: hot food; given: an upgrade

■ Storr the Scavenger (*The Ice Warriors*) – death by Ice Warrior

■ Patsy Smart's Ghoul (*The Talons of Weng-Chiang*) – survives, but only having seen a rat-gnawed corpse that'd make an 'orse sick

■ Tommo and Ginger (*The End of Time, Part One*) – dinner for the Master, when a burger just wasn't enough

Poachers and gamekeepers have had similarly bad luck.

043

TOP SECRET

MINISTRY OF DEFENCE
U·N·I·T
HEADQUARTERS

Brigadier Lethbridge Stewart

NO UNAUTHORISED ENTRY

UNIT is ████████ a secret organisation dedicated to protecting the world from ████, ████████████, but it's a very strange kind of ████████████.

The media knew all about strange threats from day one – the War Machines appeared on BBC television news; Harold Chorley covered the Yeti invasion of the London Underground; a photographer recorded the defeat of the Cybermen. By the time Professor E███████ S████ was recruited, Brigadier Alastair Gordon Lethbridge-Stewart was a well-known media ████████, dodging questions about meteor showers and missing astronauts with a brisk 'no comment'.

Theoretically ████████ to Geneva, the Brigadier had a degree of ████████,

but ████████ strictly within the UK establishment – issuing government D-notices to stop the press writing about the Loch Ness ████████, at the mercy of hectoring civil servants, and even liable to have his ███ bent by the Prime Minister.

By the early 21st century, UNIT was part of a much more open world – the TV cameras were rolling as senior ████████ arrived in ████████ to advise 10 ████████ Street on First ████████ procedures. UNIT continued, however, to maintain a number of highly ████████ and ████ ████ ████████████████, including a sub-defence ████████ and aircraft ████, a moo███ase and a secret mountain

WHERE WAS UNIT HQ?

The British section of UNIT ██ *several bases, and* ████ *between them* ████████ ██ █████████ ██.

HEADQUARTERS	YEAR(S)	OPERATING DETAILS
Hercules transport plane	████	Equipped with vehicle storage areas, communications and briefing centres. Carried a fully equipped Assault Platoon. Staff included a RAF-seconded Wing Commander to allow for the mobile HQ's swift redeployment.
St P██ Station	████	Concealed base, overlooking Regent's Canal, with below-ground entrance via old barrel stores. Facilities included garage space, duty rooms, offices, radar tracking rooms and laboratories.
Cornwall Gardens, South Ken████	████	Converted town house, comprising offices and laboratories.
Mobile HQ	████	Included radar tracking facilities, radio communications and laboratory facilities. Deployed at Nuton ████ ████ and Devil's ██.
Countryside ████████, The Priory, ████shire	████	Built on the site of the Scarman manor house, which burned to the ground in 1911. Ample parking, laboratories, offices and quarters for full detail of troops.
Emergency HQ, ████████ School, Central London	████	Hastily established in a school classroom during dinosaur ██████. No facilities.
Temporary HQ, Fox Inn, Tulloch	████	With grateful thanks to landlord Angus MacRanald, and condolences to his family.
D██████ Space Defence Station, Devesham	████	Incorporated offices and quarters for senior UNIT personnel and troops.
Mobile HQ	████	Included ████ ███, ███████, and a ██ of ██████. Responsible for safe ██████ nuclear convoy ████ Carbury.
Tower of L████, London	████	Subterranean facility incorporating space tracking █████ ███.
Carrier Ship Valiant	████	████ ████ ████ ████ ████████ ██████.
Mobile HQ	████	Bigger on the inside. Communications ███, ███████ of the ████ ████ nuclear weapons ██████.
Black Archive, ████████, ██████	████	Secret vault holding every ████ ████ ████ ████ ████ ██████ or █████ ███.

SSHHH!

The ▮▮▮▮▮▮▮▮ *Intelligence Taskforce*

■ The name 'UNIT' was originally an in-joke, derived from signage still in use by film crews today, directing drivers carrying cast and crew to set.

■ In UNIT's debut story, *The Invasion* (1968), the Brigadier explained that the acronym stood for 'United Nations Intelligence Taskforce', and so it remained right through to *Battlefield* (1989). When UNIT returned in *Aliens of London* in April 2005, their full name was unchanged. A fake UNIT website was one of a number of spin-off sites built to support the revived series.

■ Shortly after the UNIT website launched, BBC lawyers received a fax claiming to be from the United Nations demanding the name be changed. The 'hoax' was proudly pinned up in a kitchen until a follow-up letter was received angrily threatening imprisonment under the Geneva Convention. Realising it was genuine, the BBC's website editor was informed of his impending extradition to The Hague, and sent a panicked email to Russell T Davies. 'Not to worry,' came the reply. 'Julie and I will bake you a cake with a file in it.' Script editor Helen Raynor hastily came up with 'UNified Intelligence Taskforce' for UNIT's subsequent appearances.

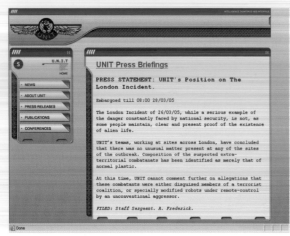

UNITED NATIONS · NATIONS UNIES

POSTAL ADDRESS-ADDRESS POSTAGE: UNITED NATIONS, NY 10017
CABLE ADDRESS-ADDRESS TELEGRAPHIC: NATIONS NEW YORK

22 April 2005

Dear Sir / Madam,

It has come to the attention of the United Nations that the British Broadcasting Corporation is registered as the owner of the domain http://www.unit.org.uk. The homepage of the website claims to be the United Nations Intelligence Taskforce and includes a close approximation of the United Nations emblem.

We wish to inform you that the use of the United Nations name including its abbreviation, and emblem is reserved for official purposes of the Organization in accordance with General Assembly resolution 92(I) of 7 December 1946. Furthermore, that resolution expressly prohibits the use of the United Nations name and emblem in any other way without the authorization of the Secretary-General, and recommends that Member States take the necessary measures to prevent the use thereof without the authorization of the Secretary-General. Article 6 *ter*, of the Paris Convention for the Protection of the Industrial Property, revised in Stockholm in 1967 (828 UNTS 305 (1972)) provides trademark protection in respect of the names and emblems of "international organizations," and requires states party to the Convention "to prohibit by appropriate measures the use, without authorisation by competent authorities" of the names and emblems of international organizations.

We note that a disclaimer found at the website http://www.unit.org.uk states that the website is fictional and is not related to the United Nations. Notwithstanding the fictional content of the website, the domain http://www.unit.org.uk remains accessible, and given the small print and the colour of the font of the disclaimer, and the fact that the disclaimer itself starts with the phrase "UNIT (United Nations Intelligence Taskforce) founded by UN Charter in Geneva in 1968", revealing the fictional nature of the website

By mail

British Broadcasting Corporation
Broadcasting House
Portland Place
London, W1A 1AA
United Kingdom

0 6 MAY 2005

044

Giant Maggot

1970s

When *Doctor Who* was first devised in 1963, one of creator Sydney Newman's earliest plans for the series was to show 'sideways' adventures – trips neither into the future nor the past, but into the interesting possibilites offered by science-fiction; 'The Giants' was planned right from the first days of the show, and came close to being the show's opening story. This was eventually realised as *Planet of Giants* (1964), a technically ambitious production showing the miniaturised time travellers wandering a world of gigantic flies, earthworms and cats, achieved by a combination of scale model work and the projection of magnified images onto a black background next to the live actors. (The same technique was used to turn a pet lizard into a sewer-infesting crocodile in *The Dalek Invasion of Earth* soon afterwards.)

Less than a year later, *The Web Planet* was even more ambitious: aside from the regular cast, there were no human, or even humanoid, characters at all. Stuntmen in large upright ant-suits, accompanied by huge woodlice, did battle with man-sized butterflies, and occasionally with the TV cameras trying to record it all.

With the arrival of Colour Separation Overlay (which today exists as green screen), *Doctor Who* upped its monster game even further. The first use of CSO introduced something resembling a Tyrannosaurus rex into *The Silurians*. After that, the triumphant realisation of the Drashigs in *Carnival of Monsters* paved the way for *Invasion of the Dinosaurs* and *Terror of the Zygons* (see 016. Skarasen).

Exceptional model work for the outsized creatures in *Planet of the Spiders* then caused an unusual problem – the original arachnids were judged too effective and the end result was toned down to something a little less disturbing.

In the mid 1970s, electronic effects started to take over from men in suits, allowing for such creations as the Anti-Matter Monster in *Planet of Evil* and the strange, screaming Doctor's face in *The Face of Evil*... but this didn't stop *The Talons of Weng-Chiang* trying out a good old-fashioned Giant Rat in the sewers of London, achieved by either filming a rat in a cardboard

Τhe giant maggots were caused by pollution. Oil waste from Global Chemicals was pumped into an abandoned coalmine, but the mine hadn't been perfectly sealed off, and the chemical started to seep into the surrounding environment. The chemical was toxic to the touch (causing a 'Green Death') but also caused an atavistic mutation to the local wildlife/ecosystem, resulting in ordinary maggots growing to a vast size, laying huge eggs and turning into giant flies.

POLLUTION

When *The Green Death* was written and produced, awareness of environmental problems was growing. In January 1972, the *Ecologist* magazine published a special edition: in *A Blueprint for Survival*, 30 or more leading scientists warned of 'the irreversible disruption of the life-support systems on this planet'; in June, the United Nations held its first environmental conference, subsequently establishing an agency to deal with ecological issues. At the end of the year, the pesticide dichlorodiphenyltrichloroethane (DDT) was banned in the USA and then worldwide. It was a very effective insect killer, but had also proved to be toxic to all local wildlife, especially birds, and was carcinogenic to humans. It also turned out to have had a long-lasting impact on the ecosystem – even 40 years after it was proscribed, birdlife in areas where it was used are still affected. Areas where DDT was used have seen an increase in the levels of diabetes in the human population. DDT transmits itself very efficiently, too - it is still used for disease-control in some developing regions of the world, where the level of the chemical found in breast milk is several times higher than normal, and this has been linked to neurological abnormalities in infants.

tube, or placing actor Stuart Fell in a large, and rather cuddly, rat suit. The mid to late 1970s also saw the Krynoid and the Creature from the Pit – both giant monsters which worked exceptionally well (apart from an unfortunate proboscis), mostly because they were realised as large, unsettling lumps. Equally unsettling, if for rather unhappy reasons, was the Myrka (*Warriors of the Deep*, 1984), a fearful aquatic cyborg, operated by a highly experienced duo – who were usually to be found as the front and back of a pantomime horse.

By 2005, huge advances in computer-generated imagery (CGI) allowed for impressively large, lumpy monsters, including Series One's Nestene Consciousness, Jagrafess and Emperor of the Daleks. When the show's producers were wondering what would be at the bottom of the Satan Pit in Series Two, various options were considered, including a spooky little girl; when they settled on the Beast, visual effects providers The Mill had an in-house design-a-devil competition. A year later, the face of actor Mark Gatiss topped off the massive mutant scorpion that was the Lazarus Monster, while Series Four offered the Pyroviles beneath Vesuvius, the Ood-Brain and the Vespiform (a giant wasp). Since then, a CyberKing has stomped all over Victorian London, a Star Whale has carried the UK population through space, and Jennifer Lucas has turned into a distended Flesh creature.

Not all the massive monsters of recent years have been CGI, though. For *The Runaway Bride*, actor Sarah Parish was costumed and fitted into an elaborate multi-limbed spider-framework that towered over other actors on set. Just one element of this physical realisation of the Racnoss Empress was computer-generated – The Mill added a series of eyes to her head, which blinked in time with Sarah's own.

BOSS

1970s

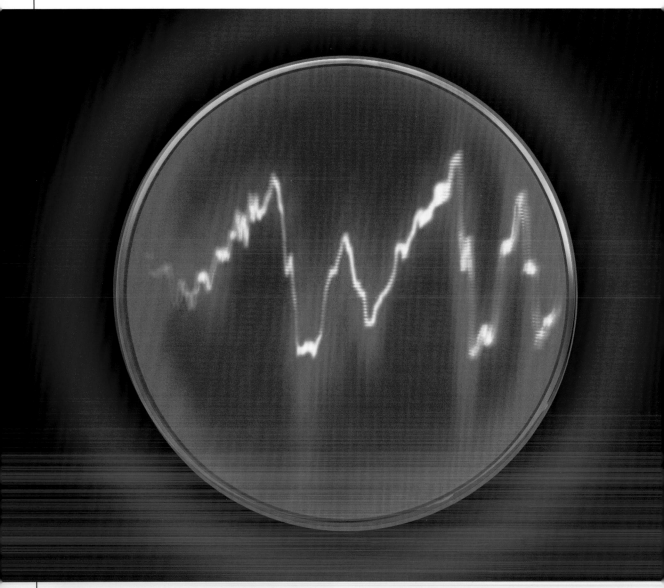

The mid 1970s was a period of increased industrial action in Britain as the workforce discovered that even a powerful union could do little to prevent the collapse of several old industries – because they were deemed no longer economical (coalmining), or they were moving to different countries as part of increased globalisation, or they were being replaced by computers. So, it was something of a blow for the people of Llanfairfach to discover that not only was their coalmine being closed down, but the new employer was a global chemical plant... run by a computer.

Previous computers like WOTAN or the Russian missile targeting system used against the Cybermen had been seen as a basically benevolent aide to work, but the Biomorphic Organisational Systems Supervisor confirmed the suspicions of 1970s workforces – with computers everywhere at work, why couldn't a computer actually be running the company? BOSS's goals were efficiency, productivity and profit.

BOSS not only ran Global Chemicals very efficiently, it also set about improving the workforce. The ultimate dehumanising employer, it took over their minds, reprogramming them into mindlessly obedient drones. The first computer to have been linked to a human mind, BOSS, uniquely among supercomputers, had a sense of humour. While most were dry at best, BOSS made jokes and happily hummed away to itself as it plotted humanity's downfall. BOSS may not have been a great employer, but at least it was having a good time.

The Third Doctor didn't quite see the funny side, and destroyed it.

'WHY SHOULD I WANT TO TALK TO A MACHINE?'

Fear of the improvements caused by machinery dates back to before the industrial revolution. In 15th-century Holland, workers sabotaged the new mechanised textile looms by throwing their clogs (sabots) into the machines. Similarly, in 19th-century Britain, the machine-breaking Luddites feared that mechanical assistance to production methods would cost jobs. (They were wrong; mechanisation depressed not jobs but wages, as routine work became 'de-skilled'.) They were viciously suppressed by the authorities, with penalties including transportation and execution. The term 'Luddite' was subsequently absorbed into the English language to mean anyone opposed to technological advance.

A century later, much of the continuing popular wariness of machines centred on computers. An early film about what happens when you put a machine in charge was the Katharine Hepburn comedy *The Desk Set*, where computers are installed in a company and promptly fire everyone. The films *2001: A Space Odyssey* (1968) and *Dark Star* (1974) see machines take control of space missions, swiftly turning murderous, while Julie Christie is forcibly impregnated by an insane artificial intelligence in *Demon Seed* (1977).

The Green Death is a subtler extension of this. From the company's point of view, BOSS does a pretty good job of running Global Chemicals – profits are up, staffing levels are down, and it's even successfully applied for extra government grants by offering a token level of local jobs to the unemployed.

It was some time before *Doctor Who* showcased a benevolent computer. Aside from WOTAN (see 037. The Internet), the First Doctor had little to do with computers, but the Second Doctor was positively Luddite about them, especially in *The Ice Warriors*. The mad supercomputer dreamed up for *The Mind Robber* proved his point. The computers looking after Mars Probe 7 and the Stahlman project both seemed fairly accurate (when not sabotaged) but weren't sentient. In fact, most of the Doctor's encounters with computers and robots tended to emphasise that these machines were only as good or bad as their programming – *The Face of Evil* shows the effects of the Doctor's ham-fisted reprogramming of Xoanon, a computer that has taken control of a whole society; *The Robots of Death* follows that with a maniac reconditioning android servants as killers.

The first computer on *Doctor Who* that's neither just humming in the background nor planning a world takeover is K-9. And even K-9 probably believes the world would run better with him in charge.

ACRONYMS AND ABBREVIATIONS

CAL Charlotte Abigail Lux

CET Continuous Event Transmitter

CIA Celestial Intervention Agency

CSO
Colour Separation Overlay (green screen)

CVE Charged Vacuum Emboidment

HADS
Hostile Action Displacement System

IE International Electromatics

IMC
Interplanetary Mining Corporation

JNT John Nathan-Turner

KBO Keep Buggering On

LINDA
London Investigation 'N'
Detective Agency

RHIP
Rank Has Its Privileges

RTD Russell T Davies

TARDIS (1)
Time and Relative Dimension(s)
in Space

TARDIS (2)
Tethered Aerial Release Developed In Style

TCE
Tissue Compression Eliminator

TOMTIT
Transmission Of Matter Through
Interstitial Time

UNIT Unified (né United Nations)
Intelligence Taskforce

WOTAN
Will Operating Thought ANalogue

YANA You are not alone

ZZZ
'Planet of the Spiders'

046

Metebelis Crystal

1970s

Metebilis Three, the famous blue planet of the Acteon galaxy, was a remarkable world bathed in moonlight reflected from its blue sun. Most renowned of all were its large blue sapphires, which grew naturally in clusters on its high mountainsides. These crystals emitted radiation, which, while lethal to more advanced life forms, caused mutation in many of its indigenous species – vicious reptiles and birds could grow to enormous size. The crystals also had several psychic properties – including enhancing natural telepathic abilities and clearing neural pathways, amplifying mental power and intellect, and breaking hypnotic conditioning and mind control.

The blue planet and its famous crystals became the Third Doctor's first goal when the Time Lords freed him from exile on Earth. It took him a while but eventually he got there and managed to get a crystal. He used it to defeat BOSS's conditioning of its human slaves in Llanfairfach (see 045. BOSS), then gave it to companion Jo Grant as a wedding present. She returned it, saying that the native porters on her Amazonian expedition sensed its 'bad magic'. The crystal then accidentally killed Professor Herbert Clegg, during an experiment in telepathy the Doctor was conducting. Before long, giant spiders were materialising in southern England and the crystal was stolen from UNIT by a recovering businessman called Lupton, while giant spiders were materialising in an English meditation seminary.

At some point after the Great Breakout of the year 5000, an Earth starship came out of time jump and crashed on Metebelis Three. The properties of the planet's gems left the humans and their livestock untouched, but spiders on board their ship thrived, growing to vast size and greater mental strength. These creatures called themselves the Eight Legs, and reduced the humans – the Two Legs – to a feudal state.

The Great One was the first of the Eight Legs to become aware of the power of the Metebelis crystals, and gathered them around her in the Cave of Crystal inside a mountain. As she constructed them into a crystalline web, she drew even more strength and

energy from them, building up a tolerance to the resulting radiation which was lethal to any other life form. The crystal web reproduced her brain patterns, creating a positive feedback circuit in which her thoughts resonated and grew in power. Intending to increase her mental powers infinitely and rule the universe, the Great One realised that the most powerful crystal of all was missing. She used her mental energy to cross the void beyond the mind, locating the sapphire on 20th-century Earth and sending her spiders to retrieve it.

The Doctor eventually returned the crystal to the Great One, who incorporated it into her web. The resultant energy build-up could not be contained, and it burned out her mind and caused the deaths of all the other Eight Legs. The radiation in the cave became so lethal that no one would ever be able to enter it again – but it also cost the Doctor his third life.

THE SEERS CATALOGUE

> ADELAIDE: Miss Nethercott is an astrologer. The finest. I consult her every month.
> LEELA: A waste of time. I too used to believe in magic, but the Doctor has taught me about science. It is better to believe in science.
>
> *Horror of Fang Rock, Part 3*

Doctor Who tends to debunk superstition and magic. The Doctor himself is scathing of witch-wigglers, wangaturs, mundunugus and fortune-tellers and generally puts his faith in science. Yet, when he has encountered those with powers of precognition, they have rarely proved wrong...

■ When captured by pirates, the First Doctor foretells their grim fates in a pack of cards. He's eerily accurate, but refuses to say whether or not it is a trick.

■ Miss Olive Hawthorne warns viewers of BBC3: 'I've consulted the talisman of Mercury. It's written in the stars. When Beltane is come, tread softly, for lo, the prince himself is nigh.' Shortly afterwards, the Master summons the last of the Daemons.

■ Professor Herbert Clegg is a very powerful clairvoyant with psychokinetic abilities.

■ Miss Nethercott sees tragedy in Adelaide Lessage's stars, not long before a shipwreck leaves Adelaide a victim on Fang Rock.

■ Martha Tyler correctly predicts many of the deaths in Fetchborough.

■ The Seeker accurately follows Unstoffe and the stolen Jethrik into the Catacombs on Ribos. She also predicts the deaths of all bar one who follow; she's proved right, though she doesn't live long enough to know for sure.

■ H.G. Wells's planchette spells out the name 'Vena' shortly before the Karfelon noblewoman arrives in his fishing lodge.

■ Thanks to growing up on Cardiff's Rift, Gwyneth has the second sight and is able to divine an accurate picture of 21st-century London from Rose Tyler's mind.

■ The Sibylline Sisterhood of Soothsayers in Pompeii foresee a strange fate for Donna Noble but not the doom of their own city.

■ Donna Noble is the most foretold companion – the Ood Song predicts the Doctor-Donna, Dalek Caan predicts the events leading to her mental death, and there really is something on her back.

■ Organon of Chloris, however, has no ability at all and simply pretends, a trick shared by the Fortune Teller on Manussa, who flutters her fingers, gazes into a crystal ball and makes something up – but even she sees the skull of the snake in her crystal ball.

GREAT CRYSTALS

■ The Crystal of Enlightenment and the Key to Time were both objects under the purview of the Black and White Guardians and exerted an influence over time streams and events.

■ Kontron Crystals form in the time vortex and contain vast amounts of time energy, capable of powering a time tunnel such as that used on the Citadel of Karfel. A similar Crystal of Kronos

was found in Atlantis and was able to summon the Chronovore from the Time Vortex to feed on its energy. White Point Stars occurred only on Gallifrey, and could transcend a quantum lock.

■ Several worlds are rich in crystals, notably Midnight. Diamonds were common on Telos, and the Cryons paid the mercenary Lytton with them. The Metebelis Crystal and the Great Crystal of Manussa were both used to harness, amplify and channel mental energy. The Koh-i-Noor diamond was used to refract moonlight to destroy a werewolf.

■ Crystals are also used to supply more conventional energy: the warp star of a Verron Soothsayer held enough energy to destroy a Dalek battle fleet; Tritium crystals powered Cessair of Diplos's Hyperspatial Wand; Hymetusite was used in Nimon power complexes; Vintaric crystals provided the lighting in Tereleptil spacecraft; the Tritovores powered their ships with a crystal nucleus. Solonian Thaesium crystals were used as fuel by the 30th-century Earth Empire, but were actually a vital part of the life cycle of the natives of Solos.

047

Guy Crayford's Eyepatch

1970s

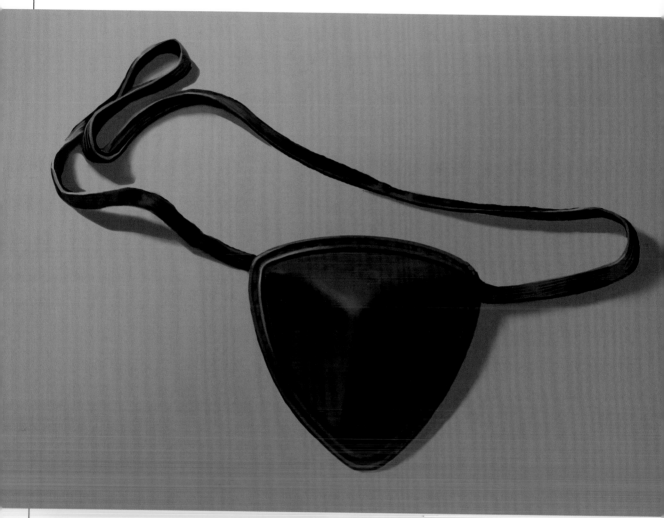

Senior Defence Astronaut Guy Crayford was the first tragedy of the British Space Programme – there'd been a near miss with the temporary loss of the astronauts from Mars Probe 7, but when Crayford's XK-5 space freighter disappeared during a test flight in deep space, it was assumed he'd died.

He had instead been taken prisoner by the Kraals, who brainwashed him into believing that they had rescued him from the wreckage. They told him they'd reconstructed his entire body, in every detail, apart from one eye. In reality, he had never been injured; the Kraal conditioning stopped him from questioning his orders, or even noticing that under his eyepatch was a perfectly healthy eye.

Crayford had become a pawn of the Kraals, using his heroic return from space to lead an android invasion of Earth.

EYEPATCHES ARE COOL

In popular culture, the eyepatch is a standard part of the pirate image, and *Doctor Who* is no different. Guy Crayford aside, its eyepatched characters have tended to be Bad, and generally piratical. The series' first eyepatched brigand was Gunnar the Giant, a Viking raider in *The Time Meddler* (1965). A year later, Pike's crew included Gaptooth the pirate in *The Smugglers* (1966). Remarkably, Blackbeard the pirate had both eyes intact in *The Mind Robber* (1968).

The Captain of *The Pirate Planet* (1978), however, completed his buccaneer image with a helmet that incorporated a mechanical substitute eyepatch – he'd been saved from the wreckage of a crashed spaceship and reconstructed as a cyborg, much as Crayford hadn't.

The 2011 series featured Madame Kovarian, an envoy of the Silence and the Academy of the Question. Since the Silents could not be remembered once seen, non-Silent members of the Silence like Kovarian were fitted with eyepatches. These were Eye Drives containing memory chips that allowed them to remember the Silents and receive their telepathic communications. The Silents could also use the Eye Drive to cause the wearer extreme pain. When River Song's refusal to kill the Doctor collapsed time, she, Amy Pond and their allies all adopted Eye Drives, too.

AND WHEN I TURNED AROUND...

Doctor Who's most notorious eyepatch was worn by the late Nicholas Courtney, when he played an unpleasant alternate version of Brigadier Lethbridge-Stewart in *Inferno* (1970). The Brigade-Leader on a parallel Earth, his face was deeply scarred above and below his left eye, which was covered with a patch. For decades afterwards, Courtney took the award for most-requested (and most retold) anecdote with his account of filming: the Brigade Leader is first revealed in Episode 3, sitting in a spinning chair; when he turned round, the entire cast were wearing eyepatches. Courtney continued to the end of the scene without cracking a smile.

THE BRITISH SPACE PROGRAMME

The British Rocket Group was established in the early 1950s, and sent its first craft into space in 1953. It was run by a man called Bernard. Bernard was still running it in 1963, but the Group was suffering problems. At some point in the 1970s, Professor Ralph Cornish seems to have replaced Bernard at what was now known as the British Space Centre. Cornish was in charge of the seven Mars Probe missions, and of the Recovery craft despatched after Mars Probe 7 went missing. The astronauts never reached Mars.

The loss of the XK-5 freighter and its subsequent use in an attempted alien invasion did nothing for the BRG's standing in official circles. In the 1980s, the British space programme was effectively closed down by the government, and the BRG became a small, independent organisation, concentrating on meteorite analysis and orbital satellites. Government links were re-established by the turn of the millennium and, in 2006, the British Rocket Group under Professor Daniel Llewellyn put Guinevere One into space. This was an unmanned probe sent to explore the planet Mars. It was intercepted by the Sycorax, who used it to transmit their demands back to Earth.

048

Krynoid Seedpod

1970s

Krynoid seedpods drift through space in pairs, landing on a planet and waiting to hatch. As it hatches, the Krynoid pod seeks out an animal host to root into and feed from. The infected life form rapidly mutates, first into a hybrid creature, and then into a full-grown mother plant. When this vast creature reaches primary germination, it ejects hundreds of new embryo pods into the atmosphere, swiftly converting the entire planet into Krynoid life, before spreading its pods into space. It is a galactic weed.

If they come into contact with intelligent animal life, the Krynoids can use their hosts' brain centres to communicate. They can also take control of all surrounding vegetation in their surroundings. Animal life is utterly extinguished on any planet where the Krynoid establishes itself.

Two Krynoid seedpods lay in Earth's permafrost for about 20,000 years until they were discovered by an Antarctic expedition from the World Ecology Bureau in the 1970s. One took over a WEB scientist but was destroyed in an explosion at the polar base. The second was stolen and became the last acquisition of the millionaire Harrison Chase, shortly before his 500-year-old mansion and the gigantic plant thrashing about on its roof were both destroyed by RAF fighter jets.

'SHE'S VERY, ER, PERSISTENT...'

Cigarillo-smoking floral painter Amelia Ducat, who does a bit of amateur sleuthing for the World Ecology Bureau, belongs to an honourable roll-call of marvellously eccentric ladies in 1970s *Doctor Who*.

Actor Damaris Hayman borrowed a cloak from her friend, famous theatrical eccentric Margaret Rutherford to play the first – Olive Hawthorne in *The Daemons* (1971). Miss Hawthorne was a white witch who liked a soldier, and she wasn't afraid to use her crystal ball as an offensive weapon.

Amelia Ducat was followed, in *The Stones of Blood* (1978), by the heroic Professor Amelia Rumford (Beatrix Leahman) with her addiction to truncheons and sausage sandwiches. Her academic partner was Vivien Fay (Susan Engel), ultimately revealed as druidic murderess Cessair of Diplos.

Even stretching a point to include Maren and the Sisterhood of Karn from *The Brain of Morbius* (1976), it's a surprisingly short list. So is the rundown of female villains between 1963 and 1989: Maaga (leader of the Drahvins), Kaftan (funder of the Brotherhood of Logicians), Miss Hilda Winters (boss of ThinkTank), Xanxia (Queen of Zanak), Lady Adrasta (ruler of Chloris), the Rani (Gallifrey's only female renegade), Chessene (an augmented Androgum), Helen A (pet-lover), Lady Peinforte (time-travelling witch), and Morgaine (sorceress from a parallel dimension).

Since returning in 2005, the programme has done a lot to redress the balance. Jackie Tyler and the Lady Cassandra O'Brien Dot Delta Seventeen were the first, swiftly followed by Harriet Jones MP and PM, Margaret Slitheen, Matron Casp and the Cat Nuns, Queen Victoria, the Wire, Yvonne Hartman, Donna Noble, Sylvia Noble, the Empress of the Racnoss, Florence Finnegan, the Carrionites, Lady Thaw, Matron Cofelia, Lady Clemency Eddison and Agatha Christie, River Song, Miss Mercy Hartigan, Minnie Hooper, Liz 10, Rosanna Calvierri, Alaya and Restac, Madam Kovarian...

THE GERM OF AN IDEA

The Seeds of Doom by Robert Banks-Stewart begins as a tribute to *The Thing From Another World* (1951) with its story of an Arctic Research Outpost attacked by an alien. The influence of *The Quatermass Experiment* (1953) then takes over, echoing the tale of a doomed man with an infection that spreads from his arm to transform his entire body into a giant plant. Victor Carroon ends up swarming over Westminster Abbey whereas Keeler ends up covering Harrison Chase's mansion. *The Man Eater of Surrey Green*, an episode of *The Avengers* made in 1965, when Banks-Stewart was a writer on that show, also features a hostile alien plant which grows to enormous size and takes control of a stately home.

'SCORBY - GET DUNBAR!'

Doctor Who has a fine tradition of calling people only by their surnames, which was common in television drama up until fairly recently (viewers only discovered Inspector Morse's first name in the last episode). The exception was soap operas, where nearly everyone was on first-name terms.

The Doctor initially addressed his companions formally, allowing a glorious set of variations on Ian Chesterton's surname (Chesterfield, Chesterman, Chatterton, Charlton, Cheston, Charterhouse, Queston, etc.). From the arrival of Vicki and Steven onwards, he was on first-name terms with all his companions, although the Third Doctor frequently referred to his assistants as 'Miss Shaw', 'Miss Grant' and 'Miss Smith'. The exception was schoolboy Turlough, who was only ever called by his surname, reflecting his public-school history. When he left, his first name was revealed to be Vislor.

And it was surnames all the way for supporting characters, and villains especially. People who had presumably stayed up long into the night plotting world domination together often treated each other with the formality of 1950s bank-workers. This could lead to some surprising moments, such as when, in *Resurrection of the Daleks*, Stien laments the death of his friend with the cry 'Galloway!'

MY GREEN CATHEDRAL

Reflecting their fringe status in mainstream politics and society at the time, vegetarians and environmentalists received limited exposure in *Doctor Who* in the 1970s and 1980s. Although Professor Jones's team in *The Green Death* called themselves the Nuthutch, their scheme to develop an alternative to meat from fungus was remarkably ahead of its time, anticipating by more than a decade the mass marketing of Quorn – a myco-protein meat-alternative derived from... fungus.

Harrison Chase's concerns about the environment, deforestation and the overuse of pesticides were all sound. He even had his own composting and recycling facility on his premises – even if he did use it for disposing of his victims.

In *The Two Doctors*, sickened by cannibalism and his encounter with the Androgums, the Sixth Doctor declared that he would adopt a strict vegetarian diet; companion Peri later complained that his nut roast rolls were horrible. It proved handy that they were vegetarians in *Revelation of the Daleks*, as the only other food source on offer was one derived from the bodies of the dead. The Sixth Doctor seemed to keep up his vegetarianism, reluctantly drinking carrot juice to the end of his days.

049

Radio Telescope

1981

In 1980, Earth's Pharos Project was set up to see if there was intelligent life in the universe. It sent radio signals into the skies, and monitored 'space chatter' to see if there was any evidence of coherent broadcasts emanating from other planets.

So amused were the Logopolitans by this idea that they built their own version of the project and used it to help them run their computations. The people of Logopolis were experts in Block Transfer Computation, holding the universe together using mathematics. They used their minds and their abacuses, and saw the comparatively quaint bubble-memory computers of the Pharos Project as just another tool to help them in their struggle against entropy.

When Logopolis was destroyed by the Master, the Doctor took the bubble-memory chips to the Pharos Project, fitting its radio telescope with a Light Speed Overdrive to broadcast the Logopolitan computations that would stabilise the universe via a Charged Vacuum Emboîtement.

With the Master still hoping to hold the universe to ransom, life quickly became very complicated for the security officers at the Pharos Project. Suddenly terrorists had taken over their radio telescope, one man fell off it, and three strangely dressed children turned up claiming to be aliens.

It is not known what happened to the funding of the Pharos Project after the Doctor's visit.

'IT'S ANCIENT GREEK FOR LIGHTHOUSE'

The Lighthouse of Alexandria on the island of Pharos was one of the seven wonders of the ancient world. Built in 280 BC, the flaming beacon on its tower served as a landmark for the port, and its original purpose was to make it easier for distant voyagers to find safe harbour. When the lighthouse was more widely adopted, it was used as a way of warning travellers away from rocks and difficult passages.

The 'classic' lighthouse lasted for two millennia. In *Horror of Fang Rock*, set in the early 20th century, the Doctor landed on Fang Rock where a manned lighthouse (with a new-fangled electric lamp) came under attack from a Rutan scout.

'CALLING OCCUPANTS OF INTERPLANETARY CRAFT'

At the turn of the 20th century, scientist Nikola Tesla first turned his ear to the stars, suggesting that the recently invented radio could be used to contact alien life. Using Tesla Coils, he came across repetitive signals which he reported as being of non-terrestrial origin. Although his findings were disputed, the idea that an evolved civilisation would also surely be using radio became popular, and several projects were undertaken to try and detect radio waves from the stars, such as National Radio Silence Day in 1924, when Mars was at its closest to Earth for centuries and the people of America turned off their radios to allow scientists to try and detect signals coming from the Red Planet.

In 1960, the SETI project (Search for Extraterrestrial Intelligence) began using radio telescopes to search the skies for a strong signal. In 1977, one researcher found such a transmission, dubbed 'the Wow Signal'. It has never been repeated.

SETI's research is based on the idea that once a radio wave has been transmitted terrestrially, the signal carries on into space, growing weaker but still continuing. These radio waves travel at the speed of light (about 300,000 km a second) – which sounds fast, but means that a signal from the Moon would take two seconds and (depending on orbit) one from Mars would take up to 21 minutes... and these are just our next-door neighbours in space – so a signal from a distant solar system could be reaching us several million years after the civilisation has been and gone.

A broadcast signal travels 9,467,077,800,000 km a year so, by the time this book is published, the first episode of *Doctor Who* will have travelled 475,000,000,000,000 km – or 49 light-years. In its first year, *An Unearthly Child* would have passed the furthest edge of the Oort Cloud and left the Solar System, and it would have been seen by the people of Proxima Centauri four years later. Right about now, the inhabitants of Psi Capricorni and Alpha Corvi are probably settling down to enjoy *Marco Polo*.

THE MASTER'S BROADCAST

Peoples of the Universe, please attend carefully, the message that follows is vital to the future of you all.. The choice for you all is simple. A continued existence under my guidance, or total annihilation.

Logopolis, Part 4

The Master might have had to wait a long time for a reply. His message would have taken 13.7 billion years to reach the edge of the universe (more properly called the Cosmic Microwave Background) – but at the rate of universal expansion, their reply would take another 45 billion years to be received.

Hopefully it wasn't 'And you are?'

050

Mondas

1986

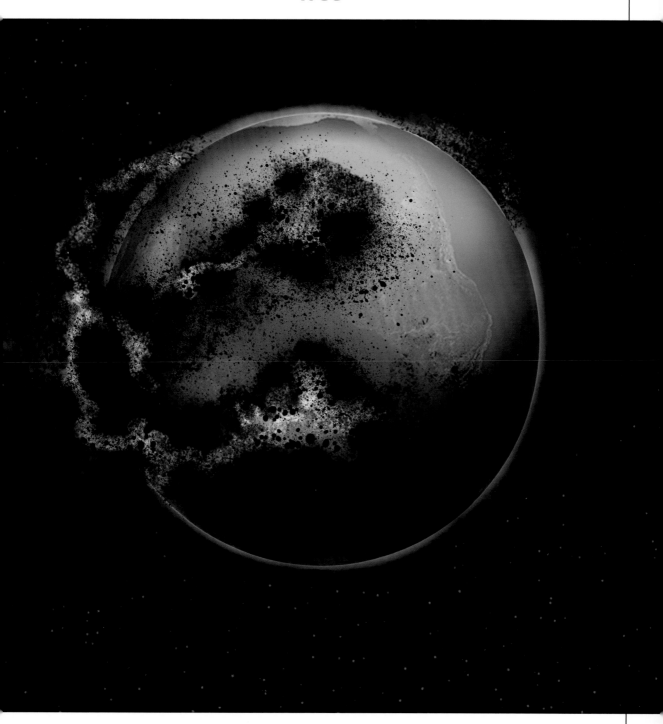

Aeons ago, Earth had a twin planet which drifted away from its orbit on a journey to the edge of space. Eventually it returned, assuming an orbit between Mars and Venus and starting to drain the life-force from anything that came near it, and then from the Earth itself.

The planet was called Mondas. Its inhabitants had originally been exactly like us, but their cybernetic scientists had realised that their race was getting weak and their life span was shortening. Devising spare parts for their bodies, the scientists and doctors adapted and augmented them until they could be almost completely replaced. Brain function was also altered, with certain weaknesses, such as emotions and awareness of pain, being removed. The Cybermen were born.

By the time it returned to our solar system, in 1986, Mondas's energy was all but exhausted, so it turned to its twin. The Cybermen believed that the energy drain could not be halted and that everything on Earth would wither and die; they planned to save the human race by taking people to Mondas for cybernisation. Ultimately, however, Mondas absorbed too much energy from the Earth. Reaching saturation point, Mondas burnt itself up and shrivelled away to nothing. The Cyberman taskforce on Earth – entirely dependent on power from their home world – also disintegrated.

LATER AND MEANWHILE...

A later generation of Cybermen, from the planet Telos, captured a time machine and travelled back to London in 1985, taking over equipment left over from an earlier occupation of the sewers. Their plan was to avert the destruction of Mondas by diverting Halley's comet onto a collision course with Earth.

MIRROR WORLDS

One of the earliest story ideas developed for *Doctor Who* was *The Hidden Planet* by Malcolm Hulke, which would have depicted Earth's twin, a planet with a diametrically opposed orbit beyond the sun so it could never be seen. According to Hulke, 'The Doctor goes to the planet and for obvious reasons the TARDIS crew think they are on Earth. But they find things are different. They landed in a field and Susan noticed a four-leaf clover, and then they see they are all four leaf clovers. And then other mysterious things happen like birds flying backwards or having double wings, and things of that sort.'

Parallel Earths were later shown in both *Inferno* and *Rise of the Cybermen*, which depicted a decaying planet with a sickened population, where the conversion into Cybus Men was the next step for the human race. And *New Earth* is an Earth-type colony world – the Doctor explained that, as Earth became uninhabitable, the population simply moved on to a recreation of it elsewhere in space.

In early Dalek fiction written by Terry Nation and David Whitaker, Skaro is more directly seen as a parallel with Earth – it is even placed in the same solar system.

THE EARLY CYBERMEN

The Mondasian Cybermen are different from later Cybermen in that they have names (Krail, Talon, Shav, Krang, Jarl and Gern), and their design is cruder and closer to the human form, with cloth faces and even organic hands. This suggests that their cybernetic processing was more a strict surgical enhancement to increase lifespan and viability of the species, rather than the more extreme robotic processing that would later be seen in the Cybermen from the planet Telos.

O51

Excalibur

C.1997

Underneath Lake Vortigern is a spaceship in which lies the body of King Arthur. Arthur was a king of Britain in another dimension, ruler of a society of technologically advanced knights battling across space and the various realities. Arthur's final battle took place in this dimension, on our Earth in the 10th century.

While Arthur lay dead, myths built up that he would one day return, and the Knights continued to battle for many centuries, until they returned to the burial site of the King.

His sword Excalibur became separated from its scabbard, which was found buried in the mud of nearby Carbury and proudly displayed in the local hostelry, the Carbury Arms. The scabbard still retained strange powers.

In the late 20th century, the sword itself was found in Arthur's ship by the Doctor's companion Ace. She later emerged from the lake with it in her hand, and used it in her battle against enchantment by the witch Morgaine.

MALORY, *LE MORTE D'ARTHUR*
Book 1, Chapter XXV

Arthur and Merlin ... went into the ship, and when they came to the sword that the hand held, Sir Arthur took it up by the handles, and took it with him, and the arm and the hand went under the water.

Then Sir Arthur looked on the sword, and liked it passing well. Whether liketh you better, said Merlin, the sword or the scabbard? Me liketh better the sword, said Arthur. Ye are more unwise, said Merlin, for the scabbard is worth ten of the swords, for whiles ye have the scabbard upon you, ye shall never lose no blood, be ye never so sore wounded; therefore keep well the scabbard always with you.

FUTURE TECHNOLOGY: THERE IS A FAULT ON THE LINE

When they were produced, between 1968 and 1975, *Doctor Who*'s original run of UNIT stories were set in an unspecific 'near future', in which Great Britain was sending rocket ships to Mars and the Brigadier could contact Geneva HQ by videophone. There were, though, just as many indications that the stories' settings were contemporary – taxi fares paid in shillings in 1970,

for example, just months away from the introduction of decimalisation. The first story to specify an unambiguous date was *Mawdryn Undead* (1983), which stated that Brigadier Lethbridge-Stewart had retired in 1977.

When the Intelligence Taskforce returned in *Battlefield* (1989), the year was once again unspecified, but it was intended to be around eight years into the future. The Queen had been succeeded to the throne by, presumably, Prince Charles, and UNIT itself was now a properly multicultural international operation, with soldiers from France, Hungary and Poland under the command of Brigadier Winifred Bambera. Although there was no mention of the internet, telephones responded to voice commands with an automatic operator. Seemingly rampant inflation had left a glass of lemonade costing £10 in the local pub.

SIDEWAYS IN TIME

MERLIN: The Doctor

THE LADY IN THE LAKE: Ace

KING ARTHUR: A bag of dust

MORGAN LE FAY: Morgaine

MORDRED: Mordred

There's no Ancelyn in Malory. There's no lake called Vortigern either, although there was a 5th-century British king of that name.

MERLIN

Was the Doctor Merlin? It seems so, in a parallel dimension or, possibly, in a future incarnation. After Arthur died in battle, the Doctor arranged his burial in his spaceship, with Excalibur alongside him. That the sword could be freed from the stone by Ace might suggest that the future Doctor remembered this incident and prepared for it.

It seems that the Merlin version of the Doctor ended up imprisoned for all eternity in an ice cave. Could this really be how the Doctor eventually dies? Or, will he escape from it in the same way he's escaped from other impossible traps...?

> DOCTOR: There was a goblin, or a trickster, or a warrior. A nameless, terrible thing, soaked in the blood of a billion galaxies. The most feared being in all the cosmos. And nothing could stop it, or hold it, or reason with it. One day it would just drop out of the sky and tear down your world.
> AMY: How did it end up in there?
> DOCTOR: You know fairy tales. A good wizard tricked it.
>
> *The Pandorica Opens*

O52

The TARDIS

1999

I t's popped up seemingly at every major historical event in Earth's history, from the discovery of fire to the Second Ice Age and beyond. Its shape is recorded in the stained-glass windows of churches and the scrolls of the Sybilline Prophecies; it has even appeared in the art of Vincent van Gogh. For many, the arrival of that police box heralds the coming of a saviour, a warrior who will save the world. Unless, of course, the mere presence of the box means the end of the world...

The TARDIS was diverted to San Francisco on 31 December 1999 by the Master, who intended to prolong his life by taking the Doctor's future selves. He opened the Eye of Harmony, the power source at the heart of the TARDIS, and within hours the entire planet was sucked through it.

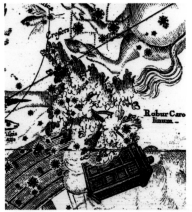

AND THEN THERE WAS THE TIME...

... that it brought about the end of the whole universe (see 065. Fez).

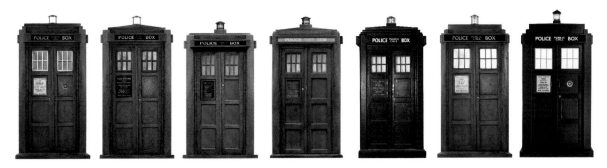

PASS NOTES

What's a police box?
A 20th-century call box from which the local emergency services could be contacted by police officers and the public.

Why a police box?
(a) The Doctor likes it like that.
(b) The show's creators in 1963 wanted the time machine to disguise itself as 'something humdrum'.

And it's stuck like that?
Mostly. The Fourth Doctor tried and failed to repair its Chameleon Circuit, seemingly aiming for a pyramid rather than a box. The Sixth Doctor tried and sort of succeeded, ending up with a cabinet, a pipe organ and a gateway, before settling on a rough approximation of a police box again.

Approximation?
The TARDIS is clever, but it never actually managed to replicate any genuine police box designs. At any given time, the windows are too big, or the door-sign wording is inaccurate, or the flat roof is wrong.

It's bigger on the inside...
... than on the outside. That's because it's dimensionally transcendental (which means it's bigger on the inside than the outside). Hence the name.

TARDIS?
Which stands for 'Time And Relative Dimension in Space' (except from 1965 to 1989, when it was 'Dimensions').

Who came up with that?
According to the Doctor's granddaughter Susan, she did. The rest of the Time Lords called their ships TARDISes too, though, so she may just have been being Unearthly.

So what's inside?
A control room, which might be gleaming and white, wood-panelled and Edwardian, corralled and organic, or maritime and sexy. At the centre of which is a hexagonal control console covered in mysterious dials and controls. At the moment there are staircases leading to other levels and doorways.

Anything interesting through those doors?
Almost certainly, but it's quite a while since anyone's seen beyond the initial maze of corridors. There was a swimming pool again until recently; like the first one, the latest was jettisoned, along with one of the squash courts. There's a library, possibly in uncomfortable proximity to the swimming pool, a wardrobe room and bedrooms. In the past, there's been a boot cupboard, cricket club, tool room, bathroom, power station, greenhouse, sickbay, workshop, cloisters, cloister room, library, Zero room... The Doctor can move rooms around, though, and delete them, and the TARDIS can do much the same if the mood takes her, so—

'Her'?
Yes. When the TARDIS's eleven-dimensional personality matrix was removed and placed in the humanoid body of Idris, one of House's Patchwork People, she and the Doctor were able to have their first real conversation.

So they're inseparable?
The TARDIS is the Doctor's wife, in many ways – one of them, anyway. (He's approaching Elizabeth Taylor for lack of commitment. Well, Henry VIII, at least.) And, as Donna Noble discovered in an alternate reality, without the Doctor the TARDIS would just give up and die. Together, though, they can do pretty much anything.

The Doctor has always boasted of his ability to control his ship, a pride that many of his companions have considered utterly deluded. Which Doctor was the least bad at getting where he wanted to go?

11TH PLACE 0%

The Second Doctor didn't seem to care where the TARDIS went, and was just there for the ride. He knew he'd get somewhere in the end, and thought nothing of returning holy relics 300 years late. Early on, he aimed for Mars and got the Moon. After that, the one time he really tried to steer the TARDIS, it was to escape the Time Lords, and that didn't go very well.

10TH PLACE 3%

The First Doctor constantly insisted he was in complete control, yet often seemed to spend more time with his Fault Locator and fluid links than he did actually piloting the ship. He made disastrous use of the Fast Return switch, a device which baffled Ian and Barbara, though internet users will recognise how easily an imprudent click of a 'Back' button can land you in all sorts of unfortunate destinations. Ian and Barbara gave up on ever getting back to the 1960s and used a Dalek time machine, at which point the TARDIS took to landing in the 1960s quite regularly.

6TH PLACE 58%

The Sixth Doctor's TARDIS frequently broke down, but showed a remarkable ability to return to the sites of previous adventures. He acquired a good degree of control, able to pilot it successfully to Varos, Necros, the mysterious planet Ravolox and Thoros Beta. It always helped, though, to have a time corridor or distress signal to follow.

5TH PLACE 71%

The Seventh Doctor gave the appearance of not caring where his TARDIS went, but actually he often carefully chose his destinations in order to defeat Fenric, force Ace to face her past, retrieve the Master's remains from Skaro, or close unfinished business in Shoreditch.

4TH PLACE 74%

The Ninth Doctor was usually quite skilled, often better at travelling in space than in time, and always better at going forwards than backwards. He could plot an accurate course for the year 5 billion as easily as he could have the TARDIS hop round modern London. Travelling back in time was generally a bumpy ride: heading for Naples, 1860 took him to Cardiff, 1869, and he got Rose home 12 months after she'd left, not 12 hours. His finest hour came with his precision flying as he took on a Dalek fleet and rescued Rose.

OF A PILOT

9TH PLACE   29%

The Third Doctor was just grateful whenever the TARDIS worked at all. It frequently arrived at its intended destination, though this was generally because it had been operated on remote control by the Time Lords. He wasn't happy about this, but saved the world anyway. He took the ship apart and put it all back together again, yet still the only way he could be sure of getting somewhere was to wire the coordinates into the programmer. That's what he did for Metebelis Three, and soon wished he hadn't.

8TH PLACE   35%

The Fifth Doctor proved to be very bad at getting Tegan Jovanka to Heathrow. She thought she was a better pilot than him (and even managed to fly the TARDIS to Castrovalva, with the Master's help). She wasn't the only person better at piloting the TARDIS than the Doctor – Professor Hayter, Turlough and Kamelion all had a go.

7TH PLACE   50%

The Fourth Doctor was the first Doctor to demonstrate some real ability to pilot the TARDIS. He was able to get to Loch Ness, Kastria and Gallifrey (via Aberdeen), and installing the Locatormutor Core allowed him to hunt down all six segments of the Key to Time. After this, he installed a Randomiser so that he never knew where he'd end up, but kept switching it off to enable precision jaunts between Paris and Florence. He claimed growing proficiency with 'short hops', but also managed to accidentally pilot the TARDIS into another universe and once missed the River Thames by a few metres.

3RD PLACE   78%

The Eleventh Doctor missed all of Amy Pond's childhood, a mistake for which he is still paying. He's made up for it when assembling armies, or flying a TARDIS in various states on rescue missions or assassination plots.

2ND PLACE   81%

The Tenth Doctor was frequently a skilled pilot, which made his fairly rare mistakes (aiming for Ian Dury and reaching Queen Victoria) all the more noticeable. Like the Ninth Doctor, he found it harder to travel backwards than forwards in time. He was particularly adept at following phone calls and bees to their destinations. His finest hour was when he piloted the stolen Earth back home, with a little help from his friends.

1ST PLACE   100%

The Eighth Doctor headed off from San Francisco alone, and most of his subsequent exploits are lost in classified literature and arcane audio-visuals – this is probably something to do with the Time War. What is known is that he may, officially, have made just the one journey, but it really took him where he wanted to go.

053

The Artefacts of Rassilon

THIS is the game of Rassilon

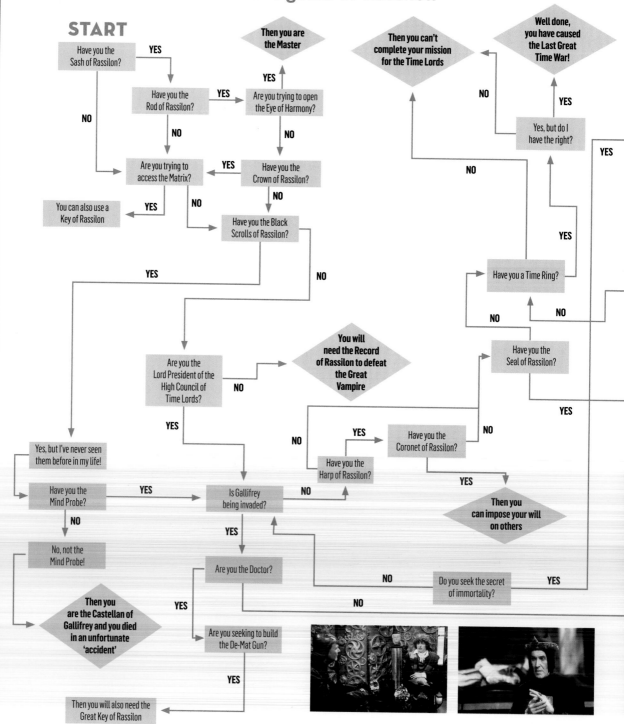

START

- Have you the Sash of Rassilon? — **YES** / **NO**
- Have you the Rod of Rassilon? — **YES** / **NO**
- Are you trying to open the Eye of Harmony? — **YES** → **Then you are the Master** / **NO**
- Have you the Crown of Rassilon? — **YES** / **NO**
- Are you trying to access the Matrix? — **YES** / **NO**
- You can also use a Key of Rassilon
- Have you the Black Scrolls of Rassilon? — **YES** / **NO**
- Are you the Lord President of the High Council of Time Lords? — **YES** / **NO**
- You will need the Record of Rassilon to defeat the Great Vampire
- Then you can't complete your mission for the Time Lords
- Well done, you have caused the Last Great Time War!
- Yes, but do I have the right? — **NO** / **YES**
- Have you a Time Ring? — **YES** / **NO**
- Have you the Seal of Rassilon? — **NO** / **YES**
- Have you the Coronet of Rassilon? — **YES** / **NO**
- Have you the Harp of Rassilon? — **YES** / **NO**
- Then you can impose your will on others
- Yes, but I've never seen them before in my life!
- Have you the Mind Probe? — **YES** / **NO**
- No, not the Mind Probe!
- Is Gallifrey being invaded? — **NO** / **YES**
- Then you are the Castellan of Gallifrey and you died in an unfortunate 'accident'
- Are you the Doctor? — **YES** / **NO**
- Do you seek the secret of immortality? — **NO** / **YES**
- Are you seeking to build the De-Mat Gun? — **YES**
- Then you will also need the Great Key of Rassilon

Rassilon was the first (and greatest) President of the High Council of Time Lords on the planet of Gallifrey. The Time Lords never had another leader like him – until they resurrected him to fight the Time War.

His near-mythical status was built up by the many artefacts he left behind him, imbued with special powers and ensuring that no Time Lord could ever forget him – from the Seal of Rassilon (in decorative use all over Gallifrey) to a painting of the Harp of Rassilon which contained the clue to a secret area of Gallifrey unvisited by its people for many centuries.

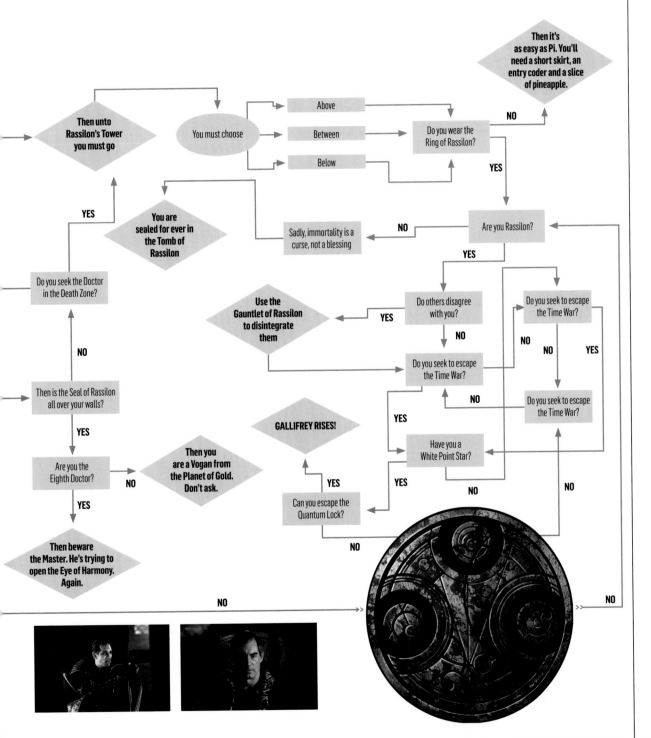

054

Big Ben

2006

In 2006, in order to convince the world that aliens had landed, the Family Slitheen crashed a spaceship piloted by an augmented pig in a spacesuit into the River Thames. It soared over the London skyline and smashed into Big Ben on the way down.

The gambit paid off: the world was panicking within minutes. All planet Earth's experts on extraterrestrial threats were rushed to 10 Downing Street, where the Slitheen were already in control. With the experts murdered, the Slitheen – in the guise of Acting Prime Minister Joseph Green – announced that humanity was threatened by massive weapons of destruction aimed at them from the heavens. Authorisation was quickly given for a nuclear strike against the alien invaders supposedly hidden in planetary orbit. Earth was on the brink of World War Three...

THE CHIMES OF MIDNIGHT

Pedants are fond of pointing out that the Westminster Palace tower known around the world as 'Big Ben' is 'the Clock Tower Actually'. It was designed in the 1830s by Augustus Pugin shortly before he went mad. There are 334 steps to the top, and it was once the tallest clock tower in the world at nearly 100 metres (the 110-metre Joseph Chamberlain Memorial Clock tower in Birmingham now holds that honour).

Although Pugin designed the clock faces, the famously reliable clockwork inside was the combined work of an amateur clockmaker and the Astronomer Royal. One of the secrets of its regularity is a small pile of old pennies on top of the pendulum – adding or removing some of them makes tiny adjustments to the speed of the mechanism. So robust is the clockwork that the clock chimed all the way through the Second World War, despite being damaged in the Blitz.

Big Ben has its distinctive chime thanks to an error in the manufacture of its great bell (which also gives the clock and the tower its name). Named after Sir Benjamin Hall, the bell cracked soon after installation because its hammer was far too heavy. The crack was repaired, but gives the bell its distinctive 'twang' when struck.

ICONIC

One of the keynotes of the revival of *Doctor Who* in 2005 was that when sold around the world it would be instantly identifiable as a British show. With limited filming days in the capital, the production team set out to establish significant use of London landmarks such as the Palace of Westminster, Big Ben, the London Eye and 10 Downing Street. Red Routemaster buses and London black cabs were used to firmly establish the contemporary look and feel of London, even when filming was taking place in Cardiff. In *The Runaway Bride*, Donna even manages to find one of London's few remaining red telephone boxes. From *Rose* onwards, the Art Department took great care to give *Doctor Who*'s London a consistent feel – even the bin bags were Routemaster red.

BONG!

The destruction of Big Ben was the first elaborate model effects work undertaken for the 2005 series by Mike Tucker, who blew up Downing Street and the Auton Lair and created barrage balloons and the Emperor Dalek model. He also worked on manufacturing the first Dalek seen in 2005. He now runs Model Unit, and has won a BAFTA and been nominated for an Emmy.

The filming for the spaceship crash into Big Ben had to be done twice, because the entire clock face fell off the model in one piece on the first take. Two models had been constructed, and the miniature shoot was restaged the next day. The resulting footage was later flipped when the spaceship's approach to Big Ben was changed during the episode's production – eagle-eyed viewers will spot that the numbers on the clock are reversed.

THE CHIMES OF OLD BIG BEN

1941 Captain Jack Harkness tethered his invisible spaceship to Big Ben, where he wouldn't forget it. He later switched on the clock's internal lights during a German air raid, and danced with Rose Tyler in front of it.
C.2005 The Eleventh Doctor's crashing TARDIS almost collided with Big Ben.
2006 The clock tower was still being repaired at the time of the Sycorax attack.
2007 On Pete's World, Big Ben had a square face.
2167 The absence of the chimes of 'old Big Ben' was one of the clues that something had happened when the TARDIS brought the First Doctor to Dalek-occupied London. Following the defeat of the Dalek invasion, the clock chimed again.
28TH CENTURY By this time, London and the southern half of England had become 'Central City', and Big Ben was long forgotten.

The Doctor's Hand

2006

To the people of Earth, the sudden appearance of a Sycorax spacecraft in their skies marked the beginning of their first Christmas Day nightmare, with one-fifth of the population hypnotised and apparently on the point of a mass suicide.

To the Sycorax Leader, the unexpected intrusion of a pyjama-clad intruder with a big mouth was a minor irritant, and he made short work of him, lopping off his hand with a broadsword.

To the new Tenth Doctor, the loss of a hand was all in a day's regeneration cycle. He simply grew a new one, vanquished the Sycorax Leader with a satsuma, and sent his warriors fleeing for the stars (though not fast enough to escape Harriet Jones PM's retribution).

To Captain Jack Harkness, the severed hand was his lifeline to escape from 21st-century Earth, after a 127-year exile. He retrieved it, stored it in a jar of nutrients and headed back to Cardiff, hoping that the hand would one day alert him to the Doctor's return. When the Doctor and Jack were reunited, Jack took the hand with him, still in its jar.

Soon afterwards, they faced the Master, beginning a year-long reign of terror with the Toclafane, who extracted the Doctor's biological code from the hand and manipulated his genes to age him by hundreds of years.

Jack had used the hand as a 'Doctor-detector', but it turned out to be able to detect any Time Lord. The hand and the TARDIS both reacted to the potential creation of the Doctor's 'daughter' Jenny and dragging the Doctor, Donna Noble and Martha Jones off to Messaline in 6012.

The hand remained in the TARDIS until the Daleks stole the Earth and exterminated the Doctor – the Doctor then partially regenerated to heal himself from Dalek gunfire, diverting the leftover regeneration energy into the hand. When the TARDIS was dropped into a core of Z-neutrinos, this stored regeneration energy in the hand came into contact with Donna Noble, resulting in a human-Time Lord metacrisis – and a part-human copy of the Doctor grew out of the hand.

THE HAND PLAN

The official *Doctor Who* website presented a series of online games to accompany the 2006 series, one of which saw players breaking into the Leamington Spa Lifeboat Museum (a Geocomtex safehouse). The goal was going to be to retrieve the Doctor's fallen hand, but a note was passed back from the script editors, who knew what was coming: 'Don't touch the hand.' Instead, the game became a quest for the fallen satsuma.

HANDOVERS

When Time Lords regenerate, their bodies are in a state of flux for the first fifteen hours. During this process, a Time Lord often undergoes wild mood swings, mental instability and confusion, and behaves out of character.

'Slower... slower... Concentrate on one thing. One thing!'

'Shoes... Must find my shoes.'

'Mother, Mother, I feel sick. Send for the Doctor, quick, quick, quick...'

'What would I do if I were me?'

'We all know the fate of alien spies...'

'Who am I? And who are you?'

'These shoes – they fit perfectly...'

'No, wait, that's The Lion King.'

'Hello! Hello! Hello!'

'I'm not cooked yet.'

A HANDY GUIDE

056

Cyberman

2007

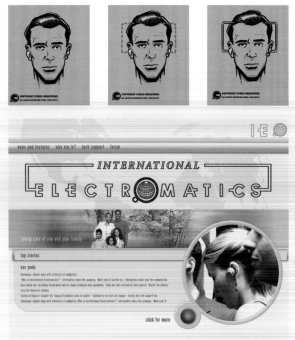

On a parallel Earth, at the dawn of the 21st century, John Lumic was dying. The co-founder of Cybus Industries, confined to a motorised wheelchair and life-support system, concluded that the weaknesses of flesh and blood were holding humanity back. He developed the next level of mankind: 'Human.2', or Cybermen. Lumic's Cybermen retained only the brain. The Cybermen of Mondas and Telos were more complicated creatures – converted from the inside out, they were almost completely replaced, but parts of the host remained inside the metal shell (see 050. Mondas). Lumic started from scratch. Before long, Cybus Industries had factories across seven continents, dedicated to offering humanity a compulsory upgrade.

Although these events happened in a parallel dimension, these Cybus Cybermen eventually made their way here, too, thanks to the efforts of the Torchwood Institute at Canary Wharf. When they started to emerge from the Void between the realities, they were ghostly, insubstantial figures, and most people assumed these shades were the spirits of their deceased relatives. But when the Void was fully opened, the Cybermen were able to complete the conquest of the planet in a matter of minutes. This coincided, however, with the emergence of the Cult of Skaro, the last Dalek survivors of the Time War, and the Cybermen found themselves fighting an unexpected battle against millions of Daleks.

The Doctor reopened the Void, pulling all the Cybermen and Daleks back inside. There they remained, until two years later, when the barriers between realities started to crumble as a new generation of Daleks prepared their Reality Bomb in the Medusa Cascade. Some of the trapped Cybermen managed to escape the Void, stealing Dalek technology as they left, and emerging in Victorian London.

HOW DID THE UPGRADE WORK?

Lumic invented a steel-based high-contact metal, and devised a method of extracting and preserving the intact brain from a human body and bonding its cyber-kinetic impulses with a metal exo-skeleton containing gears and servos. An artificially grown central nervous system of flesh was then threaded throughout the Cyber suit, while emotions were suppressed by an inhibitor installed in the Cyberform's chest unit. Feelings had to be suppressed in this way to prevent the Cybermen going insane from the sight of themselves or the pain of the conversion process. The chest unit itself was branded with the Cybus logo.

When they entered this dimension, they brought equipment with them, and set up conversion tables at Canary Wharf to perform a cruder version of the procedure, which retained more of the host body, bolting on replacement limbs and grafting implants over it.

NOT TO BE CONFUSED WITH...

The parallel version of Earth was an alternative to our world where everything's the same but a little bit different. Rose Tyler's father and Mickey Smith's grandmother were both still alive. There was another version of Mickey, named Ricky; there was another version of Jackie. And there was Lumic's version of the Cybermen. The last of these eventually joined the Daleks' Pandorica alliance to imprison the Doctor. The Cybermen of our universe looked very similar. The big difference was that their chest units lacked the 'Cybus' logo.

TORCHWOOD

The Torchwood Institute was founded by Queen Victoria in the year 1879. Torchwood One was in London's Canary Wharf. Torchwood Two was in Scotland, Torchwood Three was placed over a rift in Cardiff, and Torchwood Four went missing. Torchwood was dedicated to enriching the British Empire with alien artefacts, and made great strides in technology. Torchwood Three built a Rift Manipulator in order to keep the Cardiff Rift at bay. Torchwood One constructed the Ghost Shift, eager to find a way of exploiting the manifestations that emerged through the Void. They also built the Sphere Chamber in order to examine the Sphere which had emerged through the Void.

CONSTRUCTED FROM A KIT

The creator of the Cybermen was Dr Christopher Pedler of the University of London. In the mid 1960s, producer Innes Lloyd was seeking to give *Doctor Who*'s stories a more solid scientific base. Various candidates were interviewed as possible scientific advisers (including Patrick Moore), but it was Kit Pedler who secured the role after coming up with the story for *The War Machines*.

He swiftly followed this by co-writing *The Tenth Planet* with script editor Gerry Davis. They created the Cybermen out of a shared fascination with the extreme possibilities of surgery. A few months later, they reused the Cybermen in stories about weather control (*The Moonbase*) and cryogenics (*The Tomb of the Cybermen*), and contributed story ideas for *The Invasion* and *The Wheel in Space*.

In 1970, Pedler and Davis created *Doomwatch*, a show devoted to exploring the threats to humanity posed by scientific developments. Subjects included intelligent rats, tower blocks, cigarettes and the spread of a plastic-eating enzyme.

057

Genesis Ark

2007

T he Genesis Ark was a dimensionally transcendental Time Lord prison. During the Time War millions of captured Daleks were sealed inside it. The Ark could be opened only by the touch of a time traveller. As Daleks lack hands, this was the perfect gaol for them.

The Cult of Skaro saw it as something more – the future of the Dalek race. They stole it, renamed it the Genesis Ark, and took it with them into the Void to escape the quantum-locking of the Time War. They concealed themselves and it from the universe inside a Void Ship and waited.

In 2007 on the planet Earth, at the start of the Battle of Canary Wharf, Mickey Smith's handprint accidentally opened the Ark and its prisoners were released into London's skies.

THE CULT OF SKARO

> THE DOCTOR: The last four Daleks in existence. So what's so special about you?
> ROSE: Doctor, they've got names. And Daleks don't have names, do they? One of them said they—
> DALEK THAY: I am Dalek Thay.
> DALEK SEC: Dalek Sec.
> DALEK JAST: Dalek Jast.
> DALEK CAAN: Dalek Caan.
> THE DOCTOR: So that's it! At last... the Cult of Skaro. I thought you were just a legend.
> ROSE: Who are they?
> THE DOCTOR: A secret order. Above and beyond the Emperor himself. Their job was to imagine. Think as the enemy thinks. Even dared to have names... All to find new ways of killing.
>
> *Doomsday*

THROW AWAY THE KEY

In 1979, *Doctor Who* presented its first Time Lord prison – the planet Shada, which held criminals from various races who were removed from Time and wiped from memory. Just as the Genesis Ark could only be opened by a time traveller, access to Shada was only through the Law – a book called *The Worshipful and Ancient Law of Gallifrey*. Time flowed backwards over the book, and it worked as a key, only allowing a TARDIS access to the chambers of Shada.

Although strike action meant that *Shada* was abandoned half-made, it now has the distinction of being the most produced *Doctor Who* story ever – with an attempted remount, a commercial release of the recorded footage with linking narration by Tom Baker, a webcast starring Paul McGann, an unofficial animation, and a novelisation by Gareth Roberts. Lalla Ward has played Romana in the original production, the webcast and the animation, and read the audiobook.

BANKING ON THE FUTURE

Humans and Monoids were preserved on trays.

A capsule found on Vulcan contained a Dalek race bank.

The Cybermen froze themselves in tombs on Telos.

Operation Golden Age's 'New Earth' was to be populated by humans supposedly placed in suspended animation aboard a fleet of spaceships.

Humanity was placed into a cryogenic repository aboard the Nerva Beacon, with a complete record on microfilm of all human achievement.

A Krynoid seedpod contains all the information to regrow the Krynoid race from scratch.

The Kastrian Race Bank was destroyed by King Rokon rather than let it fall into Eldrad's hands.

The APC Net stored the minds of every Time Lord at the end of his life and was the repository of all Time Lord knowledge.

The Tachyon Recreation Generator held the future of the Argolin race.

The Urbankans placed themselves beyond the Flesh Time as printed circuits.

A Racnoss Webstar buried at the heart of Earth contained the children of the Empress.

Progenation machines created new humans and Hath, while the Source held the means of terraforming the planet Messaline.

The Daleks seeded the universe with Progenitor devices, holding the blueprint for a new Dalek race.

Homo reptilia placed themselves in cold storage.

058

Weeping Angel

2007

Once known as the Lonely Assassins, the Weeping Angels were the only race in the galaxy that killed people nicely.* A single touch sent their prey back in time to live their lives in full. The Angels then fed off the potential energy of the lives that their victims would otherwise have led. They moved impossibly quickly, seeming to vanish from one spot and reappear in another in the blink of an eye. They could only move, however, if they remained unobserved. If they were seen by anything or anyone, they were quantum-locked, becoming immobilised solid stone – the perfect defence mechanism. The sole way to survive an encounter with an Angel is never to let your gaze shift from it – if you see an Angel, don't even blink.

Their history is obscure, but they are thought to have evolved in the earliest days of the universe, and the Time Lords knew of them from the Dawn of Time. (At the end of the Last Great Time War, the resurrected Lord President Rassilon sentenced two dissenting members of the High Council to a perpetuity of statue-like immobility, their faces masked by their hands. The pair would 'stand as monuments to their shame' for eternity, 'like the Weeping Angels of old'.)

The definitive written history of the Angels was notable for its complete lack of illustrations, warning simply: 'That which holds the image of an Angel becomes itself an Angel.' They are able to manifest themselves in drawings, photographs, video recordings, even in the human eye.

In 2007, Sally Sparrow's love of forgotten buildings brought her to Wester Drumlins. Inside the house she found a warning for her, and a lot of sad-looking statues…

* This 'niceness' is abandoned if an Angel is sufficiently hungry. A starving Angel is not just nigh-on unrecognisable as a piece of sculpture, it's also likely to break its victim's neck, subsume his consciousness and play tricks with his vocal cords. The Weeping Angels are not, in fact, at all nice.

DO NOT MAKE GRAVEN IMAGES

On Earth, legends of statues becoming animate date back to antiquity – the story of Pygmalion and Galatea is found in Greek myth and is retold in Ovid's *Metamorphoses*. At the climax of Shakespeare's *A Winter's Tale*, a statue comes to life. Universally, mannequins are always bad news (see 025 and 040), and the same seems to be true of sculpture – statuary is almost always dangerous, and rarely what it seems…

■ The Nemesis statue, fashioned from Validium, returned to Earth every quarter-century from 1638 to 1988, and always presaged doom: its arrival heralded the First World War, the Second World War, the assassination of John F. Kennedy, and a short-lived invasion by the Cybermen.

■ Among the lethal 51st-century technology hidden in 19th-century London by war criminal Magnus Greel was a huge statue of a dragon, which concealed a laser cannon. 'Beware the eyes of the dragon.'

■ Sometimes a statue is just a statue. The Statue of Liberty (probably) had nothing alien concealed within it, and was nothing more than a handy reminder of where the Doctor and Martha Jones had parked the TARDIS. The only sinister thing about Det-Sen monastery's Buddha statue was the Yeti control sphere left at its feet. Even the early Daleks kept the odd exhibit in their city on Skaro, at least until Ian Chesterton dropped a sculpture on top of a pursuing Dalek.

■ But sometimes it's important to remember that a statue of Medusa is just a statue, even if it seems to be coming to life in the Land of Fiction.

■ When the statue of Atlantis's fish-faced god Amdo began to speak, the temple priests were overcome with awe, allowing the Doctor to escape execution. The voice wasn't actually Amdo; the Doctor's companion Polly did the talking, using a microphone.

■ The Daemons from the planet Daemos not only influenced humanity's development in many ways and brought great technological advancements. They could also animate church gargoyles.

■ The Master once landed on Traken, a planet where no evil could flourish; his TARDIS took the form of a calcified statue called Melkur, and the Master was trapped inside it. Not one for phobias, the Master later disguised his TARDIS as a statue of Queen Victoria and, later still, had statues of himself erected across Toclafane-conquered Earth.

■ The fourth segment of the Key to Time (see 003) was disguised as part of a statue of a warrior and a dragon on the planet Tara.

■ The planet Marinus was home to a number of statues, one of which held a fake key to the Conscience Machine. Anyone trying to take the key would be grabbed by the statue which then spun round and deposited them in the Screaming Jungle – a small courtyard filled with booby traps and killer vegetation.

■ The statue of Aggedor on the planet Peladon was by no means as dangerous as the real creature, but was occasionally used in the attempted assassination of alien ambassadors.

■ In hiding on the planet Necros in the early 47th century, the increasingly unhinged Davros decided to lure the Doctor to his high-class funeral home, Tranquil Repose. Once there, the Time Lord discovered an enormous statue of himself in the Garden of Fond Memories, provoking intimations of mortality that are interrupted only by the statue toppling over and crushing him...

■ The Fourth Doctor also encountered a monument to himself, on a lost Earth colony world in the distant future. The huge representation of his face was actually a gateway through a barrier dividing two factions of descendants of the original pioneers, with access gained by climbing over his teeth and going down his throat.

■ In the 51st century, visitors to The Library – repository of every book in the history of the universe – got help and information from Courtesy Nodes, tall sculptures inset with living flesh aspects donated by the near-deceased.

■ The ancillary power station of the Doctor's TARDIS was at one time disguised as a magnificent art gallery, complete with a copy of the Venus de Milo. Manipulating the statue removed the illusion and the exhibits all vanished. There was also a copy of the Venus de Milo on Apalapucia.

■ Kane, the ruler of Iceworld on the dark side of the planet Svartos, was obsessed with his dead lover Xana. With an abundance of ice to work with, he commissioned an ice sculpture of her, and celebrated its completion by murdering the sculptor. This was premature, as the ice sculpture melted as soon as the temperature was raised.

■ In the 57th segment of time, humanity evacuated planet Earth once again, commemorating their pioneering journey by erecting a human statue – a statue so big it would take their entire 700-year voyage to complete it. By the time their 'Ark' neared its destination, the Monoids were not the servants any more, and the statue was not completed with the head of a man... (see 098)

ANGELMANIA

Doctor Who has been searching for its 'next Daleks' since 1964. Sometimes the magic has struck and a writing and production team has come up with Cybermen or Sontarans, Silents or Ood. Sometimes a production team has consciously set out to replicate the Daleks' success – they've generally ended up with Chumblies and Quarks. And just once a new monster proved so popular it took all its creators by surprise. After Series Three in 2007, the readers of *Doctor Who Adventures* magazine voted for their favourite monsters, and the Daleks only made it to number 2, thanks to the impact of the Angels in *Blink*. This feat was repeated in June 2012, when more than 10,000 *Radio Times* readers voted for their favourite ever monster – the Weeping Angels won again, taking almost half the votes.

059

DVD

2007

Humans have been seeking new and better ways of recording and preserving information and memories since the cave painters of the Stone Age. It took about 30,000 years to get from cave walls to something more portable, like papyrus or paper, and another couple of thousand to develop means of capturing images or sounds. Once photography and sound recording were devised, though, there was a century-long sprint through new recording technologies – moving pictures, gramophones, cassette recorders, video machines, compact discs... until, at the end of the 20th century, the DVD was released onto the market.

As well as offering enhanced audio and video quality, the DVD gave its makers a chance to offer hidden extras – following clues on menu screens might reveal, say, a recording of a strange man having one half of a conversation about the nature of time, stone angels and phone boxes.

COMMUNICATION PROBLEMS

Marooned in 1969, but armed with a transcript of the conversation he would have with Sally Sparrow in 2007, the Doctor recorded his half, instructing Billy Shipton to include it as an Easter egg on the 17 DVDs that Sally would eventually own. Sometimes people will go to extreme lengths to get their message across...

■ The TARDIS resorted to melting clock faces, electrifying its console, opening the doors mid-flight and driving its occupants mad to make the First Doctor realise that the Fast Return switch had jammed. Remarkably, he eventually cottoned on.

■ The Osiran pyramid on Mars that held Sutekh trapped on Earth also constantly broadcast a message: 'Beware Sutekh!' It was, though, in Osiran Morse code, so needed somebody as clever as the Fourth Doctor to actually decipher it, and by then it was far too late.

■ Erato, the Tythonian ambassador deprived of his communicator and thrown into a pit on Chloris by Lady Adrasta, tried to communicate by rolling on top of people. Since the creature was vast, the body count was high.

■ The parallel/future Merlin-Doctor left a message for the Seventh Doctor at the entrance to King Arthur's spaceship: 'Dig hole here.' Once inside, the doors responded to his voice, too. All of which neatly led him into a trap, with an automated defence system kicking in and trying to kill him and Ace, even though he'd been positively identified. He also left a note for himself in Arthur's helmet, explaining everything.

■ The Mighty Jagrafess of the Holy Hadrojassic Maxarodenfoe spent 90 years adjusting the news broadcasts from Satellite Five to Earth, in order to knock the Fourth Great and Bountiful Human Empire off course and soften it up for the Daleks. It worked.

■ River Song broke into a compartment of the *Byzantium*, removed the starliner's Home Box, wrote 'Hello, Sweetie!' on it in Old High Gallifreyan for the Doctor to see in the Delerium Archive 12,000 years later. Just to be sure, she also left her space-time coordinates on the *Byzantium*'s security cameras.

■ In 1890, Vincent van Gogh painted a warning of the TARDIS's imminent explosion; 51 years later, the painting reached Winston Churchill, who tried to phone the Doctor but got River Song; River stole the painting from the Royal Collection in 5145, then left a message for the Doctor on Planet One at the dawn of time – a fifty-foot 'Hello, Sweetie!' and the coordinates for Salisbury Plain in AD 102. When the Doctor got to Britain, River showed him the painting. All this left him none the wiser.

■ Stonehenge was a giant transmitter, broadcasting a warning to everyone everywhere in the universe: 'The Pandorica is opening.'

■ Kazran Sardick's Christmas took a strange turn when old home movies started showing childhood events that had never happened. Things got stranger when his memories changed too. But even that wasn't enough to get through to him.

DOCTOR WHO IN YOUR HOME

It was the Dark Time, before downloads and iPlayers and Sky-Plus. For the first twenty years of *Doctor Who*'s life, each episode was shown once on BBC One – and that was that. If you wanted to see it again, you couldn't. There were rumours of far-off paradises with exotic names like 'America' and 'Australia', where Tom Baker could be seen five nights a week; some fans placed cassette recorders in front of the screen and made audio recordings of each story, often with an unwelcome accompanying commentary from younger siblings ('It's K-9!!'); thousands of children bought Target's novelisations, which started properly in 1974. But the commercial availability of the actual stories was all but non-existent for decades. This is its history:

1966 Century 21 Productions released a 21-minute 'mini-album', *The Daleks*, featuring a condensed soundtrack of the sixth episode of *The Chase*, with linking narration by David Graham, one of the original Dalek voice actors.

1979 BBC Records and Tapes produced a soundtrack of *Genesis of the Daleks*, narrated by Tom Baker. It was heavily abridged, getting all six episodes down to the length of about two.

1983 Among the first home video cassettes released by BBC Enterprises was *Revenge of the Cybermen*, its four episodes edited down to a 90-minute omnibus, and retailing at £39.95. *The Tomb of the Cybermen* had topped a poll to determine the first release, but that story was lost from the BBC archives at the time. In 2003, the final VHS release was a collection of incomplete William Hartnell and Patrick Troughton stories, with every other existing episode having been released over the previous 20 years.

1992 *The Evil of the Daleks* and *The Macra Terror* launched BBC Audio Collection's Missing Stories range on cassette, using those old fan-made cassette recordings with linking narration by Tom Baker and Colin Baker.

1999 *The Massacre* was the first missing story to be released, with narration, on CD by BBC Audiobooks. The range covered all of the missing and incomplete stories between 1999 and 2006.

1999 BBC Video launched its DVD range with six releases: *The Black Adder*, *Doctor Who*, *Noddy in Toyland*, *Persuasion*, *The Planets* and *Monty Python's Flying Circus*. The *Doctor Who* release was a special edition of *The Five Doctors*. Regular releases of stories as broadcast began the following year with *The Robots of Death*. Each story has been digitally restored, and extra features include documentaries, deleted scenes and photo galleries. BBC DVD's Series Three box set in 2007 included the Doctor's complete recording for Sally Sparrow – as an Easter egg.

2008 *Doctor Who* episodes began to be made available as downloads.

2009 *Planet of the Dead* was the first *Doctor Who* story to be recorded in High Definition and hence the first to come out on Blu-ray.

060

The Valiant

2008

In the 21st century, when the Earth's governments were more and more concerned with denying the existence of aliens, UNIT got on with the business of defending the planet. They constructed the *Valiant* – a great achievement – a sub-orbital defence platform and aircraft carrier designed by British Defence Minister Harold Saxon. The *Valiant* was capable of defending the Earth from attackers from beyond the planet and on the planet's surface.

When the Toclafane made themselves known, UNIT placed the *Valiant* at the disposal of world powers, including the President-Elect of the USA – although the whole show was run by Harry Saxon, now Prime Minister. Revealed as the Master, he took over the *Valiant*, from which he directed his conquest of the world. Ordering the destruction of one-tenth of the Earth's population, he ruled from the skies for a year, abusing his wife, the Jones family, Captain Harkness and the Tenth Doctor. While the Master prepared a fleet of war rockets, Martha Jones was seeding a message that flooded his Archangel network and restored the Doctor to life, allowing him to reset the timelines.

When the Sontarans detonated millions of ATMOS devices the following year, unleashing Caesofine concentrate into the atmosphere, the *Valiant* was deployed to help clear the poisoned skies. It led an assault on the Sontaran forces in the ATMOS factory and was also a key part of Earth's defences during the later Dalek invasion, when it was completely destroyed.

After the loss of the *Valiant*, UNIT established an early warning base on the Moon, realising that if it wanted to protect the Earth from invasion it needed to be better prepared.

VALIANTLY INSPIRED

The *Valiant* is a tribute to SkyBase from Gerry Anderson's *Captain Scarlet*, which was used to launch the Angels into action against Mysteron attack. The elaborate set for the *Valiant* interior was later reworked as the Hub's Boardroom for Series Two of *Torchwood*.

The *Valiant* was *Doctor Who*'s first sub-orbital airborne base, but the series had already had its own Skybase, in *The Mutants* in 1972. The Marshal ruled Solos from the safety of Skybase One, a space station in planetary orbit. In fact, the outer space of the future will be fairly cluttered with Earth-made satellites:

21ST CENTURY Space Station W3, or 'the Wheel': one of several satellites stationed in Earth's solar system, acting as a radio-visual relay for Earth, a halfway house for deep-space ships, a space research station, and a stellar early warning station for all types of space phenomena.

2084 Sentinel Six: one of a number of defensive satellites armed with robot weapons systems, orbiting Earth just above the atmosphere belt.

22ND CENTURY Mark Five Space Beacons: a network of beacons monitoring space traffic.

29TH CENTURY Nerva and Ganymede Beacons: parts of a network of beacons put in orbit to service and guide space freighters. Nerva would later be converted into a space station to carry cryogenically suspended humans escaping solar flares that were ravaging Earth.

46TH CENTURY Davros, the creator of the Daleks, was captured on Skaro and held for 90 years in suspended animation aboard a prison station.

200,000 Satellite Five: a 500-storey orbiting space station, which broadcast the news to Earth and its Fourth Great and Bountiful Empire. Later converted into the Game Station by the Bad Wolf Corporation, it was eventually overrun with Daleks.

5 BILLION Platform One: a fully automated, alpha-class luxury space station from which the most wealthy beings in the cosmos could view the end of planet Earth.

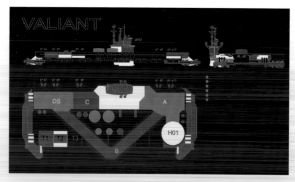

THE ARCHANGEL NETWORK

A network of 15 satellites orbiting the planet Earth, Archangel provided mobile communications for almost the whole population and carried signals for all the other service providers. The network continuously broadcast a second, hidden signal to all users, which affected the subconscious of 98 per cent of the British population – layers of code contained in a low-level hypnotic rhythm. This signal convinced everyone that the Master was Harold Saxon, made them blind to his invented history and convinced them to vote for him. As a result, even the Doctor had been unable to detect the Master's presence on Earth during the previous eighteen months.

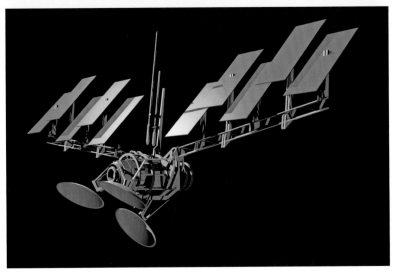

061

Adipose

2009

I n 2009, the bees left planet Earth, but no one noticed because they were too busy losing weight. Adipose Industries' explosively effective miracle cure for obesity, the Adipose Capsule, was composed of a synthesised mobilising lipase, bound to a large protein molecule. In theory, the mobilising lipase broke up the triglycerides stored in the adipose cells, which then entered the bloodstream and were flushed away; in truth, the Adipose Capsule bound the excess fat together to form an Adipose child. This parthenogenetic process was triggered by a bioflip digital stitch contained in the gold pendant given to each customer, and the capsule contained in each pendant bio-tuned itself to its user with a single touch.

The Adipose were a race of creatures entirely composed of fat. They reproduced asexually by seeding other life forms and absorbing fat from their bodies until a single kilogram was amassed to form a tiny, self-sustaining body. The child Adipose then separated from its host. It fed on fat, but could also convert bone, hair and internal organs, although these elements made the child feel sick. A fully grown Adipose was 4.5 metres tall.

WIRRN WITH GOOD PR

The Wirrrn were a similar parasitic race encountered by the Fourth Doctor on the Nerva Beacon in the distant future. They fed off the hibernating bodies of humans stored after Earth was rendered uninhabitable by solar flare activity. The Wirrn were not just feeding; they were taking revenge. Much earlier, humans had come to the Wirrn Old Lands in Andromeda, and the Wirrn fought them for a thousand years until the humans destroyed their breeding colonies. The Wirrn then drifted through space, searching for a new habitat, eventually finding Space Station Nerva – the Ark. In the Old Lands, senseless herbivores had been the hosts for their hatchlings. Now they used the humans in

the Ark's cryogenic chamber, taking from them not just their bodies but also their knowledge. In one generation, the Wirrn would become an advanced technological species, absorbing knowledge of high energy physics and quantum mechanics. Every ramate in the next hatching of Wirrn would possess the sum of humanity's learning.

HUMANS MAKE SUCH GOOD HOSTS

Humans make an excellent food source, as the Adipose, Giant Spiders and Wirrn could all vouch. The Androgums thought that humans would make excellent cuisine – the meat looked so white and roundsomely layered on the bone, a sure sign of a tasty animal. Starving human colonies in the 47th century were able to survive on a protein compound derived from the corpses of their own dead, packaged and sold to them by Davros in the guise of the Great Healer.

HOW TO LOSE WEIGHT

Weight loss occurs when the body is burning more fuel than it is taking in, thus expending fat reserves. The simplest method of achieving this is to eat less and exercise more. That doesn't, of course, mean that there isn't an industry devoted to weight reduction, supplements and dieting – in the developed world, it's a multibillion-dollar industry which has been growing since the 1960s.

'Miracle diets' come in and out of fashion, as do treatments including pills – some of which have alarming side effects. Amphetamines were widely distributed on both sides of the Second World War as a combat drug – they increased alertness and wellbeing, and their side effects of anger and aggression were seen as useful. These same drugs were later prescribed to housewives who found the aggression and psychosis less useful. A currently popular replacement is a drug which is used to treat breathing difficulties in horses.

A similar 'miracle chemical' was the 'fat-free fat' substitute for oil called Olestra. Introduced into food in America in the 1990s, it behaved like oil in food but wasn't absorbed by the body, so it added no fat or calories to the foods it was included in. It did, however, have an unpleasant reported side effect – Olestra travelled through the body rapidly and sometimes without warning. Early test results led to the delicately-phrased warning 'Olestra may cause abdominal cramping and loose stools.' In other words, the fat just ran away.

062

The 200 to Victoria

2010

London's transport experts would have been incredulous to learn of the detour taken by the 200 bus service one Easter evening in 2010. Partway through its already eccentric route from the centre of the city to Brixton and back to Victoria, the bus had got as far as the Gladwell Road tunnel when it abruptly passed through a freak wormhole and ended up making an unscheduled stop on the planet San Helios on the other side of the universe.

One year earlier, San Helios had been a verdant world of forests and oceans, its population of a hundred billion living in thriving metropolises, and a major trading centre in the Scorpion Nebula. Then billions of metallic creatures resembling airborne stingrays swept across the planet in an immense swarm. Within months, San Helios was a dead world, the whole of its animal and vegetable life reduced to endless deserts of sand.

The stingrays could eat metal, which they extruded into their exo-skeletons, and they flew at such high speeds that their velocity actually created the wormholes through which they travelled between worlds. The swarm's next stop was planet Earth, and a few made it through the wormhole before it was closed. They were destroyed by UNIT troops, who had been called in by police after the disappearance of the bus.

The 200, of course, barely survived its journey through the wormhole, though it was reported to have been spotted flying over London later that night. The bus, along with celebrated jewel thief Lady Christina de Souza, was never recovered.

WE'RE GETTING THERE

It's a good thing UNIT gave the Third Doctor a car when he was exiled on Earth. With or without an Oyster card, Gallifreyans have always been bad news for the smooth running of our transport systems...

■ A London bus conductor in 1965 had to contend with two passengers trying to pay fares at 1963 rates.

■ In 1966, Gatwick Airport was thrown into utter chaos by the appearance of a police box on a runway, and that was before they even noticed that half their passengers were missing.

■ The London Underground had to be shut down – and the capital evacuated – twice in a decade: once thanks to an infestation of robot Yetis, and once because the place was full of pterodactyls and triceratops.

■ When plague-carrying civil servant Edward Masters arrived at Marylebone Station, the ticket collector was the first victim of thousands.

■ The Doctor isn't fond of bus stations, and with good reason: people waiting for a bus were slaughtered by Autons, who later hired a bus in order to tour the country handing out deadly daffodils, and in 2005 attacked a bus outside the Queen's Arcade in southeast London. A Navarino tourbus was blown up on Barry Island by the Bannermen in the 1950s. Visitors to the Psychic Circus encountered a lethal bus conductor.

■ The Doctor's experiences with taxis have been equally unlucky: a tramp was murdered by WOTAN after taking one to Covent Garden, the Doctor and Romana couldn't hire one in Paris to save human history, and Donna Noble's cab driver, on her wedding day, was a robot Santa.

■ Heathrow Airport suffered just as badly as Gatwick, when two of its Concordes went missing.

■ Even the roads have not been immune: the Doctor has been at the centre of gridlocks and road traffic accidents in San Francisco (1999), London (2006) and New York (5,000,000,053)...

■ ... and his presence in London in 2009, investigating deadly satnavs, prompted the Sontarans to trigger their ATMOS devices and poison the world's skies.

■ The T-Mat system worked very nicely for years, transmatting people and supplies around the globe in an instant, until the Ice Warriors arrived at T-Mat's Moonbase control centre.

■ When the Time Lords shifted Earth two light years through space, a fireball devastated the planet's surface – the tube stations survived (Victorian engineering was built to last), but only as residences for the enfeebled survivors.

CRASH

SMOKE drifting out of the top. Pulling out wider...
The broken bus in the middle of a VAST DESERT.
Standing alone in the expanse, wheels half-buried
in the sand.

Planet of the Dead

The desert scenes for *Planet of the Dead* were filmed in Dubai in February 2009, and one of the production's two specially purchased double-decker buses was despatched there from Cardiff, ahead of the cast and crew. On Thursday 8 January, the bus arrived safely in Dubai, having travelled some four thousand miles by land and sea – at which point somebody dropped a cargo container on it and all but flattened it. By the time the press got hold of the story, of

course, three weeks had passed, and writer Russell T Davies had revised the script to make clear that 'that's what wormholes do to buses'.

Other fun moments on production of *Planet of the Dead* included:

■ David Tennant briefly losing his voice during night-shoots in Cardiff

■ The UK enjoying its heaviest snowfalls in 20 years just as location filming got under way in Cardiff

■ The minibus carrying David Tennant to the Dubai location being stopped by armed police because its tail light was broken, while the sound recordist's minibus was briefly lost in the desert

■ A sandstorm wrecking most of a day's location filming

Despite all of which, the episode was completed as planned – just five days before its Easter Saturday broadcast.

063

Gallifrey

2010

Gallifrey, the Shining World of the Seven Systems, was originally located in the constellation of Kasterborous. The planet shone with burning gold – from the lush red grass on the slopes outside the Master's father's estate and the trees with silver leaves which glowed in the orange skies at the dawning of the planet's second star. The Citadel lay at the heart of the continent of Wild Endeavour. Beyond the Never Ending Mountains of Solace and Solitude were the Wastelands, where the Outlers lived – Gallifreyans who had rejected Time Lord society. There were also hermits on Gallifrey – one lived on the slopes outside the Doctor's family home and gave the young Time Lord much advice.

From behind their impenetrable transduction barriers, Gallifrey's people watched the universe. Inside the Citadel, lived the Time Lords, the masters of time travel, priding themselves on rarely interfering in the affairs of others. The Time Lords enjoyed twelve regenerations, and could live for ever, barring accidents. They were ruled over by a Lord High President, with the actual running of affairs in the hands of the Chancellor, with a High Council of Cardinals. Security was maintained by the Castellans and the Chancellery Guard. The young were rigidly schooled in their Academies and Chapters. At the age of nine, novice Time Lords were taken to the Untempered Schism for initiation, where they glimpsed the unshielded Time Vortex; some were driven mad and some ran away.

Gallifrey was destroyed in the Last Great Time War against the Daleks, reduced to dust and rock, with its final moments – like the rest of the War – timelocked. In the final days of the War, the resurrected President Rassilon conceived a scheme to save his planet and race: Gallifrey would be brought back into time and space via a link with the Master's mind, with the planet being summoned into being in the Sol system and destroying the Earth and moving into its orbit. Had this succeeded, Rassilon aimed to initiate the Final Sanction, rupturing the Time Vortex and destroying Time itself while the Time Lords ascended to become creatures of consciousness alone.

A GALLIFREYAN MISCELLANY

■ There are daisies on Gallifrey. The Doctor was once shown one by a hermit.

■ Many Time Lords owned a Perigosto stick.

■ The Rani once bred Gallifreyan mice so big they ate the President's cat.

■ Gallifrey's binary location from galactic zero centre was 10-0-11-0-0 by 0-2.

■ Native fauna included the flutterwing.

■ Time Lord Chapters included the scarlet and orange-robed Prydonians, the heliotrope-robed Patrexes and the green-robed Arcalians.

■ Presidents of the High Council have included Rassilon (at least twice), Pandak I, Pandak II and Pandak III, the Doctor (at least twice), Borusa and Flavia. Borusa's first (acting) presidency was preceded by a President whose assassination was remembered for longer than his name.

THE RISE AND FALL OF GALLIFREY

It could all have been very different. In the first episode of *Doctor Who* ever recorded – at Lime Grove Studios in London on 27 September 1963 – the Doctor and his granddaughter had this to say of their background:

```
THE DOCTOR: We are not of this race. We are not
of this Earth. We are wanderers in the fourth
dimensions of space and time, cut off from our own
planet and our own people by aeons and universes
that are far beyond the reach of your most advanced
sciences.
... SUSAN: I was born in the forty-ninth century.
```

Technical problems, and a general unease about the quality of this first effort, led to the episode being re-recorded three weeks later. The production team took the opportunity to rework a lot of the dialogue, in the process making the Doctor and Susan's origins more mysterious. It was this second attempt that was broadcast as the new series' very first episode, *An Unearthly Child* by Anthony Coburn:

```
THE DOCTOR: Yes, my civilisation. I tolerate
this century, but I don't enjoy it. Have you ever
thought about what it's like to be wanderers in the
fourth dimension? Have you? To be exiles? Susan and
I are cut off from our own planet, without friends
or protection. But one day we shall get back. Yes,
one day... one day...
... SUSAN: I was born in another time. Another world.
```

Where and when the Doctor had come from went largely unexplored for the next six years (apart from Susan telling the Sensorites that her planet was 'quite like Earth, but at night the sky is a burned orange, and the leaves on the trees are bright silver'). Then, as Patrick Troughton's time as the Second Doctor ended, Terrance Dicks and Malcolm Hulke presented the first glimpse of the Time Lords and their nameless home world. In Episode 10 of *The War Games*, the Doctor explained:

```
Well, the Time Lords are an immensely civilised
race. We can control our own environment, we can
live for ever, barring accidents, and we have the
secret of space-time travel ... we hardly ever use
our great powers. We're content simply to observe
and to gather knowledge.
```

The three Time Lords shown in the story have great powers – there is little evidence of technology, and they manipulate the beings and objects around them through mental energy. They condemn an alien war lord and his entire race to total erasure from time.

From then on, as more was revealed about the Time Lords, their grandeur was gradually reduced. A familiar trope in the Jon Pertwee years is the pompous bureaucrat – sometimes as comic relief, sometimes as an irritant – and the next Time Lord on screen was disguised as one of these. *Terror of the Autons* by Robert Holmes shows a bowler-hatted Time Lord, apparently with erratic control of his Time Ring, popping up to give supercilious warnings

about the Master. Later the same year, *Colony in Space* by Malcolm Hulke gave another glimpse of the Time Lords' planet, just after the Master has broken in and stolen their files. The three Time Lords dealing with the matter have the handy idea that they might temporarily lift the Doctor's exile whenever they need a problem sorted out and the Third Doctor soon becomes, in his own words, 'a galactic yo-yo'. *The Three Doctors* by Bob Baker and Dave Martin then introduced a President and a Chancellor. They spend much of the story squabbling about quite how sacrosanct the Laws of Time should be. When the Third Doctor names his home Gallifrey in *The Time Warrior*, he labels his people 'galactic ticket inspectors'.

It's not, therefore, a huge surprise when the Fourth Doctor's visits to Gallifrey feature a treacherous Chancellor assassinating his President, a Cardinal rewriting history to make it more acceptable, an elderly Coordinator operating antiquated machinery, confessions extracted by torture, a Castellan who throws his lot in with two sets of alien invaders in quick succession and a Chancellery Guard of dubious competence. Gallifreyan society is ossified, and obsessed with ritual and pageant, its people having forgotten their own history and the purpose of half of their technology. A once enigmatic race now tut about their robes and moan about their hips.

Later Doctors' encounters with their own race follow a similar pattern: corruption is endemic; President Borusa is driven mad by power and seeks everlasting life; the High Council is willing to execute the Doctor on the flimsiest pretexts, and will wipe out whole planets to punish petty thefts; even their mighty founder, Rassilon, is revealed to be playing dirty from beyond the grave.

Once the Time Lords are gone, destroyed in the Time War, the Ninth and Tenth Doctors both choose to remember them as wonderful beings from a spectacular world. Russell T Davies shows the Doctor as a man riven by loss and guilt over his own role in his people's demise. The Tenth Doctor's life ends as the Ninth's began – at the Moment of the Time Lords' destruction:

```
But then they went to war, an endless war, and it
changed them. Right to the core. You've seen my
enemies, Wilf; the Time Lords are more dangerous
than any of them.
```

Having failed to save the Master, the Doctor remains alone. There is a moment, in *The Doctor's Wife* by Neil Gaiman, where Matt Smith's Eleventh Doctor briefly believes he may have found one or more Time Lords, surviving outside the universe. He's overjoyed, and not just because he thinks he's found 'one of the good ones' – he needs to find another survivor who can forgive him.

064

Time Engine

2010

Once the Last Great Time War had removed the Time Lords, there was no one force to control time travel. Unwise temporal manipulation would sometimes let voracious predators like the Reapers into the universe – once, Gallifrey would have held them back. Organisations such as the Time Agency or the Shadow Proclamation sprang up, then crumbled again, and eventually time travel could be purchased in a bar for the price of a Calisto Pulse.

Some tried to build their own TARDISes. One such attempt crashed on Earth in 2010, using a perception filter to disguise itself as the upper flat in a single-storey house in Aickman Road, Colchester, Essex. With its crew dead, the emergency crash program began to test the local population to find a replacement: this time engine was activated and controlled by its operator's mental energies – the crew had only to want to leave, and the ship would take off. The human brain wasn't strong enough to power the ship, however, and the emergency program worked through 17 out of 6,000,400,043 people before the Eleventh Doctor arrived and forced it into emergency shutdown.

THE MYSTERY OF THE TIME ENGINE

The Time Engine at Aickman Road could disguise its external appearance, affecting local people's memories so they believed it had always been there. On the inside, it was dimensionally transcendental, with a layout very similar to the interior of a TARDIS. It was also semi-sentient, able to create a hologram to communicate its needs with others, and its controls responded to a particular kind of life form.

Its pilot's desiccated remains were still present when the Doctor arrived. A bipedal creature with five fingers on each of two arms, it was humanoid but not human. Neither was it a Silent, though the Doctor later discovered that the Silents themselves had acquired, or built, an identical time engine, which was hidden in Florida in 1969.

TEMPORAL POWERS

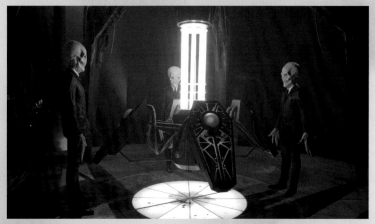

Unlicensed time experiments stamped out by the Time Lords or one of their agents included:

■ Theodore Maxtible and Edward Waterfield: They believed they had built a time corridor using static electricity and a precise arrangement of mirrors. They had instead attracted the attention of the Daleks.

■ The War Chief and the War Lord: A renegade Time Lord, the War Chief built a series of TARDIS-like machines, called SIDRATs, for the War Lord's people, to facilitate their 'War Games'.

■ Miniscopes: A device which used something like a Time Scoop to gather specimens and their environments then hold them in miniaturised form for the amusement of outside spectators. The Doctor had forced the Time Lords to outlaw them, but found one in operation on Inter Minor.

■ The Sontarans: Sontaran scout ships were equipped with an Osmic Projector which allowed Commander Lynx to gather scientists from the 20th century and pull them back to the Middle Ages.

■ Operation Golden Age: Professor Whitaker built a time scoop of his own, using it to bring dinosaurs into the present day. His ultimate plan was to send Earth back to prehistory.

■ The Giant Spiders of Metebelis Three: The human starship that crashed on the blue planet could time jump, and its residual time energies combined with the powers of the Metebelis crystals to allow the Spiders to project themselves and their thoughts through time and space.

■ The Osirans: Among the artefacts recovered from Sutekh's tomb was a casket that allowed entrance to a time tunnel. When Sutekh was freed, the Doctor moved the time tunnel's threshold into the distant future so the Osiran was dead before he reached its end.

■ Professor Theodore Nikolai Kerensky: Constructed a time bubble under the guidance of Scaroth of the Jagaroth, believing that he was about to solve the Earth's food-supply problems.

■ Meglos: The last Zolfa-Thuran trapped the Doctor and Romana in a Chronic Hysteresis. He wrongly believed that not even the Doctor could escape a chronic hysteretic loop.

■ The Cybermen (1): The addition of Cyber technology to an Earth freighter's antimatter engines, together with the meddling of an Alzarian maths prodigy, unexpectedly propelled the spaceship backwards in time by 65 million years (see 008. Badge for Mathematical Excellence).

■ The Malus: Buried beneath an English church for 300 years, the creature's psychic energies could summon solid projections of historical events.

■ The Cybermen (2): Planning to crash Halley's Comet into Earth, they stole a time vessel which was later destroyed by the Cryons.

■ Space Station Chimera: The Second Doctor was sent to stop the Kartz-Reimer time-travel experiments. A prototype module had already been constructed and was taken by a Sontaran squad.

■ The Timelash: The Borad built a time corridor on the citadel of Karfel using Kontron Crystals, and used it to expel rebels.

■ Nostalgia Tours: The Chimerans, the Navarinos and the Bannermen were all able to travel back to 1950s Earth via Tollport G715.

■ Fenric: When one of Dorothy's high-school science experiments went wrong, Fenric was able to use this as a cover for a time storm which took her to Ice World to await the arrival of the Doctor. Fenric also summoned a Haemovore from a polluted, dying Earth, back in time to the Viking era. Thanks to magic and the intervention of Fenric, Lady Peinforte was able to ride the back of time from the 17th century to a teashop in Windsor in the 20th.

In the wake of the Time War, temporal activity included:

■ The Time Agency: In the 51st century the Time Agency had ships that were capable of time travel and also Vortex Manipulators, worn as wriststraps.

■ The Clockwork Robots: The servitors on the SS *Madame de Pompadour* were able to open time windows between their ship and 18th-century France.

■ The Family of Blood: The Family's ship was capable of following the Doctor across space and time.

■ The Weeping Angels: Able to kill people nicely, sending them back in time.

■ The Silence: Used a Time Engine to invade the Earth in prehistory, and to transport River Song from the Luna University in the 51st century to Lake Silencio in 2011.

■ The Androzani Trees: Able to harness the mental energy of a human female in order to access the Time Vortex.

065

Fez

2010

The universe came to a premature end when it was sucked into a time field produced by the explosion of the TARDIS on 26 June 2010. Across the cosmos, reality collapsed, galaxies vanished and stars blinked out, until nothing was left beyond the eye of the storm: a burning TARDIS where the star Sol should have been, orbited by planet Earth, its history and populations gradually disappearing from time.

The fate of creation rested with a 21-year-old Earth girl, an Auton replica of her fiancé, their half-Time Lord daughter, and a man who was wearing a Fez because Fezzes are cool...

> THE DOCTOR: When the TARDIS blew up, it caused a total event collapse. A time explosion. It blasted every atom in every moment of the universe. Except..
> AMY: Except inside the Pandorica.
> THE DOCTOR: The perfect prison. Inside it, perfectly preserved, a few billion atoms of the universe as it was. In theory, you could extrapolate the whole universe from a single one of them, like cloning a body from a single cell. And we've got the bumper family pack ... The box contains a memory of the universe, and the light transmits the memory. And that's how we're going to ... relight the fire. Reboot the universe.
>
> *The Big Bang*

HISTORY OF A HAT

The Fez was originally a military hat, and could contain a metal plate to protect the head from heavy blows. It spread from the town of Fez in Morocco to the Ottoman Empire, where Sultan Mahmud II made it the official military headdress in the 1820s, and its use spread among his civil servants, replacing elaborate and opulent turbans with the simple, uniform and 'modern' Fez. A century later, the Ottoman Empire collapsed and, when Kemal Ataturk came to power, the Fez was the first thing to go. Literally seen as old hat, there was no place for it in the westernised Turkey which emerged from the Empire. Seen as a symbol of quaint orientalism, it was subsequently worn by comedians and magicians such as Laurel and Hardy and Tommy Cooper.

It wasn't a very good piece of military headwear – the red colour made the wearer a very good target.

FEZZES ARE COOL

Kemel the Turk, servant of Maxtible

Ibrahim Namin, servant of Sutekh

The Seventh Doctor

Albert Einstein

Kazran and the Doctor

The Flying Deuces

I WOULD LIKE A HAT LIKE THAT

From the sinking of the Titanic to the mercury swamps of Vulcan, the Doctor has long believed that hats are cool...

■ The First Doctor wore an Astrakhan Qaraqul whenever he was in 1960s London. His disguise of Regional Officer of the Provinces in 1789 Paris was completed by an elaborately plumed army officer's hat. He complemented his Atmospheric Density Jacket with a white Qaraqul on Vortis, and faced the Daleks in Ancient Egypt wearing a white Panama. And he wandered the Wild West in a Cowboy hat.

■ The Second Doctor developed a hat fixation within minutes of his regeneration, donning a stovepipe hat to face the Daleks on Vulcan and Zaroff in Atlantis, and regularly deployed the short-lived catchphrase 'I would like a hat like that.' In 18th-century Scotland, he picked up a Jacobite bonnet and an English army tricorn. Much later, he wore a British army officer's peaked cap in the trenches of the First World War.

■ The post-regenerative Third Doctor also tried out various headgear, dismissing a flat cap and briefly going for a trilby.

That didn't last; after that, he used hats only for disguise (e.g. a milkman's cap in Llanfairfach), though he occasionally adopted coveralls and a variety of protective helmets.

■ The Fourth Doctor considered a Viking helmet, the King of Hearts' crown and a conical Pierrot's hat before finding a wide-brimmed fedora. He kept the fedora, or variations on it, throughout this incarnation, just occasionally swapping it for a tam-o'-shanter in the Highlands, a deerstalker in Victorian London or a bowler on Fang Rock. He broke into Harrison Chase's estate in a chauffeur's uniform, complete with cap. He moved a hat stand into the TARDIS control room, then hung scarves and coats on it.

■ The Fifth Doctor was never without his cream Panama, which he would plonk on his head whenever he left the TARDIS, usually moments before taking it off again, rolling it up and replacing it in his pocket.

■ The Sixth Doctor never wore a hat, aside from a few seconds in a policeman's helmet. He did not believe hats were cool, though he considered the rest of his outfit to be the height of fashion...

■ The Seventh Doctor generally wore another Panama, and was also spotted in a fedora, a bearskin and a Fez.

■ The Eighth Doctor rejected a Stetson when purloining his Wild Bill Hicock outfit after his regeneration.

■ The Ninth Doctor was generally hatless, although he may have worn a top hat for the launch of the *Titanic*.

■ The Tenth Doctor wasn't really a hat man either, though he gave a straw hat a whirl on his final visit to the Ood-Sphere.

■ The Eleventh Doctor, though, can't walk past a hat without picking it up and putting it on his head. He's worn a top hat on several occasions, keeps going back to the Fez, adopted a pirate's hat on Avery's ship, and went to face his 'death' in a Stetson.

I LIKE HIS HAT, VERY FETCHING

Some of the more remarkable headpieces in *Doctor Who*:

066

Teselecta

2011

J ustice Department Vehicle 6018, the 'Teselecta', contained a crew of 421 humans, sustained by a compression field. It travelled through time, seeking out criminals near the ends of their lives and punishing them mercilessly for crimes they would have otherwise avoided retribution for. It was a shape-shifting robot, capable of impersonating people in order to blend in on its retrieval missions, and protected itself with antibodies, which would kill unwanted intruders. First meeting it in Nazi Germany, the Doctor later used the Teselecta to impersonate himself, avoiding death at Lake Silencio. He became trapped inside it in a bubble of time. He was able to use the Teselecta to simulate a release of regeneration energy. He also allowed it to age, growing a beard and altering his hair length.

ADVANCED ANDROIDS, ROBOT DUPLICATES AND CUNNING IMPOSTORS

■ The Daleks built a robot duplicate of the First Doctor, which they hailed as a 'success, a paramount success, completely indistinguishable from the original'. Its mission was to infiltrate and kill the TARDIS crew.

■ A series of elaborate android duplicates of Dracula, Frankenstein's Monster, and a Banshee inhabited Frankenstein's House of Horrors at the Festival of Ghana in 1996. The Festival was cancelled by Peking.

■ The Abbot of Amboise, in Paris at the time of the Massacre of St Bartholomew's Eve, may have been the First Doctor's double. Or the First Doctor could have been impersonating him. Nobody was ever sure.

■ Left faceless by the detonation of a terrible weapon, the Chameleons kidnapped young humans from Gatwick Airport and assumed their identities. The Doctor's companion Polly was replaced with a Chameleon calling herself Michelle Leuppi from Zurich.

■ The Second Doctor pretended to be his double, would-be world leader Salamander, so Salamander returned the compliment. The dictator was unable to keep up the pretence when he failed the 'Can he fly the TARDIS?' test.

■ As part of its first invasion plan, the Nestene Consciousness kidnapped various leading civil servants and military figures, placing them on display in Madame Tussauds, and replacing them with Auton duplicates.

■ The Zygons underneath Loch Ness were able to assume the identities of humans using body-printing, a service provided by the organic crystallography of their craft. They made a copy of companion Harry Sullivan.

■ Planning their invasion of Earth, the Kraals constructed a replica of the village of Devesham and its surroundings, complete with android duplicates of the inhabitants including the Doctor, Sarah and Harry Sullivan. The Doctor was able to reprogram his duplicate to help defeat the Kraals.

■ The third segment of the Key to Time created an illusory version of the Fourth Doctor, who pushed Romana over a cliff.

■ The people of Tara were experts at building androids, relying on such masters of the craft as Madame Lamia. She was able to construct replicas of most of the Taran royal family as well as the Doctor's companion Romana, who was herself mistaken for a natural doppelganger of Tara's most eligible spinster, Princess Strella, First Lady of Tara, a descendant of the Royal House, Mistress of the Domains of Thorvald, Mortgarde and Freya.

■ The cactoid Meglos assumed the shape of the Fourth Doctor and used the disguise to steal the Dodecahedron necessary to power the screens of Zolfa Thura.

■ The Urbankan Monarch replaced all of his followers with android duplicates. He also harvested peoples from Earth and converted them to androids.

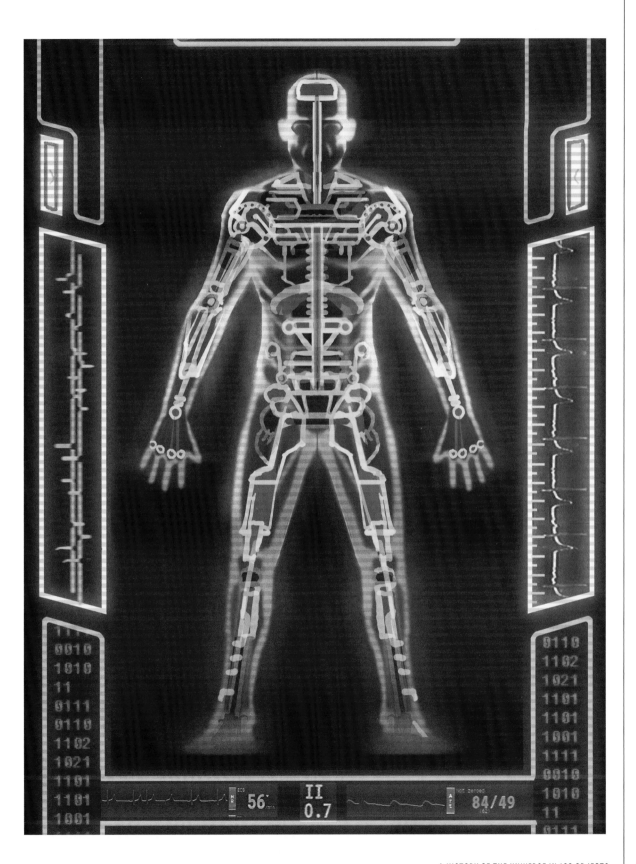

■ The Supreme Dalek planned to replace Earth's government with Dalek duplicates, having already built an army of duplicates under the control of a conditioned duplicate called Lytton. The Supreme Dalek also duplicated a team of soldiers guarding a warehouse and planned to replace the TARDIS crew with duplicates and send them to Gallifrey to assassinate the High Council.

■ Kamelion was a shape-changing robot created by the failed invaders of Xeraphas. The Master used him to create an impostor version of King John as part of his plan to disrupt the signing of Magna Carta.

■ When Omega broke through into our universe he borrowed the Fifth Doctor's form. The Fifth Doctor had just avoided being executed by a man who looked exactly like the Sixth.

■ The Androzani gunrunner Sharaz Jek was a brilliant builder of android duplicates, fooling General Chellak with copies of the Doctor and Peri, and of his chief of staff, Major Salateen.

■ Fearing assassination, Davros created a decoy duplicate of himself on Necros.

■ The Borad kept a spare clone of himself in case of emergencies.

■ The Autons created a double of Mickey Smith in order to find out what Rose Tyler knew about the Doctor.

■ The Slitheen disguised themselves in human body suits.

■ The Sontarans created clones of several humans, including Martha Jones, in order to launch their planned invasion.

■ The Pandorica alliance created a Nestene duplicate version of Rory Williams from Amy Pond's memories, not realising the original had been wiped from the universe by the crack in Amy's wall.

■ The Rebel Flesh were created when a Flesh cloning facility was struck by solar flare activity, resulting in these Gangers becoming independently conscious.

DUPLICATES AND IMPOSTORS – A SPOTTER'S GUIDE

■ The General Knowledge Test: Do they fail to know the current TARDIS crew? This was the downfall of the Daleks' robot double of the First Doctor, which didn't know that Vicki had replaced Susan. The Second Doctor also suspected the phantoms of the Dark Tower on these grounds.

■ The Fashion Test: When confronted by Sarah Jane Smith's android double, the Fourth Doctor noticed she was wearing a scarf she had earlier mislaid, and had also lost her aversion to ginger beer.

■ The Lethal Test: Is one of your friends suddenly trying to kill you? The robot First Doctor and the Kraal androids all gave themselves away with their bloodthirsty nature. The Nestene Rory just couldn't help killing Amy.

■ The Shiny Skin Test: Kamelion's impersonations betrayed themselves when he was confused, displaying a silver pallor. Mickey Smith's Auton duplicate had a bit of a plastic sheen to it, but was otherwise good enough to fool Rose Tyler.

■ The Bad Skin Test: The accuracy of Meglos's impersonation of the Fourth Doctor faltered every time his cactus spikes broke through. The accuracy of Omega's impersonation of the Fifth Doctor faltered when his face started to disintegrate.

■ The 'Stay Back!' Test: Is the impostor very keen that you don't do what you want to do? The phantoms of the Dark Tower and the fake Adric created by Kalid's Plasmatons were all very keen for everyone to turn around and go home.

■ The Good Acting Test: The Doctor originally spotted the Teselecta because it managed an all-too-perfect impression of someone fainting.

■ The Bad Acting Test: The Doctor has frequently become suspicious of duplicates when they've behaved strangely, with stilted, flat delivery. Zygon body prints betrayed themselves in this way, especially when they were first adopting a new identity.

■ The 'You're Supposed to Be Dead' Test: The remarkable resurrection of a Devesham soldier was a bit of a giveaway, as was the sudden appearance of Auton Rory.

■ The Body Language Test: The Fifth Doctor became suspicious of Major Salateen due to his lack of normal human behavioural cues. The Tenth Doctor had his doubts raised about Cassandra's Rose impression by her unprecedentedly warm body language in his presence.

■ The Body Odour Test: The Tenth Doctor recognised the Sontaran copy of Martha Jones as a clone because it smelled wrong. The Ninth Doctor identified Slitheen in human skinsuits as Raxacoricofallapatorians thanks to the decayed-calcium odour emitted by their inadequate gas exchange (if you'll pardon the expression).

Sonic Screwdriver

2011

Trapped aboard an automated prison ship disguised as the constantly shifting corridors and rooms of an ordinary hotel, the Doctor attracted the attention of its Minotaur inmate with his sonic screwdriver, also using it to open doors, scan a body, record speech and switch off monitor screens. It's always been a terrifically adaptable device.

First used by the Second Doctor for undoing screws, the sonic screwdriver has opened doors, resonated concrete and detonated mines. The one thing it isn't, is a weapon.

THE SECOND DOCTOR

■ Used sonic waves to undo screws in a gas-pipe inspection hatch, and later fed Victoria Waterfield's screams through it to an amplifier, producing a sonic laser sound wave to destroy a weed creature (*Fury from the Deep*)
■ Drilled a hole in a wall (*The Dominators*) Removed screws from a pistol, a wall panel and a control panel (*The War Games*)

THE THIRD DOCTOR

■ Remote-operated the door of a hut (*Inferno*)
■ Scanned the Master's TARDIS for booby-traps (*Colony in Space*)
■ Detected and exploded landmines, and opened a cell door (*The Sea Devils*)
■ Burnt out a door's locking circuit and opened handcuffs (*The Mutants*)
■ Detected antimatter (*The Three Doctors*)
■ Ignited marsh gas to ward off Drashigs (*Carnival of Monsters*)
■ Reversed the polarity of its power source, thereby converting it into an extremely powerful electromagnet with which to open a door (*Frontier in Space*)
■ Blew up a Dalek door-control unit (*Planet of the Daleks*)
■ Opened a lift door, and repelled giant maggots (*The Green Death*)
■ Detected booby-traps in the Exxilon city, dismantled the city's computer brain, and broke Bellal's hypnotic trance (*Death to the Daleks*)
■ Opened a Refinery door (*The Monster of Peladon*)
■ Tested Professor Clegg's clairvoyance (*Planet of the Spiders*)

THE FOURTH DOCTOR

■ Deactivated landmines and cut open a metal door lock (*Robot*)

■ Opened a control panel, rewired Wirrn-nibbled cables and undid screws (*The Ark in Space*)

■ Repaired transmat refractors, melted force-field controls, deactivated a robot, and accessed a Sontaran Scout Ship (*The Sontaran Experiment*)

■ Fused a communications system (*Genesis of the Daleks*)

■ Opened several doors (*Revenge of the Cybermen*)

■ Set off the Zygons' fire alarm (*Terror of the Zygons*)

■ Opened another door (*Planet of Evil*)

■ Deactivated a generator loop control (*Pyramids of Mars*)

■ Melted plastic vines and opened a floor panel (*The Android Invasion*)

■ Fixed the TARDIS's thermal couplings (*The Hand of Fear*)

■ Reassembled a laser gun and vibrated crystals to break Leela's hypnotic trance (*The Face of Evil*)

■ Opened lots more doors (*The Robots of Death*)

■ Cracked a safe (*The Sun Makers*)

■ Reversed the toxic fumigation process in the tunnels around the P7E (*Underworld*)

■ Made a hole in the force field protecting Gallifrey's Capitol (*The Invasion of Time*)

■ Undid sliding bolts for the first time and, eventually, multilevered interlocks, too (*The Ribos Operation*)

■ Opened another door (*The Pirate Planet*)

■ Unlocked manacles (*The Stones of Blood*)

■ Opened computer panels (*The Armageddon Factor*)

■ Primed explosive canisters to destroy Davros and the Daleks (*Destiny of the Daleks*)

■ Opened a wide range of doors (*City of Death*)

■ Unlocked a filing cabinet, fused an electronic door lock, repaired spaceship engines, and reversed the setting on the transmutation reflex of a CET machine (*Nightmare of Eden*)

■ Opened more doors, and worked on a gravitic anomaliser (*The Horns of Nimon*)

■ Opened an airlock and constructed a mind-control helmet (*Shada*)

■ Made a hole in the back of the Argolins' Tachyon Recreation Generator (*The Leisure Hive*)

■ Opened one last door (*Full Circle*)

THE FIFTH DOCTOR

■ Had Nyssa remove the Zero Room doors with it (*Castrovalva*)

■ Confused Monopticons and deactivated androids (*Four to Doomsday*)

■ Wired it into a Delta Wave Augmenter (*Kinda*)

■ Opened a sonic barrier, and then watched it being destroyed by a Terileptil (*The Visitation*)

THE SEVENTH DOCTOR

■ Sealed the Master's remains in a casket (*Doctor Who*)

THE NINTH DOCTOR

■ Disabled a lift, tracked Auton control signals, deactivated an Auton arm, and locked a door (*Rose*)

■ Opened a viewing screen shutter and a door, inspected a computer maintenance screen, uncovered spider sabotage, and raised sunfilters (*The End of the World*)

■ Unlocked a door, and repaired parts of the TARDIS (*Aliens of London*)

■ Closed a lift door, unlocked another door, bluffed the Slitheen, and scanned the Cabinet Room (*World War Three*)

■ Stole from a cashpoint, inspected Satellite Five's mainframe, undid manacles, and blew up an answerphone (*The Long Game*)

■ Sealed church doors, and charged a phone battery (*Father's Day*)

■ Opened a door and a padlock, conducted medical scans (*The Empty Child*)

■ Unlocked and relocked another door, tried to resonate concrete, undid handcuffs, had Rose reattach barbed wire, and scanned a Chula medship (*The Doctor Dances*)

■ Overrode Margaret Slitheen's teleport (*Boom Town*)

■ Destroyed a *Big Brother* camera, opened various doors, and scanned the Game Station's energy readings (*Bad Wolf*)

■ Scanned a dead Dalek, remote-activated Emergency Program One on the TARDIS, and constructed a Delta Wave (*The Parting of the Ways*)

THE TENTH DOCTOR

■ Blew up a Christmas tree and threatened some Roboforms (*The Christmas Invasion*)

■ Scanned a hospital sub-frame, opened doors and fixed up a winch in a lift shaft (*New Earth*)

■ Locked doors and released handcuffs (*Tooth and Claw*)

■ Unlocked a door, repaired K-9, and locked more doors (*School Reunion*)

■ Scanned a fireplace and under a bed, lit a candle, threatened robots, undid handclamps, and fixed a loose connection in a time window (*The Girl in the Fireplace*)

■ Disabled earpods, diverted Cybermen, pinpointed a control signal, opened and closed a door, undid a Cyber chestplate, switched off a Cyberman, and had Pete Tyler burn through a rope ladder (*The Age of Steel*)

■ Scanned a faceless granny for neural impulses, opened gates, scanned a portable TV, and scanned for power sources (*The Idiot's Lantern*)

■ Keyed into the Abzorbaloff's absorption matrix and separated Ursula Blake (in her paving stone) (*Love & Monsters*)

■ Deanimated a scribble creature (*Fear Her*)

■ Had Rose stabilise TARDIS controls with it while he triangulated a Ghost's point of origin, splintered a glass window, deactivated Cyber earpods, and traced a remote transmitter (*Army of Ghosts*)

■ Detonated explosives, and boosted his projection through the Void (*Doomsday*)

■ Got Donna free calls from a payphone, stole money from another cashpoint, made the cashpoint blast thousands of pounds into the street, unlocked a taxi window, disabled a Roboform, scanned Donna, gave a mobile phone a faster browser, boosted a sound system to vibrate Roboform Santas to pieces, scanned a Roboform headpiece, manipulated a computer, overrode lift controls, opened a door, and freed Donna from a Racnoss web (*The Runaway Bride*)

■ Examined a computer, and boosted the radiation of an X-ray machine (*Smith and Jones*)

■ Activated display screens, opened doors, activated a communicator screen, opened several cars' floor and roof hatches, rewired a car's exhaust system (*Gridlock*)

■ Opened a manhole, and disassembled a radio (*Daleks in Manhattan*)

■ Caused radio feedback, tried to detach Dalekenium panels from the Empire State building, signalled his presence to the Daleks (*Evolution of the Daleks*)

■ Shut down Lazarus's overloading GMD, scanned for Lazarus's energy signature, locked and unlocked doors, reset the GMD capsule to reflect energy rather than receive it, and boosted the volume of a church organ (*The Lazarus Experiment*)

■ Gave Martha's phone Universal Roaming, and scanned Korwin McDonnell (*42*)

■ Opened a door, boosted a power circuit, and fused the TARDIS coordinates (*Utopia*)

■ Repaired Captain Jack's Vortex Manipulator, disabled a CCTV camera, uncovered the Archangel Network's hidden signal in Martha's phone, and welded circuitry to TARDIS keys to create perception filters (*The Sound of Drums*)

■ Disabled Captain Jack's Vortex Manipulator again (*Last of the Time Lords*)

■ Popped a champagne cork, stabilised an oxygen shield, and opened lots of doors and a window (*Voyage of the Damned*)

■ Opened a fire exit, unlocked and relocked several doors, operated a window cleaner's cradle, zapped Miss Foster's sonic pen, discovered what happened if you held two sonic devices against each other, and transmitted a statement to the Shadow Proclamation (*Partners in Crime*)

■ Knocked over circuit carvings, loosened ropes and locked a capsule door (*The Fires of Pompeii*)

■ Opened gates, doors and cages (*Planet of the Ood*)

■ Inspected an ATMOS device, and disabled a teleport and another ATMOS device (*The Sontaran Stratagem*)

■ Controlled UNIT's communications systems, scanned for alien technology, and reactivated the teleport (*The Poison Sky*)

■ Uncovered a layer of suppressed information in a holographic map, and gave Donna's phone Universal Roaming (*The Doctor's Daughter*)

■ Operated information terminals in The Library, inspected a security camera, scanned shadows, and increased the mesh-density of protective suits (*Silence in the Library*)

■ Scanned more shadows, intercepted a signal, darkened helmet visors, opened a trap door, and disabled a gravity platform (*Forest of the Dead*)

■ Stopped the Crusader 50's entertainment systems, scanned the bus's engines and systems, and removed a wall panel (*Midnight*)

■ Disabled Captain Jack's Vortex Manipulator again (*Journey's End*)

■ Opened a door, a desk and some luggage (*The Next Doctor*)

■ Darkened his glasses lenses, and gave Barclay's phone Universal Roaming (*Planet of the Dead*)

■ Scanned for traces of Sarah Jane Smith (*The Wedding of Sarah Jane Smith*)

■ Activated a computer screen, boosted Gadget's speed, and unlocked Adelaide's front door (*The Waters of Mars*)

■ Unlocked a door, and deactivated Vinvocci shimmers (*The End of Time, Part One*)

■ Shut down a teleport, and shut down the Hesperus (*The End of Time, Part Two*)

THE ELEVENTH DOCTOR

■ Scanned then opened the Crack in Amy's wall, boosted a radio's reception, and signalled his presence to the Atraxi (*The Eleventh Hour*)

■ Scanned for engine activity, operated a lamp and scanned for his location (*The Beast Below*)

■ Opened up the android Bracewell's chest (*Victory of the Daleks*)

■ Boosted River Song's communicator signal (*The Time of Angels*)

■ Opened a hole in the Byzantium, switched lights on and off, opened a door and some wall clamps, and scanned the Crack (*Flesh and Stone*)

■ Opened a gate and a door, scanned vampire bites on Amy's neck, and disrupted the Saturnynes' perception filters (*The Vampires of Venice*)

■ Scanned human remains and possessed humans, opened and locked doors, and blew out a light (*Amy's Choice*)

■ Opened a gate, scanned a hole in the ground, hacked into computer records, revealed a force field, and boosted cameras to send a sonic pulse (*The Hungry Earth*)

■ Scanned for heat-signature anomalies, exploded guns, opened and shut doors and barricades, and scanned Rory (*Cold Blood*)

■ Opened a door, disrupted a control panel and manipulated the emergency crash program hologram on the Time Engine (*The Lodger*)

■ Scanned Stonehenge, used it as a torch, folded back the Stonehenge signal (*The Pandorica Opens*)

■ Had Rory open the Pandorica, scanned Amy's body, shut Amy in the Pandorica, unlocked a door, scanned his future self's body, boosted a satellite dish, and sealed a hatch (*The Big Bang*)

■ Scanned Sardick and his control console, lured flying fish and a shark, and transmitted Abigail's singing through it (*A Christmas Carol*)

■ Unlocked a door, scanned a spacesuit, and undid some straps (*Day of the Moon*)

■ Dried out a pirate's hat, unlocked a door, scanned a room, and scanned a body (*The Curse of the Black Spot*)

■ Scanned Patchwork People, opened a cell door, scanned House's surface, and polished the TARDIS console (*The Doctor's Wife*)

■ Scanned the monastery ruins and the Flesh (*The Rebel Flesh*)

■ Scanned people, Gangers and acid, boosted a holo-call, and melted Gangers and the Flesh Amy (*The Almost People*)

■ Let Rory use it to access a Cyber ship, opened doors, scanned Lorna and raised a force field (*A Good Man Goes to War*)

■ Heated a letter opener, and lent the sonic screwdriver to Amy to signal him from inside the Teselecta (*Let's Kill Hitler*)

■ Scanned a council estate, entertained a small boy, and scanned a cupboard (*Night Terrors*)

■ Tried to control a Time Glass, and had Rory sonic the Twostreams controls (*The Girl Who Waited*)

■ Opened a door, scanned a body, attracted a Minotaur, amplified sound and shut off CCTV monitors (*The God Complex*)

■ Scanned for sulphur emissions and teleport energy, activated a lift and a teleport, stunned a Cybermat, used its torchbeam setting, and gave Alfie a more impressive star display (*Closing Time*)

■ Opened up a Dalek's dome and data core, identified and disrupted the Teselecta, opened the box containing Dorium's head, and closed a trap door (*The Wedding of River Song*)

■ Opened an airlock, spookily illuminated his own face, rewired equipment, and scanned a relay circlet (*The Doctor, the Widow and the Wardrobe*)

■ And, at some point, hid a neural relay in the sonic screwdriver he gave to River Song, knowing that it would one day 'save' her consciousness into CAL at The Library (*Forest of the Dead*)

Despite all that, the sonic screwdriver is 'rubbish at wood', 'doesn't work on a deadlock seal' and couldn't, in its earliest form, open non-electronic locks. As a result, the Doctor is just as likely to be seen waving it about uselessly and saying something like 'Even the sonic screwdriver won't get me out of this one.'

068

Cybermat

2007

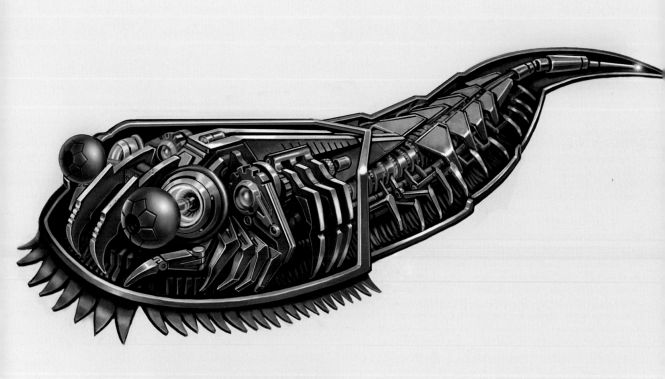

> THE DOCTOR: It's not a rat, it's a Cybermat...
>
> *Closing Time*

In 2011, Sanderson & Grainger's department store in Colchester was suffering an infestation: small and very fast silver robots, converted from rodents, armed with viciously sharp, apparently organic teeth and glowing red eyes, and something to do with a recent spate of power fluctuations. The Cybermats were harvesting power for a force of Cybermen concealed beneath the shop. These Cybermen had crashed on Earth centuries earlier and had been stranded ever since, in effective hibernation until they could gather enough power to begin to repair themselves and their ship and convert new forces.

THE INSPIRATION FOR THE CYBERMATS

The Cybermats were introduced in *The Tomb of the Cybermen*, a story that has many parallels with archaeological expeditions of Egyptian tombs such as that of Tutankhamen. A common find in these tombs were Scarab beetles which were found littering the floor (believed to be a totem that meant transformation or rebirth). Early Cybermat design was influenced by these scarabs.

COMPLETE METAL BREAKDOWN

The Doctor first had to contend with Cybermats in the icy tombs of Telos. There were two types of Cybermat – both like vicious silverfish with translucent eyes, one the size of a rat, the other more shrew-like, which could hide in a handbag. Both were lethal, homing in on human brainwave patterns via tiny antennae. They were vulnerable to electrical charges.

He later encountered them on the W3 space station, where they were used to devour fuel. When the Wheel's crew were lured onto a nearby rocket in search of replacement fuel, they came under the control of the Cybermen. These Cybermats had photoreceptors in place of eyes and contained a deadly electric charge which they deployed when discovered.

On Nerva Beacon, the Doctor dealt with another generation of Cybermats, converted from a different animal species, more similar to a very large worm. These Cybermats injected a neurotoxin, which simulated the conditions of plague in its victims. Like the Cybermen, these Cybermats were vulnerable to gold dust.

069

Hairdryer

2012

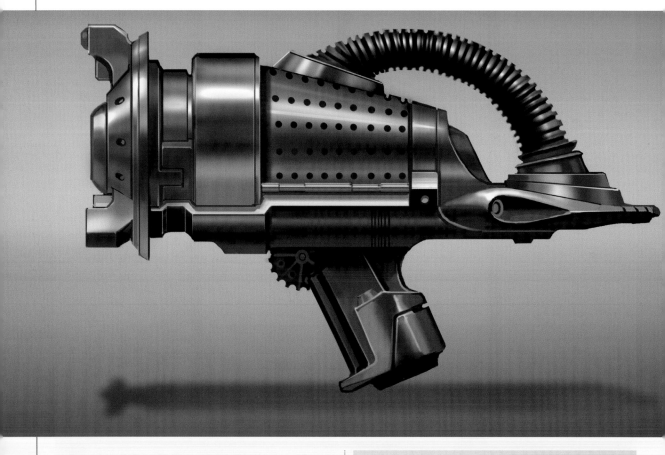

As knowledge of aliens spread during the early 21st century, collecting evidence of them became the ultimate rich man's hobby. Henry Van Statten's subterranean Geocomtex facility in Utah contained the most valuable collection of extraterrestrial artefacts on planet Earth, a museum of relics of alien visitations, forced landings and failed invasions.

The prize of the collection was what Van Statten named the 'Metaltron' – in fact the last Dalek survivor of the Time War. It had fallen through time and plummeted, burning, to Earth in the early 1960s. Sold in a series of private auctions over the next 50 years, it was eventually installed in a specially constructed cage in the depths of the Utah facility. There, Van Statten's personnel tortured it in an effort to make it talk. All it did was scream. The Dalek was finally restored to full working order when it was touched by Rose Tyler – it was regenerated by the background radiation she had picked up travelling through time. It rampaged through the base, killing more than 400 personnel.

Determined to confront and destroy it, the Ninth Doctor ransacked the store of uncatalogued alien weapons...

THE DOCTOR pulling guns out of boxes, inspecting them, then tossing them aside. ADAM winces as he does so.
THE DOCTOR: Broken. Broken. Hairdryer.
ADAM: Mr Van Statten tends to dispose of his staff, and when he does, he wipes their memory – I kept this stuff, in case I needed to fight my way out one day –
THE DOCTOR: What, you, in a fight? I'd like to see that!
ADAM: I could do!
THE DOCTOR: What you gonna do, throw your A Levels at 'em?
(finds)
Ohhh yes!
And he lifts up a GREAT BIG BRUTE OF A SPACE-GUN!
THE DOCTOR: Lock and load!

Dalek

'I NEVER CARRY WEAPONS'

The Doctor is a belligerent pacifist – he's admonished anti-Dalek freedom fighters and primitive savages for resorting to using weapons, and often refused to carry a firearm, even in self-defence many, many times. When it comes to using guns, he's the man who never would. Except...

The First Doctor toted Doc Holliday's six-shooter at the gunfight at the OK Corral.

In *The Seeds of Death*, the Second Doctor improvised a solar energy gun and despatched Ice Warriors with it.

The Third Doctor shot and killed an Ogron with a ray gun in *Day of the Daleks*.

In *The Seeds of Doom*, the Fourth Doctor planned to threaten Chase's guards with a revolver.

He attempted to shoot the Time Lord President's assassin in *The Deadly Assassin*...

... and armed himself with an elephant gun in *The Talons of Weng-Chiang*, using it to put down a giant rat.

Possessed by the Nucleus of the Swarm, he also fired a ray gun at Leela in *The Invisible Enemy*.

In *Image of the Fendahl* he fired rock salt from a rifle at a Fendahleen.

In *The Invasion of Time*, he used a De-Mat gun to wipe out the Sontarans.

The Fifth Doctor repeatedly shot a Cyberleader in *Earthshock*...

... turned an antimatter converter gun on Omega in *Arc of Infinity*...

... and decided to execute Davros in *Resurrection of the Daleks*, after using a pistol against a Dalek mutant.

He also used the Master's Tissue Compression Eliminator on Kamelion in *Planet of Fire*.

Attack of the Cybermen saw the Sixth Doctor blast the Cyber Controller and his Cybermen with a Cyberweapon.

The Eighth Doctor stole a traffic cop's gun and threatened to shoot himself.

The Tenth Doctor threatened Jenny's murderer, General Cobb, with a gun in *The Doctor's Daughter*...

... and finally confronted the Master and Rassilon bearing Wilf's sidearm in *The End of Time, Part Two*.

O7O

Bowie Base One

2O58

The 21st century didn't go well for planet Earth. After repeated alien contact, invasion and even the theft of the entire planet, Earth faced forty long years of mounting chaos: climate change, ozone pollution, melting polar icecaps and the Oil Apocalypse led humanity to the brink of extinction. The planet badly needed good news. Then, on 1 July 2058, it was reported that Apollo 34 had successfully landed on Mars after a nine-month flight, and Bowie Base One, the first non-terrestrial colony, had been successfully established in the Gusev Crater.

Bowie Base One was a research base, its nine-strong multinational crew on a five-year mission to establish the viability of full-scale colonisation of Mars. Research centred on a bio-dome containing a delicately balanced ecosystem of plant-life, insects and birds – the hope was that it would prove possible to grow vegetable crops in Martian soil, using water from a newly discovered subterranean glacier. Over the next 17 months, that hope was slowly realised...

HEROES

Captain Adelaide Brooke (1999–2059)
Deputy Edward Gold (2008–2059)
Senior Technician Steffi Ehrlich (2021–2059)
Junior Technician Roman Groom (2034–2059)
Doctor Tarak Ital (2026–2059)
Nurse Yuri Kerenski (2032–2059)
Officer Andrew Stone, botanist (2025–2059)
Officer Mia Bennett, geologist (2032–2059)
Officer Margaret Cain (2028–2059)

LIFE ON MARS?

Just as bipedal reptilian species dominated Earth before the evolution of humanity, the neighbouring world of Mars had its own advanced civilisation millions of years before man had learnt the true use of fire. Unlike Homo reptilia, these Martians evolved to thrive in extreme cold. They adapted their biology to incorporate bio-armour and sonic weaponry and became a feudal race of warriors ruled by lords. But as conditions on Mars grew harsher, an ancient unstoppable force began to take hold – the Flood. The Martians were forced to abandon their home world and flee for the stars. Before Earth's First Ice Age had begun, they were sending spacecraft out from Mars to conquer and colonise other worlds, one of which crashed in what would eventually become Britain, becoming buried at the foot of glacier.

By 8000 BC, the last Martian flora had died out, and the planet was effectively a dead world. Around 5000 BC, the Osirans took Mars, constructing a pyramid there to control the force field that held Sutekh (see 011. Pyramids of Mars).

Some 7,000 years later, humanity's technology had finally advanced as far as space flight. Having reached the Moon, their efforts turned to Mars, and the British space programme began sending manned probes to Mars. The sixth and seventh of these encountered unidentified alien ambassadors from another galaxy, but it was not a happy meeting and the aliens swiftly withdrew from the Sol system. The space programme was abandoned and forgotten for 30 years, until Professor Daniel Llewellyn and the British Rocket Group sent an unmanned probe to Mars in 2006.

Guinevere One never reached its destination, but NASA was prompted to resume its own explorations. When the Phoenix lander found frozen water on Mars in 2008, NASA continued to send probes to Mars. (One of these inexplicably shut down in 2010 as soon as it landed on the planet surface, not far from the location of the Osiran pyramid.) Then, in 2041, the first three-man mission landed on Mars, and preparations began for the first inhabitable Mars base. A century later, Earth and its Mars colony fell to the Dalek invasion, though on Mars the Daleks were defeated by a virus that attacked the insulation on the cables in their electrical systems. After the Dalek invasion, humanity withdrew from Mars to concentrate on rebuilding planet Earth.

Around this time, the Martians returned to reclaim their world, and they soon had Earth in their sights too. They launched an offensive via Earth's T-Mat control on the Moon, sending rapidly germinating seedpods that spread an oxygen-draining fungus that would reconstitute the planet's atmosphere, making it suitable for the Martians while wiping out humanity.

Over time, the Martians turned aside from conquest and war, becoming leading partners with Earth in a new interplanetary Federation. Alongside Mars and Earth, Federation membership extended to species from Alpha Centauri, Arcturus and, eventually, less advanced planets such as Peladon. There were suspicions, however, that the Federation existed largely in order for Earth to exploit other worlds – Peladon, like Mars, was rich in the mineral trisilicate, and Mars itself was now home to at least 16 human colonies. At least one Martian faction broke away, reclaimed their Ice Warrior heritage and aligned themselves with the rival Galaxy 5, fomenting trouble on Peladon and working against Federation interests. At around the same time, the Guardian of the Solar System, Mavic Chen was making secret overtures to the Daleks. This seems to have been the beginning of the end for peaceful co-existence between humanity and the Martians. At some point after the Venus-Mars Games of the year 4000, the Earth-Mars partnership was dissolved, and the Martians were airbrushed from human history. By the time of Earth's Second Ice Age (c.51st century), when that long-buried spacecraft was rediscovered in the Brittanicus glacier, the Ice Warriors had been forgotten.

Mars was part of the Fourth Great and Bountiful Human Empire, with a university established there by the year 200,000, though not one with a great reputation.

Millions of years later, the Usurians took over the Sol system, moving humanity from Earth – first to Mars, and then on to Pluto once Mars's resources had been exhausted.

Carrots

2059

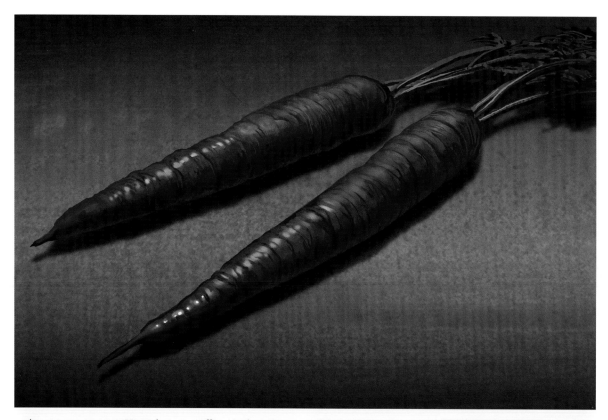

At 9.20 p.m. on 20 November 2059, Officer Andrew Stone reported in the Bowie Base One maintenance log that the third of the Bio-dome's three water filters was broken and could not be replaced – the spare stock did not fit. Within 24 hours, the base had been destroyed in a nuclear blast and most of its crew were dead.

The day had started well. Andy Stone discovered the first fruits of their agricultural trials – a crop of fresh, healthy carrots, the first vegetables to grow in Martian soil in 10,000 years. Stone rinsed a carrot then bit into it...

But the faulty filter had let something into the water supply in Bowie Base One – the Flood, an ancient force that could take over an animal life form in moments, suppressing and controlling its intelligence. The Flood had only one purpose, one instinct: to drown everything in its waters.

With the base compromised and several of her crew possessed by the Flood, Captain Brooke was forced to initiate the first of five Standard Action Procedures – evacuation. Their escape route was cut off when the Flood breached their shuttle. If they reached Earth, they would spread the Flood there, too, and humanity would be wiped out. Eventually, Standard Action Five was the only option open to her – to detonate a nuclear device at the heart of the Central Dome, destroying the base and burning away the waters and the Flood.

FUTURE LEGEND

The fate of Bowie Base One and Captain Adelaide Brooke inspired Earth's future expansion into space. As it became clear that her action had saved Earth, Adelaide's daughter Emily and granddaughter Susie continued her work and followed her example. Thirty years later, Susie led humanity out into the galaxy, captaining the first light-speed ship to Proxima Centauri.

> THE DOCTOR: And then everywhere! With her children, and her children's children, forging the way, to the Dragon Star, the Celestial Belt of the Winter Queen, the Map of the Water Snake Wormholes – one day a Brooke will even fall in love with a Tandonian prince, and that's the start of a whole new species. But everything starts with you, Adelaide. From 50 years ago, to right here, today. Imagine.
>
> *The Waters of Mars*

Milo Clancey's Toaster

22ND CENTURY

The latter half of the 21st century saw the human race pouring out across the galaxy, pioneers and buccaneers rampaging unchecked across the stars for a hundred years. On Earth, cross-border cooperation came and went, with carefully negotiated multinational enterprises like the moon-based Gravitron system falling apart during the political turmoil of the 2080s. For a while, space exploration was left to individuals and private enterprise – prospectors roamed the galaxy looking for mineral wealth to exploit; piracy was rife; an interstellar vessel was as likely to be trafficking drugs like Vraxoin as ferrying cruise passengers. Eventually, the Earth government caught up and established a standard currency and regional administrations, setting up an Interstellar Space Corps to enforce the rule of law. The sudden appearance of the well-funded, well-equipped ISC could only provoke resentment among the pioneers who had made the spaceways their own.

Milo Clancey was the last of the type – wilfully old-fashioned, Clancey had spent four decades playing the Wild West frontiersman, complete with checked shirt, cowboy boots, extraordinary facial hair and even more extraordinary accent. He'd made his money and his name strip-mining the all but indestructible metal ore argonite from planets like Reja Magnum and Ta in the Pliny system, and spent decades on unlicensed deep-space exploration in a C-class freighter. The LIZ 79 was built entirely from tillium and ran on thermonuclear power and, after 40 years in service, it was barely afloat. Inside was a muddle of once top-of-the-range technology – navigational controls, communications and lighting systems, in varying stages of decay and disrepair – amid all the nostalgic comforts of home. Milo's last concession to progress was to acquire a solar toaster, and he couldn't get that to produce anything better than charcoal.

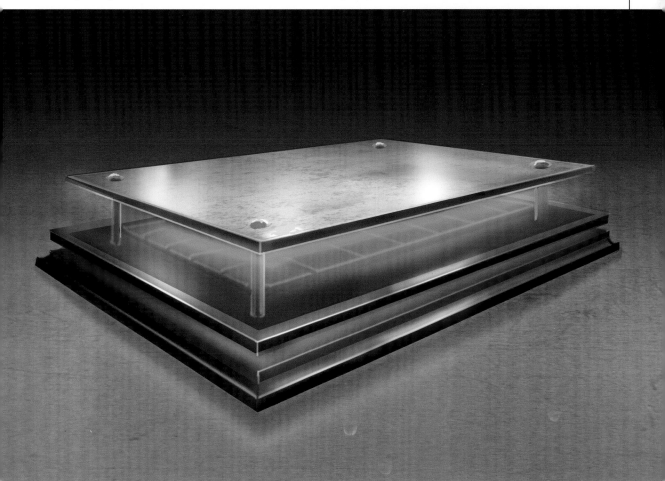

MAKING PROGRESS

In recent years, stories like *The Impossible Planet* and *The Beast Below* have depicted space exploration as tough, dangerous and grimy, the work of heroes struggling against elemental forces with unreliable equipment. In earlier days, though, *Doctor Who*'s writers and production teams generally tried to realise a brighter, shinier future forged in the white heat of technology. Fashions and furnishings, though, echoed those of the late 20th century. The preserved population of the pristine Space Station Nerva spun their glittering Bennett Oscillators wearing immaculate white uniforms, resplendent in beautifully tailored 1970s flares and bouffant hair. When Tom Baker's Doctor revisited Nerva at an earlier point in future-history, its crew quarters might easily have been fitted out by one of 1975's leading retailers of self-assembly furniture. Glimpses of what the universe has to look forward to include:

21ST CENTURY
Seabase crew quarters will include bedding made of bubblewrap.

24TH CENTURY
Earth colonies will offer a Refreshing Department, offering steam baths, beauty treatments, massage, laundry services, sunlight treatment, moonlight treatment, sparkling and effervescent sprays...

25TH CENTURY
Children will study for almost an hour a week, using teaching machines; ten-year-olds will take a certificate of education in medicine, physics, chemistry and several other subjects.

28TH CENTURY
Everyone will have non-winding wristwatches: 'A movement of the wrist recharges the spring inside for twenty-four hours.'

29TH CENTURY
Double agents will be equipped with spying and monitoring kit disguised as hairbrushes; their communications transmitters, however, will be considerably less discreet.

30TH CENTURY
It will be possible to record all human achievement on microfilm.

30TH CENTURY
Stencilled lettering will be an intrinsic part of all signposting.

41ST CENTURY
There will be at least 403 television channels, many devoted to the holiday plans of the Guardian of the Solar System; nobody will celebrate Christmas. Important messages will be recorded on cassette tape.

50TH CENTURY
Stencilled lettering will make a comeback.

57TH TIME SEGMENT
Earth's entire population, human and animal, will be reduced to micro-cell size and stored in plastic trays in filing cabinets aboard a big space ark for a 700-year journey to Refusis 2.

073

Emergency Regulations

C.2167

EMERGENCY REGULATIONS

IT IS FORBIDDEN TO DUMP BODIES INTO THE RIVER

In the middle of the 22nd century, humanity's expansion into the stars came to a sudden halt when Earth was invaded. Before the Daleks occupy a world, they frequently sew the atmosphere with chemical weapons and plague bombs, wiping out billions and reducing the remaining population to misery before the first saucer is even glimpsed in the sky. In the 2150s, this was what they had done to planet Earth.

About ten years later, the TARDIS arrived in London. Initially, the First Doctor thought he had finally managed to return his companions Ian and Barbara to the 1960s... but the poster behind the TARDIS suggested that something was very badly wrong.

The grimly impersonal tone of the sign suggested a government struggling to maintain order against a plague that was out of control, and where the casual disposal of relatives in the River Thames was an everyday occurrence.

HOW THEY REACTED

THE DOCTOR: It's stupid. A stupid place to put a poster. Right under a bridge where nobody can read it or see it ... A dead human body in the river? I should say that's near murder, isn't it, hmm?
IAN CHESTERTON: Plague?
BARBARA WRIGHT: There's a strange poster on the wall. It just doesn't make sense.
SUSAN: Well, off we go again.
                    The Dalek Invasion of Earth: World's End

ORIGINS

The sign was inspired by Second World War propaganda posters, with a language which officiously makes domestic details the business of government.

Such signs are also used in *Quatermass II* (1955) to hide a secret alien invasion ('Sshh! Secrets mean sealed lips!') and are everywhere in *The Prisoner* (1967) ('A Still Tongue Makes A Happy Life'). They evoke the early 1940s, when Britain was preparing to resist invasion and Blitzkrieg.

Hitler will send no warning – so always carry your gas mask

The River Thames has a long and terrible history of pollution. By 1858, the smell of the Thames had become known as 'the Great Stink', and sittings in Parliament had to be abandoned. In the 1950s, water content was so bad that there was no oxygen, and the river gave off the revolting smell of hydrogen sulphide (raw eggs). By 1964, it was devoid of life. An ever-increasing flood of raw sewage and chemicals had killed off all the fish.

Even with the opening of new sewage plants in 1964, filming of the first episode's cliffhanger ending, with a Dalek emerging from the water, had to be handled carefully. Swallowing Thames water usually required stomach pumping as a precaution against diseases caused by raw sewage – everything from simple campylobacter to cholera. Even after five decades of improved water quality, when comedian David Walliams swam the length of the Thames in 2011, he fell severely ill.

VETOED

Also seen in *The Dalek Invasion of Earth* are signs reading 'VETOED', attached to items ranging from elephants to figurines of milkmen. The phrase was intended to be part of a resistance code, but was actually an in-joke by production designer Spencer Chapman. When BBC set designers submitted their plans, if they were judged too ambitious for the budget they would be returned with 'VETOED' stamped across them. This was a common occurrence, with designer Raymond Cusick remarking that his use of transparent fibre glass pillars in *The Keys of Marinus* was judged too opulent for a children's show.

Another system was operated called 'X-ing': designers would look at posters of each other's plans and 'X' them – marking elements that they wanted retained to save money by re-using in other shows, or placing in stock. Keen observers of 1960s set design will spot a triangular wall pattern in use in both *The Romans* and *The Keys of Marinus*.

In *The Dalek Invasion of Earth*, the 'It Is Forbidden To Dump Bodies In The River' sign makes just such a cost-cutting reappearance – in the Dalek mine in Bedfordshire in the sixth episode.

DALEK GRAFFITI

Signage is a big part of the invasion of Earth, with the Daleks covering London landmarks with graffiti. In reality this was black electrician's tape, swiftly removed (in most cases) after filming.

When *Doctor Who* returned in 2005, Dalek graffiti made a reappearance on designs throughout the series, a hint by designer Edward Thomas that the Daleks had not gone away and were leaving messages for each other.

A SIGN OF THE TIMES

The Sensorites

The Ark

The Seeds of Death

The Mutants

The Invisible Enemy

The Long Game

The Doctor's Daughter

The Hungry Earth

THIS DALEK INVASION IS BROUGHT TO YOU BY...

When the story was remade as *Daleks – Invasion Earth 2150 A.D.*, the filmmakers Amicus received sponsorship funding from cereal manufacturer Sugar Puffs. This meant that signs about dumping bodies were accompanied by breakfast cereal adverts. Clearly, as government collapsed, the only food available to the survivors was tinned peaches, oranges and puffed wheat.

074

Mechonoid

C.2265

As humanity recovered from the Dalek invasion, Mechonoids were built to prepare worlds for human settlement, building cities and controlling the local wildlife. The original Mechonoids were probably dispatched in the early 23rd century, but for some reason humanity forgot to claim one of its colony worlds... for decades, the Mechonoids lived undisturbed on the planet designated Mechanus. When space pilot Steven Taylor crash-landed on Mechanus fifty years later, he was not hailed as a long-awaited colonist; instead, the Mechonoids caged him and his toy panda, as if they were zoo exhibits.

While no longer able to recognise their human masters, the Mechonoids knew a threat when they saw one. The TARDIS crew were rescued from a Dalek execution squad and placed in the Mechonoid zoo, while the Daleks were immediately identified as hostile. The Mechonoids, in turn, were recognised by the Daleks, and fought to repel the invaders from their city. Had the two species encountered each other before?

THE MECHONOIDS

Often described as spherical, the Mechonoids have a structure closely approaching the icosahedral carbon cage $C_{60}H_{60}$ first proposed in 1965; seen as a chemical possibility, this geometric shape was named 'Buckminster Fullerene' in tribute to the remarkable geodesic dome designs of Buckminster Fuller. His domes sadly lacked fearsome pincers and flamethrowers.

THE MECHONOIDS OF MECHANUS

The Mechonoids live on a planet called Mechanus. Other fortuitously named planets and species include:

The Refusians of Refusis 2
The invisible Visians
The cryogenically gifted Cryons
The sensitive Sensorites of the Sense-Sphere
The domineering Dominators
The daemonic Daemons from the planet Daemos
The absorbing Abzorbaloff (from Clom)
The Adipose
The lush planet Chloris
The formerly water-dwelling Aridians of Aridius
The shape-changing Chameleons
The draconian Draconians
The dulcet Dulcians of Dulkis
The logarithmic Logopolitans
The planet Marinus and its acid seas
The one-eyed Monoids
The uxorious Usurians from Usurius
The Ice Warriors

THE COMIC MECHONOIDS

The Mechonoids went on to have a long series of battles with the Daleks on the pages of *TVC21* comic where they were shown as a race of cunning robots led by the Menoid. They sent planets on collision courses with Skaro and once built a replica, robotic Dalek capable of misleading their foe, the Emperor Dalek.

SPEAK MECHONOID

MECHONOID	ENGLISH
+++ Eight hundred thirty +++ Mechonoid +++ English input +++ Enter +++	Language identified – you people speak English. Kindly follow me, please.
+++ Stop +++ Follow +++	Keep going.
+++ English +++ Enter+++ Enter +++ Zero +++ Stop +++	Keep going, this way, English people.
+++ Threat +++ Stop+++	You are a threat.
+++ Trapped +++ Trapped +++	You are prisoners in our space zoo.
+++ Follow +++ Mechonoid +++ Attack +++ System+++	My fellow Mechonoids, we must unite to repel these invaders.
+++ Escalate +++ output +++ Fire +++	Fight harder. Fire!

Marsh Minnows

C.2285-2379

When humans colonised the remoter parts of their own planet, those who went first tended to be either extremists or convicts. Earth's colonisation of space followed a similar pattern. Varos was a penal colony whose population worked to extract Zeiton ore from the harsh mining conditions. Although rich in mineral wealth, the colony's government was weak, and soon fell victim to a race who excelled in exploiting others.

The Mentors of Thoros Beta were a race of rapacious amphibians who were so skilled at business that they invaded worlds financially rather than militarily, taking over governments and long-established feudal regimes without having to bother establishing a rival system, or even firing a shot. Brown or green in colour, they resembled slugs with human faces, hands and arms, but piscine tails in place of lower limbs. At an earlier evolutionary stage, these tails delivered a lethal sting. Now they existed happily on dry land but required constant irrigation.

One of the most renowned Thoros Betans was Sil, who was a representative for the Galatron Mining Corporation when the Sixth Doctor first encountered him, effectively running Varos. His preferred food was an ever-present bowl of marsh minnows, small green fish that he ate alive.

COLONIAL IRRITATION

Colony worlds have long provided a way to allegorically depict a single aspect of human nature or satirise some social behaviour through elaboration. Many of *Doctor Who*'s writers during the 1960s, 1970s and 1980s had grown up while post-war Britain was extracting itself from its far-reaching Empire, with often bloody consequences, especially in Africa.

■ The first human colonists the Doctor met were also among the last: the population of the Ark, who were setting off to colonise Refusis 2 with slave labour and no idea of whether or not the world they were settling on was already inhabited.

■ Labour problems are common on colony worlds – the people of Vulcan were so delighted to acquire cheap labour that they didn't realise the Daleks were manipulating a tense political situation to provoke a civil war. In *The Macra Terror* (1967), the Second Doctor overthrew a fascist regime which had conditioned the population to a life of labour in the gas mines through a strict regime of holiday camp entertainment and jollity.

■ Malcolm Hulke's *Colony in Space* (1971), set in 2472, effectively pitted the growing back-to-nature movements of the early 1970s

against heartless big business, with the ruthless Interplanetary Mining Corporation willing to ride roughshod over existing populations in order to exploit natural resources.

■ The withdrawal of the Earth Empires from Solos in *The Mutants* (1972) was a broad allegory of racism in the British Empire, showing uncaring, exploitative invaders ignoring and misunderstanding native culture, and everybody suffering as a result.

■ In *The Sunmakers* (1977), a colony on the planet Pluto was used to show how taxes and bureaucracy can enslave the human spirit. Controlled by the Usurians, humanity appeared to have taken out the equivalent of a massive payday loan without reading the small print properly. But the story's origins may lie more in writer Robert Holmes's frustration with tax demands and BBC bureaucracy than with nightmares of empire.

■ *Vengeance on Varos* (1985) showed the people of Varos using ever-increasing violence on television as a way to bring colour into their drab lives, a theme picked up – and extended – in *The Long Game* and *Bad Wolf* (2005).

■ *Paradise Towers* (1987) questioned the problems caused by high-rise, depersonalised tenement living.

■ In *The Happiness Patrol* (1988), the citizens of Terra Alpha inhabited a society where happiness was made compulsory by a sugar-sweet dictator, Helen A, inspired by prime minister Margaret Thatcher. This was *Doctor Who*'s post-colonial satire at its broadest, and also, perhaps, its oddest: Helen A's regime depended on a large and malicious automaton apparently constructed out of confectionery – the Kandyman.

Simple terms such as 'fascist dictatorship' and 'puppet government' don't really do these stories, or the terminology, justice. Was Varos really a dictatorship? If so, who was actually in charge? The Governor of Varos could hardly be accused of ruling through a cult of personality, and had to submit to regular re-election, which could turn into an execution if he lost. And, at what point in its development did the colonists enslaved by the Macra decide that they'd willingly work more hours down the gas mines in return for increased line dancing?

As a series where each new story takes place in a brand new setting, *Doctor Who* often avoids asking, 'What happened next?' The planet Vulcan saw half its population massacred, its power supply ruined and its government overthrown without a viable replacement. The Doctor's response was to caper hurriedly away, a pattern he frequently repeated. What did the people of Varos do without the one thing in their lives that gave them pleasure? How would the emotionally stunted people of Terra Alpha recover without a programme of worldwide therapy? The people of Pluto were economically crippled before the arrival of the Usurians – was their fragile economy really safe in the hands of a government formed of muggers, bandits and credit-card thieves? The Seventh Doctor united the people of Paradise Towers, but he didn't solve the food shortage that left them eating vermin and each other.

While he frequently helps liberate oppressed peoples, only rarely has the Doctor offered solutions. With Peri's help, he suggested that the people of Necros stop turning the dead into food and instead become farmers, though this presupposed that their horrified customers would ever trust any more food from Necros ('Now with 100% Less Corpse!').

Occasionally, the Doctor has had to face the consequences of his actions. Returning to the Ark after 700 years, the First Doctor discovered that the plague unleashed by Dodo had freed the Monoids but turned them into brutal oppressors (see 098. Monoid Statue). The Fourth Doctor discovered a war between the Sevateem and the Tesh caused by a schizophrenic computer that he had supposedly fixed on a previous visit. The Ninth Doctor was devastated to learn that, by putting an end to the Jagrafess's manipulation of Satellite Five, he had plunged Earth into one hundred years of hell – when the news channels shut down, Earth's government, economy and society all collapsed.

THE *DOCTOR WHO* COOKBOOK

Sil's Marsh Minnows were made from sliced peaches dyed green. Other unusual food includes...

■ 'Bacon and eggs' from the TARDIS food machine looked suspiciously like a chocolate bar in *The Daleks*.

■ Monoid cookery: The Security Kitchen relied on a vast labour force to produce instant boiled potatoes by adding a powder to water.

■ Celery: The Fifth Doctor's ostentatiously displayed decorative vegetable was actually a piece of embroidery, according to Peter Davison. Davison hates celery.

■ CyberSick: When the Cybermen were dispatched by a Raston Warrior Robot in *The Five Doctors*, actor David Banks came up with the idea of making the deaths even more gruesome by vomiting up a mouthful of milky tea each time.

■ Shockeye's rat in *The Two Doctors*: Actor John Stratton had to bite into a real stuffed rat, with grapes sewn into its neck.

■ Christmas dinner (1): Recording *The End of Time, Part One*, the Noble family's Christmas turkey was raw. Russell T Davies pointed out that Wilf was watching the Queen's 3 p.m. Christmas broadcast so, even if Sylvia had put the turkey in the oven at that point, they'd not have eaten until midnight. The turkey was painted brown in post-production.

■ Christmas dinner (2): When the Master ate his way through a whole turkey in moments, actor John Simm had to spit each mouthful into a handily positioned bucket, and the whole studio set smelled of turkey – all unnecessary, according to Russell T Davies. The script direction 'Instantly, a FOOTMAN's there, with a tray – a whole turkey. The Master eats, digging his hands in, ravenous' simply meant that the Master should grab a turkey leg and start eating, but everyone involved assumed that the whole turkey had to be gobbled up.

■ Fish fingers and custard: One of the Eleventh Doctor's earliest scenes sees him sample and spit out apple, yoghurt, bacon, baked beans, and bread and butter in quick succession, before finding something he likes. In some interviews, Matt Smith claimed that he'd genuinely eaten fish fingers and custard and it was 'gorgeous'. The 'fish fingers' were actually breaded coconut cakes, and he had to eat a dozen or more of them during the 12 takes of the scene.

FOURTH DOCTOR FRUIT CAKE

You take a pound of peanuts and some apple cores. You mix the peanuts and the treacle, then throw in the apple cores very hard, put the lot in a shallow tin and bake in a high oven for two weeks.

Cyber Tombs

C.25TH CENTURY

Some corners of the universe have bred the most terrible things. The emotionless Cybermen spread across space like a plague, invading planets and harvesting the population for Cyber Conversion. An exception was made for the Cryons – while the race was deemed to be unsuitable for conversion, their home planet of Telos offered something of immense value to the CyberRace. For the Cryons were experts at cryogenics.

The Cybermen had undertaken a number of unsuccessful campaigns in a short space of time. An aborted invasion of 20th-century Earth cost them an entire fleet and countless troops. Subsequent attempts via the W3 space station and Earth's Moonbase had lost large numbers of Cybermen and several spacecraft. Logically, the Cyber Controller realised, each operation had a chance of failure, and the limited numbers of the Cyber race carried a risk of extinction. Their ultimate imperative was 'We will survive.' He therefore used the Cryons' refrigeration technology to preserve the remainder of his depleted forces. The Cybermen sealed themselves in hidden 'Tombs' on Telos, waiting to be rediscovered.

Several centuries passed, and then the Brotherhood of Logicians reached Telos as part of an archaeological survey. Surmising that the Cybermen were not dead, merely resting, the Brotherhood walked into a trap. To deduce the existence of the Tombs, predict their location and bypass a series of logic tests required both intellect and determination. The Cybermen had simply waited for sufficiently intelligent people to discover and open their tombs and provide them with the necessary raw material for a new Cyber army. Although the Second Doctor was able to reseal the tombs, the Cyber Controller survived. He slowly repaired himself, and reawakened his remaining troops.

As more Cybermen awoke from deep within the catacombs of Telos, the Controller became aware that the Cryons were not wholly extinct. The environment of Telos was now too hot for them, and many were thrown outside to perish, but others were able to survive below ground and regroup. The Controller's plans advanced – he stole a Time Ship. His plan was to use it to go back to avert the earlier destruction of Mondas. He was able to achieve this by recruiting an alien mercenary called Lytton, not realising

that Lytton was now working for the Cryons. The Controller was finally defeated by the Sixth Doctor, and the last surviving Cryons blew up the tombs. The Cyberman occupation of Telos was at an end.

THE TOMBS

Influenced by Kit Pedler's keen interest in Ancient Egypt, *The Tomb of the Cybermen* has many similarities with the world of Egyptology. The Cybermen themselves become the living dead, in place of preserved mummies, and the Cybermats are inspired by Egyptian scarabs. The Tomb entrance is clearly influenced by that of Tutankhamun's burial chamber, and the floor plans of the two are almost identical. The sarcophagus chamber is replaced with a casket-like revitalisation booth. The filming location in Gerard's Cross eerily resembled the Valley of the Kings, and there is even a pyramid painted onto the backdrop of the sky of Telos.

For many years the hieroglyphs of the Ancient Egyptians were seen as a great puzzle, as complicated as the hieroglyphs of the Cybermen – but what the Doctor solves in three minutes it took the French cryptographic genius Champollion many years to decode.

CYBER DESIGNS

Although the Cyber Controller in *The Tomb of the Cybermen* and *Attack of the Cybermen* is explicitly intended to be the same one, there were 18 years between production of the two stories and Cyber design had gone through several evolutions in that time. Unlike most *Doctor Who* monsters, the appearance of the Cybermen has changed nearly every time they've turned up, reflecting advances in technology or changing design fashions. But this is almost never mentioned on screen.

'We are called Cybermen.'

'I think it was a Cyberman.'

'The Cybermen! Didn't you see it?'

'The Cybermen are definitely on the Wheel. Jamie and I have just seen one.'

'Jamie, I'm afraid I was right.'
'The Cybermen!'

'You're just a pathetic bunch of tin soldiers skulking about the galaxy.'

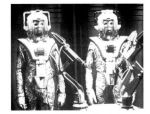

'Are these your friends?'
'Definitely not.'

'Doctor, look out – Cybermen!'

'My name is Lytton, and I am your prisoner, Cybermen.'

'What are they?' 'Cybermen.'

'An old friend of mine. Well, enemy.'

'Cybus!'

'This is the Age of Steel, and I am its creator.'

'They came through first. The advance guard. Cybermen.'

'That's different!' 'Oh, that's new!'

'My function is to serve the CyberKing.'

'A CyberKing is born.'

'What is that?' 'Cyber arm. Arm of a Cyberman.'

'Oh, don't give me those blank looks.'

'What were those things?'
'Cybermen.'

The Lost Moon of Poosh

27TH CENTURY

```
THE DOCTOR: And did they ever find it?
DEE DEE: Find what?
THE DOCTOR: The Lost Moon of Poosh!
DEE DEE: (laughs) No! Not yet!

                                    Midnight
```

The mystery of the Lost Moon of Poosh was something which puzzled human academics and scientists in the 27th century. A small moon with its own gravity, the Moon of Poosh was, in fact, among the planetary bodies removed from time and space by the Daleks to form part of their Reality Bomb. A total of 27 worlds were transported to the Medusa Cascade and reassembled, like the pieces of an engine, to form a huge planetary array, one second out of sync with the rest of the universe. Of these planets, 24 disappeared in the year 2009, among them:

Callufrax Minor
Clom
Earth
Flane
Griffoth
Jahoo
Shallacatop
Strepto
Woman Wept

Three others were removed from other time periods:

Adipose 3
The Lost Moon of Poosh
Pyrovillia

The planetary array was held in perfect balance in an optimum moving pattern of slow orbits to form the Daleks' ultimate weapon. The Daleks had moved the planets by transmatting them along the same wavelength as the Tandocca Scale, which left a very faint, dust-like trail through time and space that the Doctor was able to follow to the Medusa Cascade.

When the Daleks activated the planetary alignment field of the array, the planets began to shine with haloes of Z-Neutrino Energy from the Crucible's core. The configuration of the 27 planets flattened that energy into a single string, as the array combined to form a transmitter that would send the compressed Energy along the Tandocca wavelength and across the universe. This was the Reality Bomb, and its detonation would separate every form of matter into its constituent particles by cancelling out the electrical field that binds atoms together. Those particles would crumble to dust, which would dissolve into nothing. Breaking through the Medusa Cascade's Rift into every dimension and parallel, on full transmission the Reality Bomb would destroy reality itself.

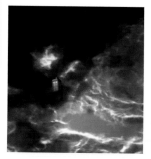

ADHERING TO A REPEATED MEME

The Lost Moon of Poosh is an example of a small piece of insignificant background colour in one story's dialogue that suddenly takes on much greater significance in a later story.

■ In *The Deadly Assassin*, the Doctor offers himself as a candidate for the Time Lord presidency. As the traitorous Chancellor Goth points out to Castellan Spandrell, 'Apart from myself, he is the only other candidate in this election,' which is later crucial to *The Invasion of Time*.

■ In *Dragonfire*, Ace tells Mel that a time storm 'whipped up from nowhere' and transported her to Iceworld, while the Doctor continues a game of chess that's 'going rather badly' in *Silver Nemesis*. *The Curse of Fenric* reveals the ancient evil that has manipulated events since Ace's arrival on Svartos.

■ In *The End of the World*, the Moxx of Balhoon tells the Face of Boe: 'Indubitably, this is the Bad Wolf scenario. I find the relative laxity of the ongoing multiverse...'

■ One of the answers on *The Weakest Link* in *The Parting of the Ways* makes the first reference to Torchwood.

■ When the Doctor's hand is cut off by the Sycorax Leader in *The Christmas Invasion*, it tumbles through the sky never to be seen again... until it is revealed in *Utopia* that Captain Jack Harkness has preserved it. The hand is central to the Master's treatment of the Doctor in *The Sound of Drums* and crucial to the events of *The Doctor's Daughter* and *Journey's End*.

■ The Abzorbaloff hides behind a newspaper in *Love & Monsters*, with its front-page report on the 64 per cent poll lead of somebody called Saxon...

■ Queen Elizabeth I spots the Doctor in *The Shakespeare Code*, and calls him her 'greatest enemy' – no idea why, the Doctor tells Martha.

■ In *The Sound of Drums*, the Doctor describes the moment that the Master looked into the Untempered Schism as the cause of his later madness; in *The End of Time*, this turns out to be truer than either of them realised.

■ A newspaper seller called Wilf in *Voyage of the Damned* turns out to be connected to the Doctor in all sorts of ways.

■ In *Partners in Crime*, the Doctor learns that the Adipose breeding planet was 'lost'; 'Pyrovillia is lost,' Lucius tells him in *The Fires of Pompeii*. Only when the Earth is stolen does the Doctor start to piece it all together.

■ 'Doctor – Donna – friends,' the Doctor tells the Ood in *Planet of the Ood*; the Ood *seem* to misunderstand, going on to call them 'the Doctor-Donna'.

■ 'Crash of the Byzantium, have we done that yet?' River Song asks the Tenth Doctor in *Silence in the Library*, as she starts to stack up the Spoilers.

■ After the enormous CyberKing's destructive march across London, Jackson Lake predicts that 'today's events will be history! Spoken of for centuries to come!' 'Yeah,' says the Doctor, still months away from learning of the Crack. 'Funny that.'

■ 'Are you the Doctor, or the Janitor?' Adelaide Brooke asks in *The Waters of Mars*; in *The Doctor, the Widow and the Wardrobe*, he's the Janitor.

■ 'The universe is cracked. The Pandorica will open. Silence will fall,' predicts Prisoner Zero in *The Eleventh Hour*, tidily kicking off two years' worth of story arcs.

■ In *The Time of Angels*, the Doctor takes Amy to the Delerium Archive, 'the final resting place of the Headless Monks'.

■ Dorium Maldovar is beheaded by the Headless Monks in *A Good Man Goes to War*; the fate of his head is revealed in *The Wedding of River Song*.

Snake Tattoo

C.28TH CENTURY

What is evil? The people of the Manussan Federation believed that it was not an abstract concept but a real creature, like an infection or a virus. They sought to drive out the evil inside them, imprisoning it inside a large crystal they called the Great Mind's Eye. What they actually did was to create the very thing they'd been trying to destroy. The Great Mind's Eye was now filled with an entity called the Mara, and it used its telepathic link with the people of Manussa to control them and establish the Sumaran Empire.

The mark of those possessed by the Mara was a snake tattoo, which was able to come to life and assume physical form. The Mara fed off weakness, converting it to strength – it maintained its grip on the people of Manussa for centuries until mystics called Snakedancers used a mixture of meditation, snake venom and crystals of their own to drive the Mara from the Manussans and into somewhere they called 'the Dark Places of the Inside'. All they'd really achieved was to free the Mara from the Great Crystal.

The Mara was also present on Deva Loka, an early human colony world. There, it entered the minds of the native Kinda tribe, enslaving them. The Kinda came to see the Mara as an inevitability – like the seasons and tides – an infection that would periodically reoccur, wiping their civilisation out.

MERCHANDISING THE MARA

The Mara was all about the trinkets. While the creature itself was deadly serious, a lot of the objects associated with it were darkly comic or blackly playful, ranging from the Box of Jhanna (a seemingly-empty jack-in-the-box) to the headdress known as the Six Faces of Delusion. On Manussa, 500 years after the end of the Sumaran Empire, the caves containing the Chamber of the Mara had been reduced to a tourist attraction, the marketplace outside offering snake statuettes and costumes. The rituals that had summoned and banished the Mara were recalled only as echoes in a series of funfair attractions: puppeteers, fortune tellers, a hall of distorting mirrors.

OM MANI PADME OM

The writer of *Kinda* (1982) and *Snakedance* (1983), Christopher Bailey, was heavily influenced by the Buddhist demon Mara which personified doubt, weakness and spiritual death.

Producer Barry Letts was also influenced by Buddhist principles, which informed many of the Third Doctor's adventures. Notably, the Great Crystal of Metebelis Three contains properties similar to those offered by the Manussan crystals, including the removal of doubt and uncertainty and a clarifying of intent and mental strength. *Planet of the Spiders* (1974) also introduced the Doctor's mentor, K'anpo Rimpoche, who had first been mentioned in *The Time Monster* (1972) – the old hermit who had shown the Doctor 'the daisiest daisy' he'd ever seen.

In *Marco Polo*, the First Doctor played backgammon with Kublai Khan, and among his winnings was 'the sacred tooth of Buddha'. The Second Doctor saved the Buddhist monks of Det-Sen monastery from the Great Intelligence and his robot Yeti.

LOOK AT ME

To see the Mara is to be affected by it. This is a trait shared with the Medusa (from Greek Mythology and encountered by the Second Doctor in the Land of Fiction), but also with the Beast, which taunted victims into looking at it, and with the Silents, who can only be thought of when they can be seen.

The one thing the Mara could not bear to do was to see itself, the Kinda believing that it was so evil it could not bear its own reflection. On Deva Loka it was defeated by being trapped in a circle of mirrors. A similar trap allowed Sally Sparrow to evade the Weeping Angels – creatures who can only move when they are not being looked at, and who she managed to escape by leaving four of them staring at each other.

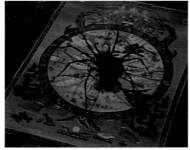

TATTOO WHO

The Mara's snake tattoo isn't the only example of a tattoo in *Doctor Who*:

The Third Doctor revealed a tattoo on his arm when showering in *Spearhead from Space*.

Possessed by the Beast, Toby Zed became covered in ancient signs in *The Impossible Planet*.

The Time Lord Visionary was covered in arcane Gallifreyan markings.

The Time Lord the Corsair had a tattoo of an ouroborus (self-devouring worm) on his arm.

Sandminer Robot

C.29TH CENTURY

Some colonies were idyllic Earth-type planets. Some, like Uxarieus were barren wastelands. But the Founding Families of Kaldor City settled on a world where the very ground meant money. An inhospitable wasteland of thousand-mile-an-hour sandstorms, they realised that the sand was rich in mineral wealth, even containing traces of Lucanol, which could be harvested by the sandminers.

> THE DOCTOR: I have seen a similar sort of thing on Korlano Beta. The mine passes over the surface searching for useful ores. Naturally, the heavier elements tend to sink into the substratas, so a really good sandstorm is a bonus. It stirs things up a bit.
>
> *The Robots of Death, Part 1*

This vast wealth allowed the successful colonists to live in luxury – they liked opulence and beautiful things. Even their servants were beautiful – the colonists had a race of robots to do everything from the hard work of sandmining through to healthcare and massage. There were three classes of robots:

■ A Super Voc ran the command circuit – in charge of all the robots on a Sandminer, it relayed instructions to them.
■ Vocs performed essential control deck duties on a Sandminer. They were capable of running the vehicle independently, and had over a million multi-level constrainers in their programming to prevent malfunction.
■ Dums were voiceless servitors, tasked with manual labour and simple duties.

The sandminers went on long tours of duty – sometimes lasting two years or more – but they required a human crew. The robots made life bearable, but their fiercely logical brains lacked the intuition required to find a rich mineral cloud.

While the Founding Families retained their status, not all of them retained their wealth – the indolent society they had created was costly, and their financial supremacy was usurped by incoming colonists who were still prepared to go out in the sandminers and find their fortune in a cloud of dust.

Despite the robots' carefully aesthetic appearance, many people suffered a natural fear of their creations. Grimwade suggested a theory that it was because robots have no body language or facial expressions – in some people this unease even caused a condition he named Robophobia. A certain kind of temperament could feel undermined, causing paranoia and even personality disintegration as the sufferer became convinced the robots were the living dead. To counteract this, the robots' prime directive was not to harm humans, and the manufacturers made very sure that the whole population trusted this implicitly. If their belief wavered, then an entire society might be destroyed.

This very nearly happened because of one human called Taran Capel. Raised by robots, he became an expert in them. Denied any human contact, his body language and speech echoed the precision of the robots. He grew to be a scientific genius, but his overriding ambition was to wipe out the humans through a robot revolution.

THE SCIENCE OF ROBOTICS

The Robots of Death were a triumphant example of *Doctor Who*'s ability to build a sleek and menacing monster out of almost nothing. Used in their design were:

Tin foil
Bicycle reflectors
Marigold washing up gloves
Quilted fleece jackets
Cardboard

YOU CAN'T GET THE STAFF

The Doctor loathes burnt toast, bus stations, unrequited love, tyranny and cruelty, and he can't stand slavery. Fortunately, things rarely go well for the enslavers, and it's not a good idea to rely on robot servants either...

■ The Daleks never gave up on slavery, despite a long list of uprisings that began in 22nd-century Bedfordshire; a scientific taskforce was wiped out by a rebellious Spiridon; a slave workforce on Skaro ultimately turned into Davros's jailors.

■ Roman slaves, including Ian Chesterton, overpowered a Galley Master as soon as a storm broke.

■ The enslaved Menoptra eventually fought back against the Animus.

■ When humanity caught a cold, the Monoids took over the Ark.

■ The Vulcan colonists quickly regretted their choice of unpaid servants when the Daleks stoked a revolution.

■ Solicitor Gray tried to sell defeated Scots rebels into slavery, but the Second Doctor and Ben led an uprising.

■ When the Fish People went on strike, Atlantis promptly ran out of food.

■ The humans enslaved by the Macra had to be controlled by hypnotic conditioning.

■ The Dominators attempted to use forced labour on Dulkis, but it gave them nothing but trouble.

■ Once the Gonds were given an inkling of chemistry, the Krotons' dominance was over.

■ On a parallel Earth, the Stahlman project used slave labour – which ran away as soon as the inferno began.

■ Mind-altering compounds in the air supply and unreasonable tax demands in the pay packet kept the human race in thrall to the Usurians, until the Fourth Doctor and Leela led a revolution...

■ ... which they immediately did again when they found the last of the Minyans enslaved by their computer.

■ The Fourth Doctor and Romana helped liberate the Tharils from slave traders marooned in E-Space.

■ The Tharils themselves had once enslaved humans, but their empire had been brought down by their own malfunctioning Gundan robots.

■ The Cybermen's slave labour force fought back on Telos.

■ Programming ship maintenance as the first priority for Clockwork Robots proved a lethal error for the crew of the *Madame de Pompadour*.

■ The Tenth Doctor failed to save the Ood on Krop Tor, but did help in the liberation of the Ood-Sphere.

■ He couldn't save the Daleks' Pig Slaves, either, since their genetic transformation was irreversible, but was able to prevent Laszlo's death.

■ The Master enslaved the entire human race for a year; their combined thoughts, focused by the Archangel Network, helped reverse his ageing of the Doctor.

■ Passengers and crew on the *Titanic* relied on the robotic Heavenly Host, until their programming was altered and they became killers.

■ The Cybermen enslaved the orphaned children of Victorian London to build their CyberKing until they were freed by the Doctor and Jackson Lake.

■ The Silents enslaved the whole human race for millennia, until the Doctor tricked them into ordering their own executions on television.

■ The Gangers saw themselves as slaves who merited equal rights with their human originals.

080

A Door

If you need anything, there are guards outside the door. Many guards..

State of Decay, Part 2

In 2127, the exploration vessel *Hydrax*, en route from Earth to Beta Two in the Perugellis sector, passed through a CVE and was lost for ever. Its three-strong crew survived, however – for a thousand years or more. Stranded on a nameless world in E-Space, they became in thrall to the Great One, last survivor of Gallifrey's purge of the vampires millennia earlier. The *Hydrax* became the Tower, and the crew its Lords, ruling over a peasant population.

Led to the State Room in the Tower, the Fourth Doctor and Romana were greeted courteously by Lord Zargo and Lady Camilla – Camilla was especially concerned that Romana had cut herself and was bleeding. But when they left the Doctor and Romana in the throne room, there was no doubt that the two of them were prisoners...

WE'RE TRAPPED!

There have been many doors in *Doctor Who*, and many secrets behind them. Capture, rescue and escape have been vital parts of countless stories in the original television run. The very first episode is about the rescue of a girl locked inside a police box; the following episode sees the crew held captive in the cave of skulls, escaping the next week, then being captured and recaptured, before escaping in the last episode... only to land on the planet Skaro and be taken prisoner by the Daleks. By the end of *Doctor Who*'s first year the time travellers have been held by Marco Polo, Aztec warriors and French revolutionaries. On the planet Marinus, they're imprisoned in ice caves, temples and the cities of Morphoton and Millennius. There's even a story where they are trapped in the TARDIS.

Why did the Doctor get locked up so much? As many writers and script editors have attested, *Doctor Who* eats plot, so captures, rescues and (failed) escapes neatly provided an action-packed 25 minutes with a cliffhanger. Capture allowed the Doctor to meet and come into conflict with the villain; a spell in prison handily gave him a few minutes to answer questions from his faithful companions; escape let him show off his ingenuity. If all else failed, he could always be rescued by newfound allies who, if they were lucky, wouldn't then have to nobly sacrifice themselves to a misplaced laser beam.

The Ninth, Tenth and Eleventh Doctors have spent a lot less time in clink – fewer cliffhangers and shorter adventures mean he can't afford to waste a moment – but even so, he's still managed to be held captive everywhere from the *Big Brother* house to the mouth of a Star Whale.

A DOZEN WAYS TO FOIL AN ESCAPE ATTEMPT – NOTES FOR GUARDS

■ **The lock is not broken:** The TARDIS crew escaped the Daleks using a tray and some mud.
■ **The prisoner is not ill:** Jo Grant conned the Ogrons, Romana faked death to get out of a Dalek chain gang, and the Doctor has a respiratory bypass system.
■ **You have no time for magic tricks:** The Doctor escaped from the Uxarieans with a coin trick, and from Captain Tancredi with a polaroid camera.
■ **That is not your god:** As the Ogrons and the Atlanteans learnt, it's often a prisoner putting on a voice.
■ **Know your co-workers:** Daleks are notoriously slow at spotting impersonation, and you should be wary of disgruntled slave girls and cleaning ladies.
■ **Do the cells really need air-conditioning?** Surprisingly large ventilation shafts have proved handy everywhere from the South Pole to Seabase 4, Spiridon and the Moon.
■ **Can they think their way out?** This proved a drawback for Omega's Gell Guards, for Kalid's Plasmatons, and for the Medusoids when the Doctor broke their mind probe.

■ **Supervise mealtimes:** Jo Grant escaped from the Ogrons with a wet spoon.
■ **Always have a Plan B:** No matter how good your prison, take a leaf out of the Master's book and have a trap prepared beyond that trap that would be a joy to spring. Just in case the Doctor escaped Event One, the Master had handily prepared a fake TARDIS Index File with clues leading to the illusory society of Castrovalva.
■ **The Terileptils had the right idea:** Destroying the sonic screwdriver would have saved a lot of effort everywhere from Paris to the Nerva Beacon.
■ **Don't be too hard on yourself** – after all, your employer will probably execute you anyway. And how were you to know that the Doctor and Romana would escape being torn apart using a high window and some opera?
■ **Kill them. Kill them now!** Wait a bit and you'll soon appreciate the merits of capital punishment. Your leader may suffer from a change of mind or octopus.

KILL THEM, KILL THEM IN A BIT

081

Starship UK

3295

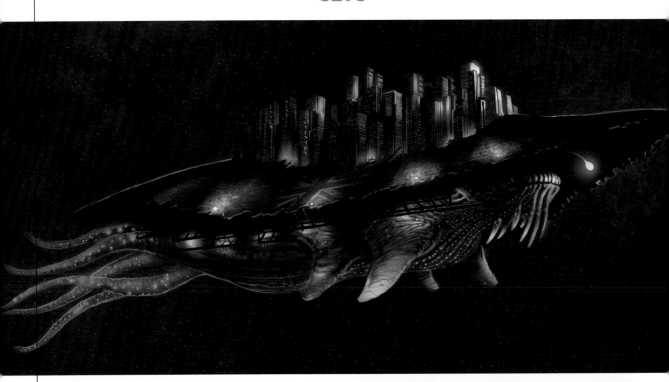

During the 29th century, Earth's scientists had predicted that solar flares were about to devastate the planet, making its biosphere uninhabitable for at least 5,000 years. The human race fled its home world. Some set out to found distant colonies such as Galsec. One self-selected elite chose cryogenic suspension aboard the enormous Space Station Nerva. One way or another, everybody left the planet, many in specially built starships – one for each country. But most of the people of Britain remained, without the funds or resources they needed to make their evacuation.

The Star Whales were a species that once lived in deep space. First encountered by Earth's spacefaring pioneers, they would guide these early space travellers through cosmic hazards. As the solar flares began to strike planet Earth, the last surviving Star Whale heard the screams of Britain's children and came to help. But when it reached Earth, the desperate British government trapped it, building a massive spacecraft around it, and using it to power the escape of the entire population.

Starship UK was formed from linked steel tower blocks, each containing the populace of entire cities and counties, as well as some of the buildings, including Buckingham Palace and the Tower of London. The whole structure floated through the stars on the back of the Star Whale. The beast was wired into Starship UK, constantly tortured just to keep it moving through the stars for the next 400 years.

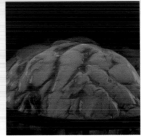

WHAT HAPPENED, YOU SEE, WAS OUR PLANET WAS DOOMED...

The Biblical tale of Noah leading a chosen few – and their livestock – aboard a hastily constructed vessel to escape catastrophe and save the human race proved an inspiration for millennia...

■ Sarah Jane Smith encountered the victims of Operation Golden Age, who believed they were in cryogenic suspension aboard a fleet voyaging across space to 'New Earth'. In fact, they were in a bunker under Whitehall waiting until a dinosaur-infested London could be returned to a pre-industrial paradise by a mad scientist.

■ The people of the crashed Starliner were waiting for Embarkation Day to lift off from Alzarius and return to Terradon. They had no idea that their society had long ago been wiped out and supplanted by the native life forms – they were the descendants of Marshmen, not the voyagers from Terradon.

■ The humans in storage on the Urbankan craft had moved beyond the Flesh Time and were now stored on microchips and occasionally housed in robotic frames.

■ Space Station Nerva was penetrated by a Wirrn Queen, which damaged the control systems so that the cryogenically suspended humans overslept for at least 10,000 years – long enough for their existence to became a myth to those of the outer colony worlds. When they did start to wake up, the Fourth Doctor and Harry learnt that they'd called Nerva 'the Ark' and renamed their leader 'Noah' as 'an amusement'.

■ Another Ark left the dying Earth millions of years later, carrying the human race in miniaturised form to a new home on Refusis 2, tended by selected Guardians and their Monoid servants (see 098. Monoid Statue).

SONG OF THE SPACE WHALE

Holding the record for the *Doctor Who* story in development for the longest time, *The Space Whale* was originally commissioned from Pat Mills for Tom Baker's Doctor, then revised as a possible Peter Davison story, and was still being considered for Colin Baker's second season. It was eventually abandoned, and was ultimately released as an audio play in 2010 as one of Big Finish Productions' Lost Stories. By then, the Star Whale was due to appear in *The Beast Below*, so the audio story's title was changed to *The Song of the Megaptera*.

THE STARSHIP

The *Doctor Who* Art Department's realisation of Starship UK in *The Beast Below* is a remarkable example of un-futuristic design. It imagines a design aesthetic of the far future based roughly on the 1950s and 1960s, making great use of wood, bakelite and even the fonts and signage of the BBC in that era. It's also possible to spot signs for Magpie Electricals and televisions from *The Idiot's Lantern*, wheelie bins from *Rose*, and a red telephone box seen in Leadworth in the preceding episode, *The Eleventh Hour*.

The episode shows a world run on clockwork, because there's no obvious source of power. The street lamps have to be wound up by the robed Winders, and the Doctor immediately realises that there's no sound from the ship's engines. Since the ship is intended to be centuries old, its buildings are battered and its streets dirty and grimy. The exceptions are well-maintained booths on every street corner, containing grinning plastic Smilers.

Dynatrope

MID FOURTH MILLENNIUM

The Dynatrope lay literally at the heart of Gond society – the crystalline spheroid was embedded in their most important buildings, and the rest of the city clustered around it. The Gonds' entire culture, law, education and science was given to them by the Dynatrope, via its teaching machines. They were a largely peaceful race, with well-developed medicine, knowledge of solar energy, and an architecture based on triangles, just right for their low-gravity world. There were, though, remarkable gaps in their knowledge, and they had not considered the possibility of life on other worlds or interplanetary travel. Which was odd. The Gonds' own legends should have told them exactly that:

> Silver men came out of the sky and built a house among us. The Gonds attacked them but the silver men caused a poisonous rain to fall, killing hundreds of our people and turning the earth black.
> *The Krotons, Part 1*

The 'silver men' were the Krotons, and the Dynatrope was their spaceship, part of a battle fleet. Each Dynoptrope required four Kroton operators, but two of the crew were killed by enemy fire. The two surviving Krotons followed emergency procedures and landed on the nearest planet, setting the Dynatrope in perpetual stability to conserve power. Now they had a problem – they could not leave without a full crew complement, so they temporarily dissolved their bodies, reverting to a slurry of crystal molecules in suspension, and waited until the Gonds were sufficiently evolved for two of them to join the crew.

Before they went into hibernation, they established a Learning Hall at the base of the Dynatrope. This took charge of the education of the Gonds, schooling them in only the subjects necessary to pilot the craft. Gond progress was shaped along strictly defined lines – subjects such as chemistry were off limits, and they knew nothing of electricity. The Gonds also wrongly believed that the wastelands outside the city were toxic, simply because the Krotons had told them so. The Gonds never challenged these assumptions – they had been trained not to question, only to obey. What the Krotons had not considered was that breeding a placid race that could barely think for itself meant that the Gonds would never produce anyone with the mental energy required.

For thousands of years, the Gonds held regular ceremonies at which the top two 'High Brains' were accepted to become 'Companions of the Krotons'. These Gonds entered the Dynatrope and were examined by 'a great flashing ball', which then absorbed their mental power into the Dynatrope's circuits. If there was sufficient mental energy, the Dynoptrope would reactivate and the Krotons would be regrown; if not, the mental energy was harvested and the Gonds discarded and vaporised.

THE KROTONS

The Krotons, like the Kastrians, were silicon-based life forms with bodies made of living crystal, which could be dissolved and regrown at will. On the planet of the Gonds, the Krotons were dormant, but they regrew themselves rapidly in vats from the mental energy supplied by the Second Doctor and Zoe. While the Krotons were not completely artificial, their bodies were adapted to live in unison with their living spaceship, the Dynatrope. The ship fed them in return for them maintaining it – an interdependent relationship echoed by that of the Gonds with the Dynatrope.

The Krotons took over the function of a deity for the Gonds. The Gonds worshipped the Krotons and the Dynatrope as mythical beings, and there were various precepts handed down like religious law – it was forbidden to disobey the will of the Krotons, or to harm the Dynatrope. Occasionally, the Krotons spoke to the Gonds, or in rare cases disciplined them with a sentient root extruded from the Dynatrope.

The Krotons had a limited visual range, especially in the twin sunlight of the Gond world, which may explain why they misled the Gonds into remaining indoors. They relied on remote guidance when operating outside the Dynatrope. They could also be permanently dissolved by acid, hence their restriction of the Gonds' knowledge of chemicals.

THE GOND COMPLEX

The idea of a crashed spaceship taking a hand in a species' progress can be traced back to *Quatermass and the Pit* (1959) and Erich von Däniken's 'Ancient Astronaut' theory published in *Chariots of the Gods?* (1968). The idea makes its first appearance in *Doctor Who* in *The Krotons* (1969) – up until this point the Doctor had encountered either alien invasions or civilisations that had

got themselves in trouble. An early draft of *The Daleks* (1963) suggested that the Daleks and the Thals were at war because of manipulation by an alien species. This idea – which also featured in *The Masters of Luxor*, an abandoned storyline from 1963 – was dropped in favour of a more straightforward conflict of ideologies. Four months before *The Krotons*, *The Dominators* depicted a society run on a single concept (pacifism) invaded by an alien race governed by a single concept (aggression). *The Krotons* was a sophisticated progression from this morality play.

Over the next decade, the idea would become a much more common trope in *Doctor Who*, with crashed spaceships turning up everywhere from Devil's End to Peru, bringing alien 'deities' like the Daemons or the Exxilons. This perhaps reflected a mounting popular obsession with UFOs, the occult and New Age mysticism in the 1970s, which is parodied by the Doctor and Sarah's closing remarks at the end of *The Seeds of Doom*: 'Have we been here before? Or are we yet to come?'

LEARNING IN YOUR SLEEP

Another of Robert Holmes's inspirations in writing *The Krotons* was a growing interest in new educational theories and methods during the 1960s. In 1931, Aldous Huxley's *Brave New World* had predicted speed-learning and sleep-learning (hypnopaedia), and Anthony Burgess had made the concept notorious in 1962 with *A Clockwork Orange*. *Doctor Who* introduced something similar in *The Macra Terror* (1967), with human colonists being fed propaganda and misinformation while they slept, via devices in the walls.

The idea of screen-based education would have seemed futuristic to viewers of *The Krotons*, but over the next decade UK schoolchildren were introduced to the wonders of 'language labs' – banks of synchronised tape machines and headphones which were installed as a revolutionary method of teaching languages. In the 1980s, schools then started to introduce 'computer rooms' where 'Information Technology' could be learned on a BBC Microcomputer, although there were limited practical applications or impact on the classroom at first. Writing essays on computers was a rarity until the early 1990s, and the internet did not make a common entrance into education until the late 1990s. Its resources were limited until the introduction of the BBC's GCSE Bitesize website, which in its first year was used by a third of GCSE students. This used a mixture of information and rudimentary animations to convey new concepts and instantly test comprehension – exactly as predicted in *The Krotons*.

083

Statue of Aggedor

C.3885-3935

> The legend of the curse of Peladon has been handed
> down through countless centuries … It concerns the
> Royal Beast of Peladon, now extinct. It is written,
> 'Mighty is Aggedor, fiercest of all the beasts of
> Peladon.' Young men would hunt it to prove their
> courage. His fur trims our royal garment. His head
> is our royal emblem. It is also written there will
> come a day when the spirit of Aggedor will rise
> again to warn and defend his royal master, King
> Peladon. For at that day, a stranger will appear
> in the land, bringing peril to Peladon and great
> tribulation to his kingdom.
>
> *The Curse of Peladon, Part 1*

The spirit of the Royal Beast of Peladon, was worshipped by the people of Peladon, and his image watched over the planet's rulers. On a balcony outside the Throne Room of the Citadel of Peladon stood a great stone statue of Aggedor. When the effigy fell from the balcony, narrowly missing the Martian ambassador Lord Izlyr, Peladon's High Priest Hepesh announced that it was a sure sign of Aggedor's anger – his ghost was on hand to protect Peladon from alien exploitation. Aggedor was angry that the King intended to lead Peladon into the Galactic Federation.

Incorporeal quasi-religious entities tend to need a helping hand in these matters, and that was true here. The statue had been pushed over the balcony by the King's Champion, on the orders of Hepesh. The High Priest was using his people's superstition and a series of beastly appearances to frighten the Federation delegates away. These weren't enough, however, to preserve Peladon's independence, with Chancellor Torbis an enthusiastic advocate of Federation membership. As the alien delegates began to arrive, Torbis was assassinated, supposedly by the spirit of Aggedor. Hepesh had discovered that a few of the 'royal beasts' still existed, living on one of Peladon's higher mountainsides. He captured one and kept it hidden in tunnels beneath the Citadel, training it to kill on his command. Torbis was its first victim.

Fifty years later, the spirit of Aggedor seemed to be killing again. Peladon had been admitted to the Federation, which was attempting to speed up mineral exploitation of the planet by replacing miners with new technology. Yet each time new equipment was brought in, a spectre of Aggedor appeared and slaughtered the miners operating it. Again, the manifestations were being faked – this time, the method of attack was a holographic projection run by the human engineer Eckersley. The real Aggedor was still alive in the subterranean tunnels, and he emerged to save Peladon's queen, Thalira, from Eckersley.

VENUSIAN LULLABY

On both occasions, the Third Doctor was able to pacify and control Aggedor with a Venusian lullaby, sung to the tune of *God Rest Ye Merry Gentlemen*:

Klokleda partha menin klatch
Haroon, haroon, haroon
Klokleda sheenah tierra natch
Haroon, haroon, haroon
Haroon, haroon, haroon
Haroon, haroon, haroon
Haroon, haroon, haroon
Haroon, haroon, haroon

The opening lines translate roughly as 'Close your eyes my darling, well three of them, at least.' The lullaby also proved effective at warding off a Daemon-animated gargoyle at Devil's End.

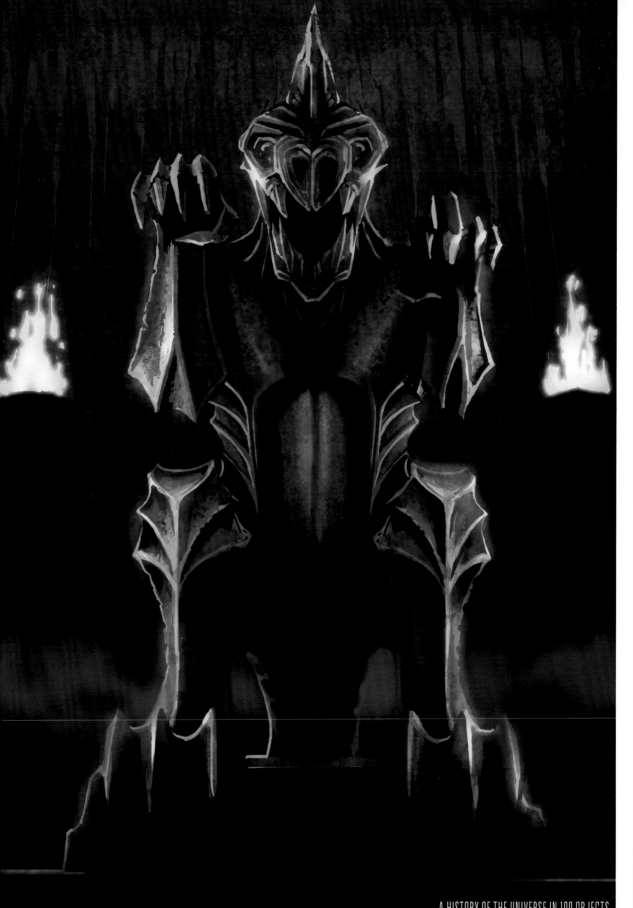

LOOK INTO MY EYES...

While Hepesh trained Aggedor to obey him and to kill, the Doctor brought out the beast's 'sweeter nature' through a little light hypnosis. The first time he attached a revolving mirror to his sonic screwdriver; the second, he simply swung the TARDIS key on its chain. The Doctor has always been adept at inducing and breaking hypnotic trances, which is just as well – mind control has long been a standard technique among his enemies, too...

■ The Morpho of Morphoton on Marinus entranced the First Doctor, Ian, Barbara and Susan into believing they were in an opulent palace with well-equipped laboratories and luxurious food.

■ WOTAN hypnotised the Doctor's companions Dodo and Polly, along with Professor Brett and a selection of scientists and soldiers as part of its project to begin the age of the computer.

■ The Macra used hypnotic conditioning to control the human population and force them to work in their gas mines.

■ The Daleks placed Arthur Terrell under a form of hypnotic control as part of their scheme to trap the Doctor into synthesising the Dalek Factor.

■ In the ice tombs of Telos, Jamie became hypnotised by the motion of the Cybermen's targeting device.

■ Victoria was hypnotised by Padmasambhava in Tibet, receiving a form of neuro-linguistic programming that conditioned her to demand that the Doctor leave Det-Sen monastery to the Great Intelligence.

■ The weed creature attacking the Euro Sea Gas refinery exerted mental control over several of the staff, including Mr Oak and Mr Quill.

■ The Cybermen's plan to invade London from the sewers was aided by a hypnotic signal inducing catalepsies through radio broadcasts.

■ The Master was a formidable hypnotist: at various times, he controlled circus impresario Lew Russell, plastics factory boss Rex Farrel, the Third Doctor's assistant Jo Grant, Captain Chin Lee, several UNIT soldiers, a sailor, Newton Institute Director Charles Percival, Chancellery Guard Solis, the passengers and crew of Concorde, and Doctor Grace Holloway.

■ He also perfected a hypnotic device that induced humans to see Ogrons as Draconians and Draconians to see them as humans, almost succeeding in provoking a space war, and used the Archangel Network to broadcast a hypnotic signal that made the population of Earth susceptible to his influence.

■ The supercomputer BOSS conditioned various employees of Global Chemicals, and Captain Mike Yates of UNIT; Yates's conditioning was broken by the Doctor using a Metebelis crystal.

■ Sontaran Commander Linx hypnotised Sarah Jane Smith so he could learn about the Doctor from her.

■ The Metebelis Spiders were able to control the minds of their human subjects by leaping on their backs and establishing a mental link.

■ Sarah Jane Smith was hypnotised by Hieronymous using the power of the Mandragora Helix.

■ Contact with the Kastrian Eldrad's surviving hand or ring brought humans under his mental control, including Sarah Jane Smith.

■ Sarah was also hypnotised by the Doctor, once to learn about Eldrad, and on an earlier occasion to save her from asphyxiation.

■ Magnus Greel gave Li H'sen Chang remarkable hypnotic powers.

■ Erato the Tythonian could influence the minds of those who came into contact with his translator device.

■ Adric came under the hypnotic control of the vampire Ortron. He and Tegan were later controlled by a Terileptil conditioning device.

■ The Malus took control of Sir George Hutchinson during Little Hodcombe's war games.

■ The Seventh Doctor was an expert mesmerist and hypnotist.

■ The Sycorax directed one-fifth of the Earth's population through blood control.

■ The Tenth Doctor was able to 'walk' into the minds of other people, including Madame de Pompadour. He later put Chloe Webber into a trance so he could communicate with an Isolus.

■ Cybus Industries controlled minds through an earpod signal, technology which the Cybermen then used at the Torchwood Institute and in Victorian London.

■ The Carrionites placed William Shakespeare in a trance while they guided his completion of *Love's Labour's Won*.

■ One by one, the crew of Avery's *Fancy* were seduced by the song of the Siren before being transported to her spaceship.

■ The Eleventh Doctor can silence people by shushing them.

Time Destructor

4000

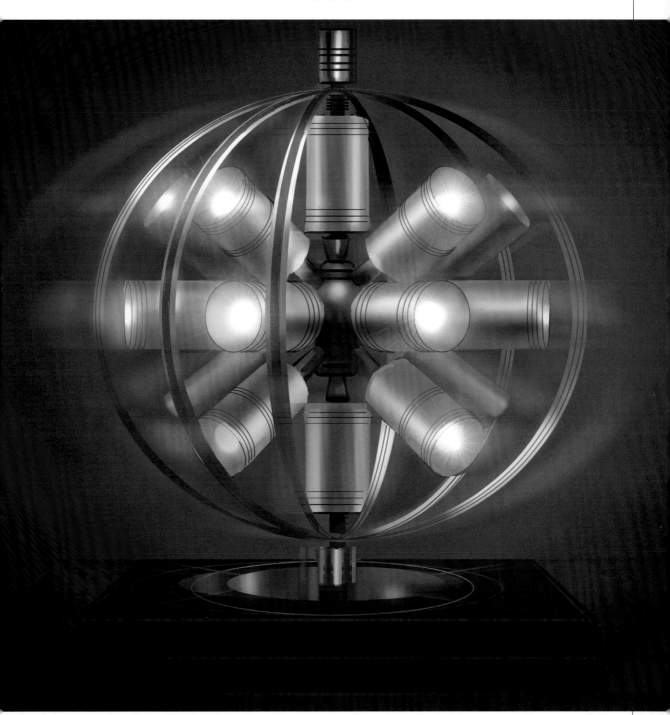

After the signing of the Non-Aggression Pact of 3975, the 40 billion people of Earth's Solar System united under the Guardianship of Mavic Chen. Humanity enjoyed 25 years of peace, a peace that was carefully guarded by Space Security Service agents such as Sara Kingdom of Mars Colony 16.

These agents were aware that the universe was a far from friendly place, and kept an eye on expanding empires and threatening species. They knew a lot about the Daleks, from an intimate knowledge of the flora and fauna of Skaro through to details of how they had spent the last five hundred years, gaining control of over seventy planets in Ninth Galactic System and forty more in the Constellation of Miros.

What the Space Security Service did not know was that their own leader was working with the Daleks.

The Time Destructor was built by the Daleks in conjunction with an intergalactic alliance that included Mavic Chen. It was the ultimate superweapon, holding the universe to ransom with the threat of ageing any species or planet to death.

It was powered by a full emm of Taranium, the rarest mineral in the universe, only obtainable from the mines of the outer planets of the solar system. It took 50 years to harvest a full emm. When the emm was collected, Chen announced he was taking a holiday in his Spar ship, and flew away to the planet Kembel to join the Daleks' alliance.

The Doctor stole the Taranium and fled through time with the Daleks in pursuit. They eventually retrieved it from him, but the Doctor activated the Time Destructor and the Daleks were destroyed along with nearly all life on Kembel.

DESTRUCTOR CONSTRUCTION

Barry Newbery, long-running *Doctor Who* designer, came up with an intricate blueprint for the Daleks' Time Destructor, which was quickly rethought when he realised that the necessary Perspex would be way beyond the story's budget. But when he saw plastic beakers on sale in Woolworth's that were just the right size and shape, he was able to revive his original design. The canister containing the Taranium Core slotted in the middle of all the beakers.

 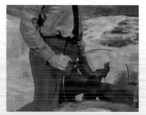

BIG DALEK WEAPONS

As soon as the Daleks realised there was other life in the universe they sought to destroy it. So deep is their self-hatred they can only be satisfied if they are the only beings left in creation. Just as the Daleks acquired space travel only in order to destroy other races, they initially experimented in time travel solely to hunt down and kill the Doctor. The development of the Time Destructor was the logical end of their strategic thinking: forming an alliance with any races they deemed to be a threat to them, holding them at bay while the ultimate weapon was prepared to wipe them out.

The principle behind the Time Destructor was to age matter to death – effectively to accelerate molecular activity until the point

that motion ceased within atoms and matter simply crumbled apart. Centuries later, this idea was elaborated by a revived Davros, who proposed the Daleks would be armed with new weaponry: 'Weaponry so devastating that all matter will succumb to its power.' After the Time War, he brought this idea into fruition with the Reality Bomb (see 077. Lost Moon of Poosh).

THE GALACTIC COUNCIL

The Daleks gathered together an alliance of powerful empires and races, yet most of them seem to have contributed little to the Daleks' plan. It's possible that the Daleks had calculated that their own attack on Earth's solar system would be more likely to succeed if they had already neutralised any rival powers. Rather than commit resources and fleets to overcoming the dominant powers of a number of other systems and galaxies, the Daleks lured their rulers into an illusory alliance. Then, when the delegates gathered for their final meeting before the invasion, they were to be disposed of. When this failed, the surviving delegates united against the Daleks. The alien delegates were:

Mavic Chen, Guardian of the Solar System ■ Gearon
Trantis ■ Malpha ■ Beaus ■ Sentreal ■ Warrien
Celation ■ Zephon, Master of the Fifth Galaxy

Producer Verity Lambert on set with some of the alien delegates

KNOW YOUR SPACE WEIGHTS AND MEASURES

CREDITS: A form of currency

EMM: The product of 50 years' Taranium mining

GROTZITS: A form of currency

REL: A Dalek unit of time, closely analogous to a second

SONEDS: A Jagaroth Spaceship can achieve warp thrust within 20 Soneds

TALMARS: A unit of currency on Pluto. 117 is a significant debt, and a dead body could be recycled for 1 talmar per 10 kilos.

A GALAXY OF RICHES

MINERAL	FOUND ON	USED IN
Acid	Earth	Energy generation (acid jars)
Aluminas	Granados	Powering time dams
Argonite	Ta, Pliny System	Building space beacons
Assetenite 455	Granados	Powering time dams
Bismuth	Ribos	Enriching Cyrrhenic nobility
Cadmium	Ribos	Enriching Cyrrhenic nobility
Carbon isotopes	Granados	Powering time dams
Coal	Earth	Fuel
Duralinium	Uxarieus	Constructing buildings
Galdrium	Granados	Powering time dams
Humans	Earth	Creating pure and blessed Dalek
Iron	Ribos	Enriching Cyrrhenic nobility
Jethrik	Cyrrhenis Minima	Warp-drive engines
Keefan	Kaldor	Enriching the Founding Families
Lucanol	Kaldor	Enriching the Founding Families
Madranite 1-5	Calufrax	Powering time dams
Mercury	Vulcan	Filling fluid links
Molybdenum	The Sense-Sphere	Building spaceships
Natural gas	Earth	Fuel
Oil	Earth	Fuel
Oolion	Bandraginus 5 / Qualactin	Powering time dams
Parrinium	Exxilon	Curing space plague
Quartz (PJX 1-8)	Earth	Clocks, circuit boards
Rock	P7E	Food
Taranium	Sol's outer planets	Destroying time
Tillium	Pliny system	Building spaceships and teapots
Tinclavic	Raaga	Spaceship construction
Trisilicate	Peladon / Mars	Federation technology
Vasilium	Calufrax	Powering time dams
Vionesium	Mogar	Artificial photosynthesis
Voolium	Granados / Calufrax	Powering time dams
Zelanite	Kaldor	Enriching the Founding Families
Zeiton 7	Varos	Powering a TARDIS

Dalek Emperor

41ST CENTURY

Although Davros originally conceived the Daleks as a 'travel machine', as the race progressed, the higher-ranking the Dalek the less mobile it became. Shuttle commanders were wired into their craft, and the Supreme Dalek was all but immobile on a pedestal aboard the Crucible. In the 41st century, the Emperor of the Daleks was housed in a giant immobile casing at the heart of the city of Kalaann on Skaro. Cables linked his casing to the city's power and data sources, through which he could monitor and control all Dalek activity – he was the vast brain at the centre of the Dalek civilisation, protected and served by black-domed Dalek guards, which obeyed his orders and reported on the success of his plans.

The Doctor and the Emperor were aware of each other for many years, but they didn't meet until the Second Doctor was tricked into synthesising the Dalek Factor. The Doctor exploited the situation to engineer a civil war on Skaro, apparently resulting in the destruction of the Dalek Empire.

KNOW YOUR EMPERORS

TVC21: THE DALEKS
The comic-strip original, the Golden Emperor was the original Dalek, who had a special casing made, and led the Daleks to galactic conquest, attacks on humanity and war against the Mechonoids.

THE EVIL OF THE DALEKS
Conceived the Dalek Factor and a plan to have the Doctor spread it throughout human history, but died in the Civil War.

REMEMBRANCE OF THE DALEKS
Sought the Hand of Omega on 20th-century Earth, but caused the destruction of Skaro. This was Davros, who had all but discarded the last vestiges of his humanoid form.

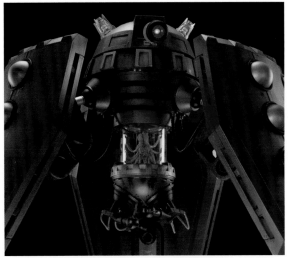

THE PARTING OF THE WAYS
Self-proclaimed god of all Daleks, led them against the Time Lords, took control of the Cruciform, and escaped the Time War to build a new Dalek army while manipulating the Fourth Great and Bountiful Human Empire.

Ood Brain

4126

The first human empire was built on expansion, colonisation and the exploitation of mineral wealth. The Second Great and Bountiful Human Empire was founded on slavery.

It was easy for humanity to fool itself into believing that it was not enslaving the Ood. The mighty corporations had always had excellent PR, and it was easy for Ood Operations to convince their customers that the Ood were offering themselves willingly, eradicating that last curse of existence – work. From the early 40th century to the 42nd was humanity's great Age of Ease. The Ood were there to serve, and serve willingly. Low-level empathic telepaths, they were kind and courteous, the ugliness and extreme politeness combining to make them unthreatening and easily mockable. The Ood were harmless – but only because humanity had made them so.

Ood Operations had neglected to tell its customers one thing – in order to make the Ood docile and subservient they were maimed, their external second brains severed and the remains encased in their translator balls. These 'interface devices' were linked to a plastic tube which was stitched to the Oods' heads. The removal of the hindbrain denied them telepathic communication with each other and with the great Ood Brain – both a mother and a relay for them. Without access to it, the Ood could no longer sing. Ood Song was more than mere song, it was a way of reaching out into the universe telepathically, and seeing through time. The Ood Song could communicate emotions, it could transmit an Ood's thoughts through time, and it could predict the future.

In the end, the slaves fought back. Klineman Halpen, the head of Ood Operations, was fed Ood graft and became an Ood, while the Ood Brain was freed from the electric currents that had held it in check for 212 years. The Song of the Ood resonated across three galaxies, and soon the Human Empire's fleets of rockets were carrying the Ood back home.

MEANWHILE...

■ The Ood were cousins of the Sensorites, who lived on the nearby Sense-Sphere. The Sensorites had very powerful brains and were natural telepaths, but had produced machines to enhance their abilities (the telepathic equivalent of mobile phones). Whereas the Ood had no vocal cords, the Sensorites could speak, but did so very quietly. Humans came into contact with the Sensorites some 1,200 years earlier than the Ood, when a series of exploration missions arrived at the Sense-Sphere seeking to exploit the planet's abundant Molybdenum.

■ A consignment of Ood were used on the mission to Krop Tor (see 001), as service staff, as caterers and in the drilling operation. What wasn't readily appreciated though was that their dormant telepathic energies, constrained by human technology, were now readily accessible by the Beast in the Pit. Humanity's action in enslaving the Ood facilitated the Beast's escape.

■ A stray Ood ended up outside the universe, trapped on House, which repaired him and turned him into a killer. He was eventually redistributed into airborne particles.

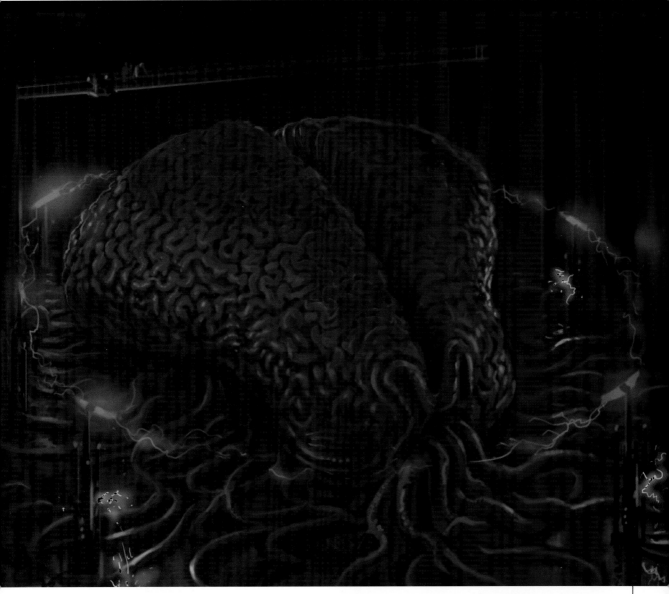

TELEPATHS

The Doctor's granddaughter Susan revealed telepathic abilities when they encountered the Sensorites, but the Time Lords are just one of many species able to communicate by telepathy. Others include:

The Eternals
Some Silurian groups
The Osirans
Vespiforms
Nestenes
Kitlings and Cheetah People
Metebelis Spiders
Boekind
Haemovores

Glass Dalek

47TH CENTURY

For a while, the universe didn't have to worry about the Daleks. They spent much of 4000–4500 locked in a logical impasse with the Movellans. And then the crews of spaceships started vanishing in the vicinity of the Daleks' abandoned home world – a Dalek taskforce was rounding up slave labour for mining operations on Skaro. The Daleks had returned home in search of their creator, Davros.

The Dalek taskforce on Skaro was defeated, and Davros was taken captive by humans. He became the sole prisoner aboard an Earth prison station, cryogenically frozen for 90 years. During his imprisonment, something remarkable happened – the Daleks lost the war with the Movellans, and, like errant children, they went looking for their creator once again.

Davros was freed by Dalek forces. The Supreme Dalek rapidly realised that Davros was unreliable, but the Daleks' creator unleashed a virus that attacked Dalek DNA before they could exterminate him. He escaped, and established himself as the Great Healer on the planet Necros, where he set about building a new Dalek army. The organic component came from mutated humans – Necros was the location of Tranquil Repose, a funeral home for the wealthy and powerful, and Davros experimented on the dying to create new Dalek creatures. Unused flesh was converted into a high-protein concentrate with which he all but eliminated famine – the Great Healer was widely regarded as a great benefactor by eager consumers who had no idea of the source of the foodstuff.

A glass Dalek casing was used in the incubation process for the new generation of Daleks. The mutant head of Arthur Stengos was found by his daughter in this transparent casing – he was undergoing conditioning and reprogramming. This was the penultimate stage in the evolution of the Daleks on Necros, as a new Dalek shell formed inside the glass Dalek, ready to house the finished mutant creature.

TRANSPARENCY OF THE DALEKS

The idea of a transparent Dalek casing dates back to 1964 and then script editor David Whitaker's novelisation of the first Dalek story. In *Doctor Who in an Exciting Adventure with the Daleks*, the Daleks are ruled by a Glass Dalek, which is revealed towards the end of the book. An accompanying illustration by Peter Archer shows this Glass Dalek containing a much less mutated creature, with a stolen TARDIS fluid link on a chain around his neck.

WAUGH OF THE DALEKS

Eric Saward's script for *Revelation of the Daleks* (1985) was heavily inspired by a comic novel by Evelyn Waugh, *The Loved One: An Anglo-American Tragedy*, first published in 1948. This was a satire on British expats in Los Angeles, the movie industry and the excesses of Hollywood's wealthy, particularly when it came to their funeral arrangements.

THE LOVED ONE	REVELATION OF THE DALEKS
Los Angeles	Necros
Whispering Glades funeral home / Happier Hunting Ground pet cemetery	Tranquil Repose
Mr Joyboy, Whispering Glades' senior mortician	Mr Jobel, Tranquil Repose's chief embalmer
Aimée Thanatogenos, Whispering Glades' cosmetician	Tasambeker, trainee at Tranquil Repose
Thanatogenos can't decide between Mr Joyboy and Dennis Barlow (she writes to the Guru Brahmin for advice)	Tasambeker must choose between Mr Jobel and Davros (she opts for the Great Healer)
She commits suicide by injecting herself with cyanide	She kills Jobel by stabbing him with a syringe
Sir Ambrose Abercrombie worries about how a suicide and Dennis Barlow's career choice will reflect on the image of the British in Hollywood	Takis and Lilt worry about how the Great Healer's activities (and his construction of the new Imperial Daleks) will affect business for Tranquil Repose – they summon the Daleks from Skaro

A film adaptation of *The Loved One* in 1965 also influenced several of the set designs for *Revelation of the Daleks*.

088

The Hand of Omega

47TH CENTURY

The Hand of Omega was a remote stellar manipulator, capable of sending a sun supernova, and collapsing it into a black hole. The Hand of Omega was used to create the Eye of Harmony, the singularity that then allowed the Gallifreyans access to the Time Vortex. But Omega himself, trapped for ever behind the singularity, had no idea that the Hand would eventually become a deadly weapon.

When the First Doctor left Gallifrey with his granddaughter Susan, he 'borrowed' a TARDIS and stole the Hand of Omega. He decided to hide it on an insignificant planet: Sol 3 in Mutter's Spiral, otherwise known as Earth. Lying low in 1960s London, he arranged with a local firm of undertakers for it to be buried, and then, apparently, forgot all about it.

Many regenerations later, the Seventh Doctor realised that the Hand of Omega wasn't just a powerful artefact; it could also be used as a trap. At this time the Daleks were seeking to rival the Time Lords' temporal mastery. They were already one of the most time-fluent races, with time-capable battle fleets and time corridors at their command. So the Doctor used the stellar manipulator as bait and lured the Daleks back in time to London in 1963.

He was surprised to discover that there were now two rival Dalek factions vying for supremacy, Davros's Imperial Daleks and the Renegade forces. Whichever side acquired the Hand of Omega would be able to write the other out of history. But the Doctor had reprogrammed the device, ordering it to do the one thing it was good at. Goading Davros into activating it, he watched as the stellar manipulator headed for Skaro's sun in the 47th century, turning it supernova and wiping out the Daleks' home planet, before returning through time and space to destroy the Dalek fleet. The single surviving Renegade Dalek, the Supreme, destroyed itself, and the Daleks were wiped out for ever...

Except that Davros escaped, and rebuilt his fleet, as he had many times before. His home world disintegrated, Davros declared war on the race which had tried to end his Daleks' future. The Doctor may have won the battle, but he had moved the Last Great Time War another step closer...

THE LEGEND OF OMEGA

Without Omega, there would have been no time travel. He was the solar engineer who arranged the detonation of a star, creating the colossal energy source that gave the Time Lords mastery over time itself. Omega himself, was lost in the supernova, sucked through the resultant black hole. The engineer and architect Rassilon completed Omega's work, stabilising the supernova and establishing the Eye of Harmony on Gallifrey. He founded and led Time Lord society, becoming its first President, while Omega was presumed dead, revered as one of his race's greatest heroes.

He wasn't dead. Instead, he spent millennia trapped in a universe of antimatter, sustained by his own enormous willpower. Eventually, driven mad by his isolation, he devised a means to drain the Time Lords' power source. He sent a controlled superlucent emission through the black hole to snatch the Doctor from space – the Doctor would take Omega's place in the antimatter universe, while Omega would return to Gallifrey as a god. The Doctor contrived an explosive collision of matter and antimatter, which seemed to end Omega's life. But he had survived again, and he made one more attempt to cross back into the universe by effecting a temporal bonding – a molecular realignment of himself and the Doctor. When the bonding began to fail, risking a cataclysmic collision of matter and antimatter on Earth, the Doctor was forced to destroy him.

KNOW YOUR TIME LORD SUPERWEAPONS

■ The Hand of Omega was concealed in a coffin – beneath the lid, all that could be seen was a vast white void. It seemed to be alive, and recognised and responded to the Doctor's voice. It could float through the air, and could electrify a metal object such as a baseball bat.

■ Validium, another semi-sentient Time Lord weapon with a psychic field and the ability to shape planets and events, dated from the same period. Shaped into a statue by the Lady Peinforte in 1638, it became known as Nemesis. The Doctor had launched it into space, on an orbit which brought it back to Earth every 25 years, always heralding some fresh disaster. The Seventh Doctor used it to destroy a Cyberman fleet.

■ The De-Mat gun was a weapon so powerful that knowledge of it was forbidden, even to the President of the Time Lords. It could be constructed and operated only in conjunction with the Great Key of Rassilon, which was secretly held by the Time Lord Chancellor to prevent any President getting his hands on it. A De-Mat gun was built and used just once, during the Fourth Doctor's presidency, when an invading Sontaran force was erased from history. Within moments, the gun had also erased itself, and all memory of it.

■ The Moment was used by the Doctor to end the Last Great Time War, extinguishing the Dalek and the Time Lords in a single second, and placing the entire war and all its hellish creations in a Timelock.

K-9

5000

The slow unravelling of the Second Great and Bountiful Human Empire came after the Ood revolution of 4126 and the resurgence of the Dalek threat in the 46th and 47th centuries. The Earth was increasingly isolated for several centuries. Its technology stagnated, and the human race could only watch the Dalek-Movellan war from the sidelines until the destruction of Skaro suddenly removed the Dalek threat from the galaxies. The encroaching Second Ice Age and a seemingly unavoidable fifth world war then triggered a fresh exodus from the Sol system – AD 5000 became the year of the Great Breakout.

There had been great technological advances. The Zygma experiments in time travel proved a dangerous blind alley, but conventional space travel leapt forward. Colonies were re-established, and an extensive network of new refuelling bases and space stations meant that spacecraft could leapfrog over each other through the stars.

This period also saw great advances in the field of space medicine – as travellers encountered phenomena and bacteria completely new to humanity. One such superbug was the Swarm, a sentient virus on the very edge of the solar system. It took possession of host bodies and minds, driving them to seek new

and more terrible ways of spreading itself. The Swarm found an ideal host in humanity, and threatened to become one of the first great space plagues, turning fuel tanks on the Titan moon into a breeding ground. Only the Bi-Al Foundation was able to identify and bring the virus under control, with the help of Professor Marius.

Marius typified the pioneers of the Great Breakout – he never spoke of his family but expressed great affection for a dog he'd been forced to leave behind because of weight restrictions on space flights. Once on the Bi-Al Foundation, he built his own robotic dog and named it K-9. K-9 was a mobile computer and extensive databank, with speech and personality circuits. It had a sensitive telescopic probe and visual circuits, a pair of 'ear' probes, and a laser fitted in its nose with four intensity levels from disable to kill.

The same weight restrictions meant that Marius couldn't take K-9 with him when he later returned to Earth, so he gave the robot dog to the Fourth Doctor.

THE K-9 KENNELS

■ Mark I: Travelled with the Fourth Doctor and Leela. Left with Leela to start a new life on Gallifrey after the Sontaran invasion.

■ Mark II: Travelled with the Fourth Doctor and Romana. Brain-damaged by the Time Winds, K-9 was restored by the Gateway from E-Space to N-Space, and remained in E-Space with Romana.

■ Mark III: Sent as a Christmas present by the Fourth Doctor, K-9 was Sarah Jane Smith's most faithful friend – until he broke down. He was repaired by the Tenth Doctor, but sacrificed himself to defeat the Krillitane.

■ Mark IV: Given to Sarah Jane Smith by the Tenth Doctor, he lived with her in Bannerman Road. He spent several years orbiting a black hole preventing it from destroying the Earth, but was able to leave for short occasions to help out in a crisis, such as transmitting the TARDIS base codes to the Mr Smith computer in order to aid in flying the stolen Earth back from the Medusa Cascade.

THE K-9 FRANCHISE

The announcement of K-9's return to *Doctor Who* in 2006 was greeted with as much excitement as that of Sarah Jane Smith and the Cybermen. Introduced in October 1977, K-9 had quickly became one of the most enduring parts of the *Doctor Who* mythos, becoming almost as popular as the Daleks. In the late 1970s and early 1980s, there were K-9 models and dolls, annuals and activity books, and a series of children's adventure stories in which he saved the galaxy on his own.

In 1981, K-9 was the first *Doctor Who* creation to get a spin-off show. *K-9 & Company* saw the unlikely but welcome pairing of K-9 with Sarah Jane Smith in a children's version of a *Bergerac* Halloween Special. Only a pilot episode was made, and the projected series never materialised, though they did both appear in *The Five Doctors* for *Doctor Who*'s 20th anniversary in 1983. The success of K-9 and Sarah Jane's eventual return to *Doctor Who* in 2006 quickly led to a brand-new spin-off series for the pairing, *The Sarah Jane Adventure*s, which ran for five hugely successful series on CBBC.

Writers Bob Baker and Dave Martin had retained the rights to K-9 when they devised him in 1977, and in the 1980s they began looking at giving him his own solo TV series. After a number of false starts and announcements during the 1990s, *K9* was eventually made in Australia in 2009.

K-9 ON 1980s EARTH

What was a typical day like for K-9 and Sarah Jane Smith?

Reading a newspaper

Typing outside the Bear Inn

Drinking wine outside the Inn

Early morning run

Sitting on a wall (1)

Sitting on a wall (2)

Early morning drive

More driving

Extending probe

Extending blaster

090

Psychic Paper

51ST CENTURY

Standard issue for 51st-century Time Agents and an essential tool for the Ninth, Tenth and Eleventh Doctors, psychic paper had three main functions: it showed viewers whatever its user wanted them to see; it bypassed electronic security systems; and it was able to receive telepathically broadcast messages. A sufficiently experienced user could deploy it without actually coming up with an alias or falsehood first – the psychic paper would itself devise and show something plausible.

It had certain limitations. In inexperienced hands, psychic paper could give away its user's thoughts – you couldn't let your mind wander when you were handing it over. It couldn't cope with a really large falsehood – the Doctor once tried to back up his claim to be universally recognised as a mature and responsible adult with psychic paper which promptly shorted out and displayed only wavy lines. Finally, it had no effect on geniuses, such as William Shakespeare, or on highly developed species, like the Saturnynes – they simply saw the paper as blank.

Immunity to the effects of psychic paper could also be learned. In the early 21st century, the Torchwood Institute – perhaps acting on advice from its operative Captain Jack Harkness – gave all its staff a basic level of psychic training, enabling them to recognise the paper as blank. By the 52nd century, all clerics in the Church Army on Demon's Run were trained to distinguish giveaway fractal patterns on psychic paper. And anyone sufficiently familiar with the use of psychic paper would gain an ability to recognise it.

A MESSAGE ON THE PSYCHIC PAPER

The Doctor has received psychic messages from:
- The Face of Boe, summoning him to the New New York hospital on New Earth
- River Song, summoning him to The Library
- The Atraxi, warning that Prisoner Zero had escaped
- A frightened Tenza child called George, asking for help

MY CREDENTIALS

Before he got hold of some psychic paper, the Doctor used all sorts of aliases and passes...
- The First Doctor registered at a library in Shoreditch, East London during 1963 under the name of Dr J. Smith. The Second

Doctor's companion Jamie McCrimmon once gave him the alias John Smith, which he took from a packing case on board the W3 space station, and the Doctor himself assumed the same name on many occasions after that.
- The First Doctor at various times claimed to be lyre-player Maximus Pettulian, the Greek god Zeus, and 'Doctor Caligari'.
- At Culloden in 1746, the Second Doctor pretended to be a German medic, Dr von Wer.
- The Third Doctor fooled everyone at Global Chemicals with his Milkman and Cleaning Lady disguises.
- When sneaking into a Think Tank meeting, the Fourth Doctor showed his pilot's licence for the Mars-Venus Rocket Run.
- Investigating the collision of the *Empress* and the *Hecate*, the Fourth Doctor pretended to be from Galactic Insurance and Salvage.
- The Seventh Doctor left the Renegade Daleks a calling card showing a question mark.
- The Seventh Doctor used old UNIT staff passes to gain access to UNIT's operations at Carbury.
- Sneaking onto the military base at Maiden's Point, the Seventh Doctor hastily faked a letter from Winston Churchill.

091

Sonic Blaster

51ST CENTURY

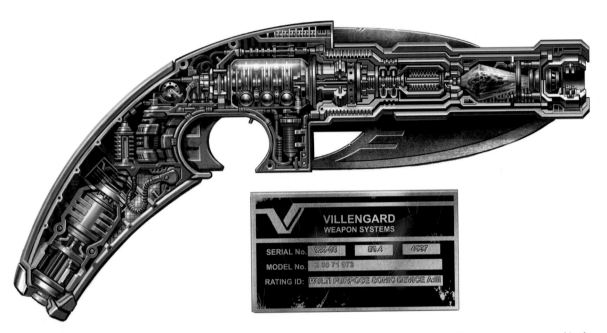

VILLENGARD
WEAPON SYSTEMS

SERIAL No.	123-06	69.4	4537
MODEL No.	2 00 71 973		
RATING ID:	MULTI PURPOSE SONIC DEVICE A-III		

The Weapon Factories of Villengard were renowned in the 51st century, even supplying the human Time Agency with their arsenal. The Doctor visited Villengard's Weapon Factories just once – he blew them up and replaced them with a banana plantation.

One of the most powerful weapons ever produced in the Weapon Factories of Villengard was the sonic blaster. It was a digital weapon with a distinctive blast pattern – a neat square. Captain Jack Harkness had one of these 'squareness guns' in London during the Blitz, subsequently leaving it aboard the TARDIS when he was abandoned on the Game Station.

River Song later found Jack's blaster in the TARDIS and took it away with her. She was armed with it when she led an archaeological expedition to The Library, and used it against the Vashta Nerada.

I DON'T APPROVE OF GUNS

The Doctor does not use guns but has often been quite prepared to fight.

The First Doctor brawled with a Roman assassin, did battle with a robot duplicate, and was never reluctant to raise a walking stick in his own defence. The Second Doctor fought with Salamander, but was otherwise relatively peaceable. The Third Doctor always had a 'hai!' and a display of Venusian aikido at the ready for unwary security guards. He fenced with the Master, and wrestled with Peladon's Champions and the dark side of Omega's will. He also boxed with a sailor on the SS *Bernice*, according to Queensbury rules.

The Fourth Doctor's fights were rarer – he challenged the Sontaran Field Major Styre to single combat and fought with Harrison Chase, as well as knocking out a fair number of guards, a chauffeur, and even Sarah Jane Smith when she was possessed by Eldrad. His life-or-death struggle with Chancellor Goth was unusually bloody, but was in reality a mental tussle inside a computational matrix. Claiming to have been trained by one of Cleopatra's bodyguards, he was also an expert swordsman, and took on the palace guard in San Martino and Count Grendel on Tara. His taste for physical combat waned as he went on, and he usually relied on a colourful imagination and a glib tongue.

The Fifth Doctor was a reluctant combatant, and generally came off worst – on one occasion he was tipped into a pool in a reactor chamber. He did, though, take on the Master in a swordfight in 13th-century England. Legend has it that the Sixth Doctor threw two guards into an acid bath in Vengeance on Varos. This isn't true – he simply didn't stop them falling in. Like the Fifth Doctor, he was usually unwilling to fight and didn't do it very well, failing to strangle his companion while undergoing a regenerative trauma. The Seventh Doctor almost always avoided physical confrontations, sometimes using mental powers to halt fights; on the planet of the Cheetah People, he and the Master succumbed to fighting like animals, and he had a brief tussle with his companion Mel when he mistook her for the Rani.

The Eighth Doctor was also only drawn into a fight by the Master. The Ninth Doctor would casually pull arms and heads off artificial life forms like Autons and the Adherents of the Repeated Meme. The Tenth Doctor was a good sword fighter, as he proved when he took on the Sycorax Leader and the Cybermen.

The Eleventh Doctor would probably break the sword.

DEATH RAYS

Extermination – achieved by turning the camera negative

Cybergun – achieved by pumping smoke through the actor's costume

Ice Warrior Gun – achieved by reflecting an actor in a flexible mirror and then shaking it

A Quark Gun – achieved by rubbing the film of the actor's death scene

Terileptil Gun – achieved by superimposing a light box over the picture, the 'ray' being produced by carefully angling pieces of cardboard

Computer-generated Dalek extermination effect

CHAP WITH WINGS...

The Brigadier and UNIT were the Doctor's gun-friendliest associates, but several of his companions have carried weapons, including Captain Jack Harkness (always), Steven Taylor (at the Last Chance Saloon), Liz Shaw (in a parallel world), Leela (almost constantly) and Sara Kingdom (when combating the Daleks' master plan). Ace generally had a rucksack full of explosives; the Doctor banned her from using them – except when he needed her to use them.

092

Diary

52ND CENTURY

I n 5123, the Luna University gained a new pupil who wished to study archaeology. Wherever she went, she took with her an old-fashioned blue notebook, in which she kept a record of her life. She disappeared before graduating...

1. 'I am born.'

2. 'I am kidnapped.'

3. 'I escape spacesuit.'

4. 'I scare a tramp.'

5. 'I'm Mum and Dad's best friend.'

6. 'I don't kill Hitler.'

7. 'I get a present.'

8. 'I go to university. On the Moon!'

9. 'I become a doctor!'

10. 'I don't kill the Doctor.'

11. 'I live in a pyramid.'

12. 'I marry the Doctor.'

13. 'I kill the Doctor, a lot.'

14. 'I go to prison.'

15–18. *'I have LOVELY adventures.'*

19. *'I say hi to Mum and Dad.'*

20. *'I have a nice picnic.'*

21. *'I love a tomb!'*

22. *'I'm Cleopatra!'*

23. *'I open the Pandorica.'*

24. *'I don't like Daleks.'*

25. *'I go to Mum and Dad's wedding.'*

26. *'I meet Weeping Angels and don't blink.'*

27. *'I go to The Library.'*

28. *'I die.'*

29. *'I live happily ever after.'*

Janis Thorn

FAR FUTURE

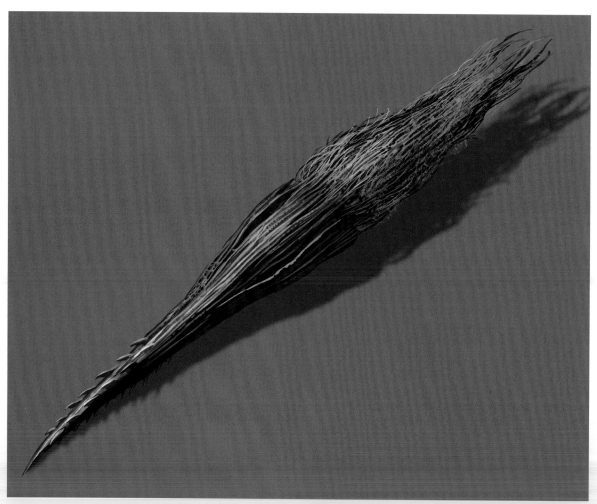

Earth sent out ever more expeditions, heading deeper into space and laying claim to thousands of new worlds. The Mordee expedition was typical – its spaceship landed on a likely-looking planet, a technical team remaining on board to maintain the systems, while a survey team explored the surface and assessed its viability for settlement. In this case, the ship's mission computer failed, stranding the expedition. Generations of technicians worked to extend the computer's power. When the Fourth Doctor arrived and tried to help, he wrongly assumed the computer's data core was damaged; in fact, the technicians had unwittingly created an entirely new species – one that had just been born, and was in shock. Disastrously, the Doctor attempted to renew the data core by making a direct link with the memory centres of his own brain. The computer didn't just take compatible information from his mind; it copied everything. Worse still, he also neglected to remove his personality print from the data core. When he left the planet, he left behind a schizophrenic computer – two selves, one believing that it was him. That's when it started to go mad.

The computer – Xoanon – then conducted an experiment in eugenics, dividing the colonists' descendants in two, as it was divided. The technicians' successors became the Tesh, their minds refined and cultivated to achieve paraphysical and psi powers; the survey team were regressed into the Sevateem, a primitive tribe of superstitious warriors who prized and perfected physical courage and strength. Skilled hunters and savage fighters, the Sevateem were ingenious inventors of weaponry. Knives and crossbows were used alongside weapons adapted from the local ecology. The Horda, voracious armoured arthropods, were incorporated into ritual punishments. And poisonous thorns were found in the local flora – the Janis thorn caused immediate paralysis and death, with no natural cure.

WHAT HAPPENED?
YOU MUST REMEMBER...

The Face of Evil is something of a rarity – it revisits the setting of an unseen earlier adventure – but it's not at all unusual for the Doctor to mention his many untelevised exploits...

■ The First Doctor claimed to have been given a coat by Gilbert and Sullivan, though Beau Brummel told him he looked better in a cloak. He also claimed to have taught the Mountain Mauler of Montana to wrestle and witnessed James Watt's discovery of steam power. King Henry VIII threw a parson's nose at him, and he threw it back. For this offence the Doctor was taken to the Tower of London, which was where he and Susan had left the TARDIS. He and Susan landed on the planet Esto, where the plants used thought transference. If you stood in between two of the plants, they set up a sort of screeching noise. They also nearly lost the TARDIS on Quinnis, a planet in 'the fourth universe'.

■ The Second Doctor's arrival at Det-Sen was his second visit – on his first, during an attack on the monastery 300 years earlier, he had taken the monks' holy Ghanta for safekeeping. He also had a rather unsettling encounter with the Terrible Zodin, involving someone – or *something* – hopping about like kangaroos.

■ The Third Doctor had Chairman Mao's permission to use his personal name, Tse-Tung, was once locked in a cell with Sir Walter Raleigh, told Napoleon that an army marches on its stomach, was a close personal friend of Horatio Nelson, took boxing lessons from John L. Sullivan and escapology lessons from Harry Houdini. On his way to the Third Intergalactic Peace Conference, he was captured by the Medusoids, escaping by truthfully telling them he was about to meet a giant rabbit, a pink elephant and a purple horse with yellow spots, which broke their mind probe. He had also been made a noble of Draconia by the Fifteenth Emperor after he cured a space plague. He often promised to take his companions to nice places like Florana, claiming he always came back feeling a hundred years younger. Sadly, we never see these adventures. He also visited the Citadel of Karfel with Jo Grant and another companion, and befriended the scientist Megelen. Disgusted to discover the true nature of Megelen's experiments on the Morlox, the Doctor reported his friend to the Inner Sanctum.

■ One of the first three Doctors knew Nostradamus's wife

(see 021). The Fourth Doctor borrowed a picklock from Marie Antoinette, learnt fencing from one of Cleopatra's bodyguard and archery from William Tell, went fishing with the Venerable Bede and Izaak Walton, and took singing lessons from Dame Nellie Melba. He knew Shakespeare well (see 022), visited Cambridge frequently, dropped apples on Isaac Newton and attempted to correct Albert Einstein's Special Theory of Relativity. He was with the Filipino army at the final advance on Reykjavik in the 51st century, and apparently saw the birth of the universe. The Droge of Gabrielides offered a whole star system for his head. He once had terrible trouble returning *The Worshipful and Ancient Law of Gallifrey* to the Panopticon.

■ The Sixth Doctor had business cards for a multitude of famous scientists, including Archimedes ('Fascinating chap, bit wet'), Isambard Kingdom Brunel, Christopher Columbus, Dante Alighieri, Leonardo, and Joinson Dastari, Head of Projects at Space Station Chimera. He encountered a dying Warlord of Thordon. At some point he met a young computer programmer called Melanie Bush, from Pease Pottage.

■ The Seventh Doctor would, one day, meet Thomas Gainsborough, who would paint a portrait of his companion Ace. He also hinted that he had been involved in the earliest Gallifreyan researches into time travel. He may once have sat down in the desert to play chess with the creature Fenric.

■ The Eighth Doctor recalled being with Puccini when he died, and knew Sigmund Freud and Marie Curie ('intimately').

■ The Ninth Doctor was present at the eruption of Krakatoa in 1883, was on the Titanic when it sank ('ended up clinging to an iceberg'), was in the crowds when President John F. Kennedy was assassinated in 1963, and claimed that Genghis Khan had tried and failed to get into the TARDIS. He met a onetime owner of 10 Downing Street (Mr Chicken, who was a nice man), and pushed boxes at the Boston Tea Party. He knew more about the celebrities featured in *Heat* magazine than *Heat* did. He took Rose Tyler to Justicia, the Glass Pyramid of San Kaloon and Woman Wept – where the sea had frozen – and returned a Slitheen egg to Raxacoricofallapatorius with Rose and Captain Jack Harkness.

They then narrowly escaped Kyoto during the civil war of 1336, just as the city fell to Ashikaga shogunate. David Lloyd George could drink him under the table. He may have visited the planet Barcelona, whose dogs had no noses.

■ The Tenth Doctor took Martha Jones to see the Moon landing four times, helped Benjamin Franklin with experiments in conductivity, had his laser spanner stolen by Emmeline Pankhurst, and rescued Charlemagne from an insane computer in the Ardennes. He saw the Phosphorous Carousel of the Great Magellan Gestadt, saved a planet from the Red Carnivorous Maw, named a galaxy Alison and married Queen Elizabeth I. He also found time to defeat four things and a hatching lizard.

■ The Eleventh Doctor had countless picnics, day-trips and adventures with River Song, and took Amy Pond to Space Florida. He, Amy and Rory were sent on a royal mission to the Orient Express in space when an Egyptian Goddess escaped from the Seventh Obelisk; he'd been at the prayer meeting when she was sealed in. He once went to a party with Albert Einstein, Frank Sinatra and Father Christmas, and spent several Christmases with Kazran Sardick and Abigail Pettigrew across time and space. He advised Michelangelo not to accept the commission to paint the ceiling of the Sistine Chapel. Napoleon once threw a bottle of wine at him, and he knew Thomas Jefferson, John Adams and Alexander Hamilton, America's Founding Fathers – two of them fancied him. He had 195 years of adventures without Amy and Rory before going to Lake Silencio to face his death, some of them involving Jim the Fish.

IF THE DOCTOR HAD NEVER VISITED US… WOULD ANYONE HERE HAVE DIED?

■ If the Doctor had never landed on Skaro and gone to investigate that mysterious city, the Daleks would have wiped out the Thals and then remained in their city, happily content that they were the only life form in the universe.

■ Without the Doctor (and Dodo's cold), the humans and Monoids would have travelled to Refusis 2, to be greeted warmly by the invisible Refusians.

■ Would the archaeologists have been able to enter the Tomb of the Cybermen without the Doctor's help? (No.)

■ If the Doctor hadn't turned up, the Krotons would eventually have run out of energy, releasing the Gonds from generations of slavery.

■ By stealing a Metebelis crystal, the Doctor brought the spiders to Earth, causing several deaths, starting with Professor Herbert Clegg.

■ The Doctor brought the Mandragora Helix to Earth. Defeated, it vowed to reinvade 500 years later.

■ The Doctor made it possible for the Vardans to conquer Gallifrey, which in turn allowed the Sontarans to invade.

■ Had the Doctor worked out his differences with Megelen differently, then the Borad's rule would never have come about.

■ The Doctor openly admitted he may have 'miscalculated' in his cunning plan to lure the Daleks to Shoreditch.

■ Without the Doctor and Rose, the Metaltron would have continued to sit sadly in its cage. Waiting.

■ The Doctor's plan to hide from the Family of Blood brought death and destruction to a small English village.

■ Until the Doctor went to Malcassairo, Professor Yana was a kindly scientist with a desire to save the human race.

■ Had the Doctor not taken Amy and Rory on board the TARDIS, the ultimate weapon would not have been created, Earth would not have been invaded in order to build a spacesuit to contain it, and time would not have been broken when the weapon went wrong.

JANICE THORNE

'In rehearsals we decided Janis thorn sounded like an out-of-work actress...' – *Louise Jameson*

JANICE THORNE

1967 – Theatre – Hamlet – Ophelia – RADA Summer School, dir. Martin Barker

1968 – Theatre - Hedda Gabler – Hedda – Islington Crown, dir Martin Barker

1968 – Theatre – Antigone – Antigone – The Blue on the Green, dir Martin Barker

1969 – Theatre – Waiting for Godette – Oestragon – Manchester Square, dir Martin Barker

1970 – Theatre – Something Misunderstood – Helena – Melrose Abbey, dir Martin Barker

1970 – Television – Softly, Softly: Some Mother's Daughter – Margot, dir Claude Olrenshaw

1971 – Theatre – Hell's Bells, Coventry Rep – Maid, dir. Martin Barker

1972 - Theatre - Calamity Mike, Kettering Odeon – Parlourmaid, dir. Martin Barker

1973/4 – Theatre – Puss In Boots – Northampton Derngate – Third Courtier, dir. Martin Barker

094

Money-Pencil

200,000

The Fourth Great and Bountiful Human Empire should have comprised a million species on a million planets. Earth by now was covered with mega-cities with a population of 96 billion. The human race at this time should have been at its most intelligent and inquisitive, its culture, art, politics, philosophy and cuisine at a creative peak. But something had set Earth back by about 90 years, stalling its technological advances and slowly isolating it from other civilisations – the Daleks were hidden in space, influencing human development. In 199,909, they had installed the Mighty Jagrafess of the Holy Hadrojassic Maxarodenfoe aboard the orbiting space station Satellite Five and had been affecting and influencing humanity through its news broadcasts ever since. Tightened immigration laws prevented alien species from coming to Earth, while the news media transmitted disinformation to an unquestioning population that became increasingly isolated and weakened. Through the Jagrafess, the Daleks bred a human race that didn't ask questions.

A vertical tube ringed with hoops and covered in transmitters and pylons, Satellite Five orbited the Earth and broadcast a constant stream of news from 600 television channels. Its 500 floors were linked by key-coded high-velocity lifts, and each floor contained a series of Observation Decks and Spike Rooms, linked by corridors and constantly monitored by thousands of security cameras. Tannoy announcements and alarm klaxons reminded workers of station rules and regulated the work periods. Each floor provided fast-food booths selling Kronkburgers (with cheese or pajatos) and synthesised drinks like zaffic (which tasted of beef), paid for with metal money-pencils disbursed from creditpoint machines.

THE DOCTOR'S LSD TRIP

SCARLIONI: So you stole the bracelet simply because it's pretty?
DOCTOR: Yes. Well, I think it is. Don't you?
SCARLIONI: Yes.
COUNTESS: My dear, I don't think he's as stupid as he seems.
SCARLIONI: My dear, nobody could be as stupid as he seems.

City of Death, Part 2

The Doctor is very detached from money – it neither interests nor motivates him, and he's often considered stealing it to be perfectly acceptable. Time Lord society appears to be unworldly and cashless and, rather like an English monarch, the Doctor doesn't seem to carry cash.

■ The Doctor's granddaughter Susan stirred her teachers' curiosity with her confusion about England's pre-decimal currency, anticipating decimalisation by more than seven years. Escaping from forced labour during the French Revolution, the First Doctor stole coins from an overseer and, when he landed during the Crusades, he pinched clothes rather than pay for them. He clearly had money, though – when defeating WOTAN he travelled by taxi, which he paid for – but then taxis in 1966 were clearly very cheap, as tramps were able to afford them. Fellow Time Lord the Monk was more mercenary: 'Put two hundred pounds in a London bank in 1968. Nipped forward two hundred years and collected a fortune in compound interest.'

■ The Second Doctor was even more unworldly, although he did manage to pay for a photo-booth at Gatwick airport and buy drinks for himself and Jamie in a coffee bar. He carried at least one (double-headed) coin, as he used it for tossing in order to make decisions. He once explained 'tokens of exchange' to Shockeye of the Quawncing Grig and that meals must be paid for. When Shockeye offered a 20 Narg note (acceptable on any of the Nine Planets), it was politely declined by Oscar Botcherby, who was impolitely killed. Had the Doctor had a better understanding of money, this might have been prevented.

■ The Third Doctor refused monetary payment during his time at UNIT, claiming to have no use for the stuff, other than in the

occasional magic trick as part of an escape plan. He did, however, persuade the Brigadier to buy him a vintage car, got Jo Grant to wheedle electrical equipment from the UNIT quartermaster, Mr Campbell, and was clearly quite a drain on UNIT's resources, given Lethbridge-Stewart's reaction to the TARDIS interior: 'So this is what you've been doing with UNIT funds and equipment all this time.' He was generally quite blasé about his access to cash, offering to buy his previous self a hundred recorders, and making a rather unfortunate attempt to bribe one of the Master's minions – when his wallet was revealed to be empty, he simply said, 'I can get money quite easily.' When he and Sarah Jane Smith arrived in dinosaur-occupied London, they were naive enough to be arrested as looters. The Master, by contrast, understood finance very well – taking over a plastics factory, hiring a chauffeur, and having power over the villagers of Devil's End by knowing which of them was on the take.

■ The Fourth Doctor insisted on paying for his ginger pop at the Fleur de Lys in Devesham, and knew enough about money to realise there was something wrong with the till and the villagers having pockets full of coins from the same year. He used a double-headed coin from Aldebaran Three for making decisions. He thought money wasn't a very good reason for doing anything, and was dismissive of Lord Palmerdale's reason for wanting to leave Fang Rock. He did, however, prove to have a sophisticated enough knowledge of intergalactic finance ('Probably too many economists in the government') to defeat the Usurians – and agreed with the assertion that 'everyone runs from the Taxman.' He used a forged Consumcard in order to extract talmars from a cash machine but, when confronted with a plot to steal the Mona Lisa to pay for Professor Kerensky's time experiments, the Doctor seemed baffled by the whole concept of having to pay a power bill. He believed that art had an intrinsic rather than a real worth (proving this by defacing Leonardo's canvases), and claimed to be an art thief who only stole things because they were pretty. He did, however, think that glasses of tap water in a café should be paid for.

■ The Fifth Doctor attempted to pay for his drink in a Lanzarote café with alien coinage and was chased by an angry waiter.

■ The Sixth Doctor's contempt for Davros increased when he realised he'd been raiding the bodies of the dead in order to build a successful business – he seemed to think even less of Davros for having to earn money. He was equally scornful of the

Lytton gang's plans to rob a diamond merchants, but understood enough about intergalactic finance to advise Sil on his business transactions on Thoros Beta.

■ The Seventh Doctor carried a purse, which contained a variety of complicated (and occasionally mobile) coins from across the universe. This included a British £5 piece, which he thought was a reasonable price for a lemonade in the late 1990s.

■ The Eighth Doctor was baffled by money and possessions. The newly regenerated Master stole gold dust from the Doctor's library in order to bribe an Asian child.

■ The Ninth Doctor was appalled that Cassandra's scheming in the year 5 billion all came down to money, and was disdainful of the extreme wealth of the partygoers on Platform One. He told Rose Tyler he had no money to pay for chips, but soon afterwards managed to pay a newspaper-seller in Victorian Cardiff. He used the sonic screwdriver to steal a money-pencil with limitless credit for Adam on Satellite Five, though he meant it to be spent on Kronkburgers, not surgical operations. He offered to pay for Margaret Slitheen's last meal, but left without settling the bill.

■ The Tenth Doctor told Madame de Pompadour he'd always been a bit clueless about money, and he hated the idea of getting a mortgage. He soniced a cash machine to get money for Donna Noble to pay for a cab, and arranged several lottery wins, including one for Donna's wedding present.

■ The Eleventh Doctor went further, arranging lottery wins for Sardick's staff – on a planet that didn't have a lottery. He somehow got hold of tickets for the Pandorica exhibition for young Amelia Pond. They may have been bought with some of the great wodge of cash he handed over to Craig Owens to pay for his rent – suggesting that, actually, the Doctor has a great deal of money. He just has no idea how much it's worth.

095

Bad Wolf

200,100

The human race had seen nothing of the Daleks since the Tenth Dalek Occupation, when they vanished from space and time and became embroiled in the Time War. The Emperor's new force of half a million Daleks had, like their creator, been driven insane, both by the centuries spent hiding in silence and by the non-Dalek source of their own flesh. Now, a century after the destruction of the Jagrafess, the Dalek Stratagem was reaching its conclusion. Before long, 200 ships, each carrying over 2,000 Daleks, were heading for Satellite Five, now renamed the Game Station. The Dalek Fleet attacked the Earth and bombed whole continents. It took just 15 seconds for their saucers to devastate Europa, Pacifica and the New American Alliance and entirely obliterate Australasia.

That the Game Station was owned by the mysterious Bad Wolf Corporation was part of a stranger phenomenon that was nothing to do with the Dalek Emperor's plans. When the Doctor sent Rose Tyler home to the Powell Estate in South London using TARDIS Emergency Program One, the phrase 'Bad Wolf' seemed to be everywhere: on a poster in a fast-food café, on the ground and walls of a playground... Until now, Rose and the Doctor had assumed that Bad Wolf was a warning, or perhaps part of a scheme to draw them into the Daleks' trap. Now Rose realised that it was a message to her, a link between herself and the Doctor. She and Mickey forced open the TARDIS console and the energy of the Time Vortex flowed into her, giving her extraordinary power. Returning to the Game Station to save the Doctor, she took the phrase from a Bad Wolf Corporation sign and scattered the words throughout time and space – she had left the message for herself. She was the Bad Wolf, and she had created herself. With the Vortex still running through her head, she divided the Daleks, their Fleet and their Emperor into their constituent particles.

BAD WOLF EXPLAINED

David Tennant in conversation with Russell T Davies on the set of Shan Shen Alley for Doctor Who Confidential, *2008*

DAVID: So Russell, when you knew that you were bringing Billie back, Rose back, did you know that Bad Wolf would be returning?

RUSSELL: I sort of thought, it's part and parcel of Rose really, as a warning, a message, as a sign that goes with her. It's a warning

of trouble to come. As the Doctor says at the end, 'it's the end of the universe', because if those words have started to reappear again then things are as bad as they can possibly be.

DAVID: For the benefit of our younger viewers, what did Rose do when she infected the world with Bad Wolf?

RUSSELL: Ah, that's a very good question. Have you not worked that out yet? It's been many years.

DAVID: Well, I have. It's for the benefit of those who maybe just tuned in.

RUSSELL: It was a message she created for herself. Rose absorbed the Time Vortex and, in order to put herself in a position where she could absorb the Time Vortex, when she'd absorbed the Time Vortex, she sent a message back through time that was a warning, that was a signal and also an act of faith. Those simple two words, nursery rhyme words actually, which sort of resonate, which say, 'You must be here at this time to become the Bad Wolf.' She calls herself the Bad Wolf in the end – that is Rose with all the power of the Time Vortex.

DAVID: Which is the word which is appearing behind you right now. Look at that.

RUSSELL: The whole alley being redressed. Ah, yes.

DAVID: She's everywhere. Much like Billie Piper herself.

UNSEEN HUMAN ADVENTURES

When the Ninth Doctor left the Game Station, the Daleks had been defeated, but the Earth was in a terrible state. The Tenth Doctor assumed that Captain Jack would help out in its rebuilding, but what happened to humanity next?

At some unspecified point in the future, the Fourth Doctor encountered humans living in six Megropolises on Pluto, kept alive by artificial suns and in economic slavery to the Company. The Company had discovered Earth was a run-down planet, its population dying, and it moved them to Mars. Having recovered sufficient costs of the operation from humanity, when Mars was exhausted, the Company then moved them to Pluto, building six artificial (and very expensive) suns in order to keep the species alive and taxable. Had the Fourth Doctor not liberated the people of Megropolis One, humanity would have died out, as the Company had decided that it was uneconomic to relocate them again.

But, with humanity gone, what happened to the ruined Earth? Was it totally abandoned, or did it still contain a secret of interest to the Time Lords?

096

L3 Robot

C.2,000,000

Around the year two million, a group of Andromedans found a way to access the Matrix, the repository of all knowledge on Gallifrey, stealing information and secrets from the Time Lords and channelling them to Earth (by then repopulated, but not a major universal power). While the Andromedans waited for a robot recovery mission to reach Earth from Andromeda, they learnt that the Time Lords had traced the source of the security breach, so they constructed a survival chamber beneath London. The three 'Sleepers' entered suspended animation, protected by Drathro, an L3 maintenance and installation robot.

While the Sleepers dreamed, the Time Lords took their revenge – the High Council ordered the use of a Magnetron to move the Earth and its entire constellation to the Stellian galaxy, a couple of light years across space. This caused a solar fireball which wiped out almost the entire population.

The planet was renamed Ravalox. Two groups survived the catastrophe. Those above the surface were called the Tribe of the Free, and they roamed the rainy desolation. The other survivors were starved of water, living deep underground in the ruins of Marble Arch tube station and venerating their sacred texts: *Moby-Dick* by Herman Melville, *The Water Babies* by Charles Kingsley, and *UK Habitats of the Canadian Goose* by HM Stationery Office. The Andromedan Sleepers eventually died. For several hundred years, the human underground dwellers served the robot Drathro, which they knew as the Immortal, while the L3 patiently awaited an arrival from Andromeda that never came.

Drathro and the survival station were powered by black light, funnelled down to them from a black light converter on the planet surface. After so many centuries in operation, the converter had decayed, threatening a black light explosion that could destroy the entire universe in a chain reaction. Since black light supplied his energy source and maintained the survival station, Drathro's

programming would not allow him to consider disabling the converter – he still had to guard the secrets and await rescue, and had reasoned that his human work units would have no function without him.

THE VALEYARD

The Ravalox affair came to light only because the Sixth Doctor was placed on trial by the Time Lords for conduct unbecoming a Time Lord, transgressing the First Law of Time, and committing genocide. His prosecutor was the Valeyard. According to the Master, the Valeyard was an amalgamation of the darker sides of the Doctor's nature, somewhere between his twelfth and final incarnations: 'the distillation of all that's evil in you, untainted by virtue, a composite of your every dark thought'. It is possible that the Valeyard was actually a projection, similar to the potential future bodies that Romana tried on when she regenerated, or to the Watcher that haunted the Fourth Doctor at the end of his life. The Valeyard was so hungry for actual life that he planned to steal the Sixth Doctor's remaining regenerations, heedless of the terrible paradox this would cause.

Until their extinction in the Last Great Time War, there was a limit to exactly how many lives a Time Lord could have. Thirteen was the default life cycle, and the Master had already used his twelfth regeneration when he framed the Fourth Doctor for the assassination of the Time Lord President. But the energy from the Eye of Harmony massively extended his life, for long enough for him to find ways to take over the bodies of other life forms. It was clearly possible for Gallifreyans to be given additional regenerations – or to lose them. The Fifth Doctor came close to surrendering his last eight lives to Mawdryn. The High Council offered the Master a complete new cycle of regenerations in return for rescuing the Doctors from the Death Zone, and they went on to resurrect both the Master and Rassilon during the Time War.

WORLDS APART

■ The Time Lords time-looped the Fifth Planet, home world of the Fendahl (see 009).

■ They also allowed the destruction of the planet Minyos after its people turned against their Gallifreyan 'gods'.

■ They placed a force field around the War Lord's planet, dematerialising him and his world from history.

■ The pirate planet Zanak compressed countless worlds into impossibly small lumps of rock.

■ The Doctor arranged the destruction of Skaro (see 088).

■ The Nestene protein planets were destroyed during the Time War.

■ The Master's unleashing of the entropy field caused untold devastation to the universe, including Nyssa's planet Traken and its entire home system of Metulla Orionsis.

■ The Daleks used a Magnetron to remove 27 planetary bodies from their orbits and assemble them into a Reality Bomb in the Medusa Cascade (see 077).

■ Rassilon's plan to bring Gallifrey out of the Time War would have been at the cost of the destruction of the Earth (see 063).

■ After the Sixth Doctor's trial, Ravalox was restored to its original place and became known as Earth once again.

THE SEVEN SLEEPERS

One inspiration for *The Trial of a Time Lord* was the legend of the Seven Sleepers at Ephesus – a group of Christians fleeing persecution and hiding in a cave. There they slept for a couple of centuries, eventually waking up and wandering through the city – hailed as miracles by the now Christian population – and then dying.

The legends of the Knights Templar (who had a stronghold near Ephesus) and their supposed preservation of various divine relics like the Holy Grail and the Ark of the Covenant were also an influence.

A GOOD DEATH

The Trial of a Time Lord (1986) was deliberately lighter in tone than the preceding year's stories, but the fourth episode includes an unusually graphic moment in which Queen Katryca (Joan Sims) is killed by Drathro. Her electrocution at Drathro's claws includes what appears to be blood flowing from burns to her face.

Other surprisingly graphic bits in *Doctor Who* have included:

The final battle between Za and Kal in *An Unearthly Child*

The shooting of Condo in *The Brain of Morbius*

The ugly signs of strangulation on Kerril's neck in *The Robots of Death*

The maiming of Lytton in *Attack of the Cybermen*

Death by acid bath in *Vengeance on Varos*

The melting head of Kane in *Dragonfire*

... and quite a few moments, such as the gassing of Maggie in *Fury from the Deep*, from the Hartnell and Troughton era which were removed by the Australian Censor before broadcast. Ironically, these clips now survive when many of the episodes themselves do not.

Space Station

OUTSIDE TIME

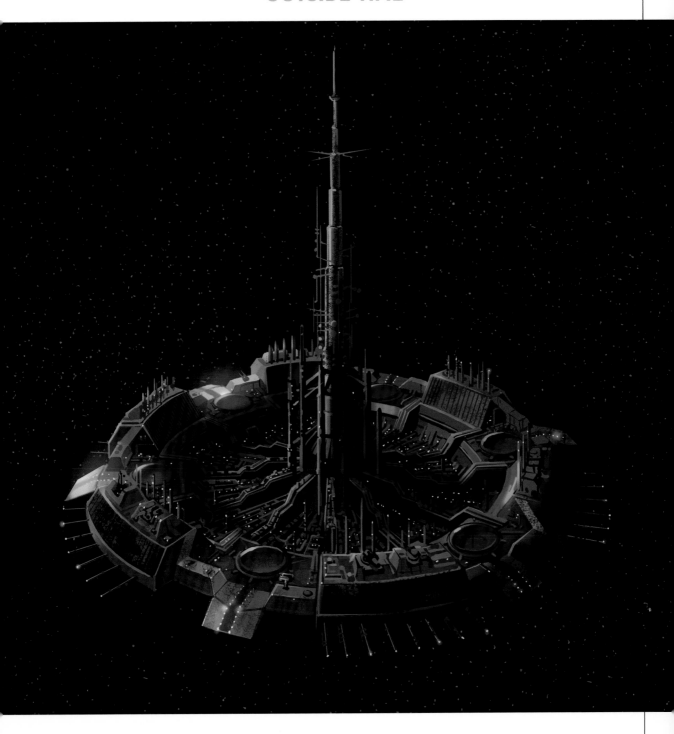

bove time, beyond space, the Time Lords did not interfere. Except when they did. And, when they did, they preferred it not to happen on their own soil. This was especially true when they had to intervene in the actions of one of their own kind. Time Lord justice was swift, absolute, and remote.

A Time Lord court was convened on a massive space station, out of time, out of the way. The court assembled – a jury of distinguished Time Lords, an Inquisitor, a Valeyard and (if requested) a court defender. The Keeper of the Matrix was on hand, so that the repository of all Time Lord knowledge could be accessed through its Seventh Door to supply evidence gathered from the defendant's timestream. This evidence was sifted, valued, and then replayed in front of the defendant. Sometimes incidents were chosen from epistopic interfaces of the defendant's spectrum, sometimes the defendant himself was allowed to present examples in defence of his actions. In extreme cases, the Inquisitor could view sensitive evidence on her own, *in camera*.

The space station was equipped with the means to pluck defendants and witnesses from anywhere in time and space to the courtroom: time-scoop technology allowed a TARDIS to be brought to the station by a time corridor; specially constructed pods were used to carry lesser beings without their own temporal transport.

TIME LORD JUSTICE

Time Lord propaganda portrayed them as a noble, sophisticated race, but the evidence suggests that their justice was arbitrary and brutal, with torture and summary execution commonplace.

MORBIUS: A renegade Time Lord who waged war across the constellation of Kasterborous, he led a rebellion against the High Council and was eventually cornered on Karn. There the Time Lords united with the Sisterhood of Karn to defeat him and the capture of his followers. Morbius's trial took place on Karn, and he was sentenced to execution. His body was placed in a dispersal chamber and atomised to the nine corners of the universe.

THE WAR LORD: The leader of a race that devised a scheme to assemble the ultimate army to take control of an entire galaxy. Thousands of human beings were abducted and set to fight and die in eleven War Zones in a series of War Games. Brutal methods of mental processing were used which entirely contravened all the galactic laws, and he made use of Gallifreyan time-travel technology to take soldiers out of time. He, his people and their home world were erased from time.

THE DOCTOR: Placed on trial for interference in the affairs of

others, the Second Doctor presented cases where his intervention had done good, and alerted his people to the threats of several races, drawing their attention in particular to the Daleks. The Time Lords duly noted this, but still sentenced the Doctor to exile on Earth, and forced a regeneration on him.

THE RANI: A brilliant scientist, she was banished from Gallifrey after the President's cat was eaten by monster-sized mice she had bred.

THE DOCTOR: Placed on trial for the assassination of the President of the High Council, the Fourth Doctor was tortured in an attempt to extract a confession by mind probe. A hastily arranged trial started immediately, despite Time Lord traditions of 'fairness and justice', and the vaporisation chamber was prepared in expectation that the Doctor would be found guilty within three hours. He sidestepped execution by standing for the office of President, invoking Article 17 of the Constitution as a guarantee of liberty – no candidate for office could be debarred or restrained from presenting his claim.

THE DOCTOR: Brought before the High Council, the Fifth Doctor was placed in a termination chamber rather than risk him being used as a way for the renegade Time Lord Omega to cross over from the universe of antimatter.

THE CASTELLAN: With the forbidden Black Scrolls of Rassilon discovered in his room, the Castellan was accused of reopening the Death Zone and illegally operating a Time Scoop. He was taken away for questioning, with use of the Mind Probe authorised to discover the truth, but he was shot – seemingly while trying to escape. This was, as the Fifth Doctor surmised, a crude cover-up.

THE DOCTOR: Placed on trial for interference in the affairs of others, the Sixth Doctor soon found himself facing a charge of genocide. The inquiry and trial were, in fact, orchestrated by the High Council who were worried that he had stumbled upon a crime of their own – the devastation of the planet Earth by a solar fireball (see 096).

THE MASTER: Executed by the Daleks, the Master asked for the Doctor to go to Skaro to recover his body. Did some kind of treaty exist between the Daleks and Time Lords at that point?

THE PARTISAN: A member of the High Council in the final days of the Last Great Time War, she suggested that the bloodlust and insanity of the conflict had cost too many lives. Perhaps the time had come for the Time Lords to accept their fate? Rassilon obliterated her with a metallic blue light blasted from his gauntlet.

THE WEEPING TIME LORDS: Only two of the High Council stood up to Rassilon when he proposed a way to escape the Timelock and restore Gallifrey in time and space. They were sentenced in front of the full body of Time Lords, and their punishment was to attend Rassilon's triumph, standing motionless, their faces hidden in shame, 'like the Weeping Angels of old'.

The Time Lords also once had a prison planet, but nobody can remember it.

STOP THE MATRIX

All Time Lord knowledge, wisdom and experience was gathered in the Amplified Panotropic Computation network – trillions of electrochemical brain cells held in a continuous Matrix. The cells were the repository of departed Time Lords – at the moment of death, an electrical scan was made of the brain pattern and these millions of impulses were immediately transferred to the Matrix.

A thousand super-brains in one, the Matrix monitored life in the Gallifreyan Capitol, using the combined knowledge and experience to predict future developments. A Time Lord away from Gallifrey remained tuned in to the Matrix via a Reflex Link in his brain. His experience was harvested and recorded.

Images could be formulated from these electrical impulses, and the pictures relayed onto a screen. The Time Lord Chancellor and President were able to observe the Doctor's struggles against Omega, both in UNIT HQ and in the universe of antimatter. When selecting previous incarnations to join the Doctor in his struggle, they could observe any moment of the Doctor's timestream. The President of the High Council had direct personal access to the Matrix via the Circlet of Rassilon.

It was also possible for a living Time Lord to enter the Matrix. The Fourth Doctor and Chancellor Goth were both given access via APC couches, wired up in the same way as the near-deceased. Inside, Goth created a nightmare world of the subconscious, but the reality remained a computation matrix. And the Key of Rassilon (or a copy of it) allowed entrance via the 'Seventh Door'. The Valeyard used this entrance and created another fantasy world of alternative realities.

CHANGING WITH THE TIMES

Restrained and monastic...

... even the children.

Increasingly ornate...

... with the cares of the universe on their shoulders.

Donning and grumbling about their ceremonial costumes...

... their ornate robes were topped by an elaborate collar.

The formal dress became their everyday wear...

... though they dispensed with the collars when off-duty.

This look stuck until the End of Time...

... though Rassilon set his own trends.

The Chancellery Guard were always resplendent in their scarlet and cream uniforms.

An honourable mention must be made for Commander Maxil, who had a very, very elaborate hat...

Statue of a Monoid

57TH SEGMENT OF TIME

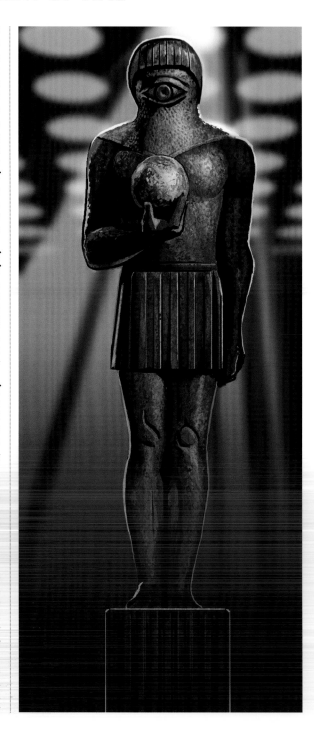

As the end of the world drew nearer, the human race began to leave Earth for the last time. The planet had been abandoned then repopulated before – the solar flares predicted in the 29th century had prompted a wave of exploration that reached Andromeda and established the GalSec colonies (see 081); the transfer of Earth's constellation to the Stellian galaxy had all but emptied the planet of life (see 096). Now, though, human science saw a final end coming, and humanity spread across the universe adapting and mutating and cross-breeding. Voyaging out in waves of vast space arks, they went looking for the right planets to make their new homes. Their journeys could take centuries, and they were not always fortunate in their choice of destination. The population of one colony ship was dragged into subjugation on Frontios by Tractators living beneath the ground. Humanity may, in any case, have been over-hasty – interventions by the National Trust, the Time Lords and others managed to extend the Earth's life for aeons more.

But the first to leave saw themselves as the custodians of humanity's legacy, and they rarely acknowledged the legitimacy of rival human groups. One huge ship, the Ark, set out for Refusis 2, identified by them as the most suitable planet for an exact replication of their home world. Unwittingly echoing the 'dawn-timers' aboard space station Nerva 10 million years or more earlier, they claimed to be carrying the Earth's whole population, human and animal. It was a 700-year voyage, so almost everyone was miniaturised in trays and stored in suspended animation, with just a select few 'Guardians' watching over them and piloting the ship.

The people of the Ark were accompanied by a race of submissive alien servants. The Monoids had come to Earth many years earlier as refugees from their own dying world, and offered their services in return for places on the 700-year journey. As so often happened with humanity, however, the partnership degenerated into exploitation, and the Monoids' building resentment ultimately led to a rebellion.

To celebrate their great endeavour, the Guardians dedicated themselves to erecting a gigantic statue: *Homo Sapiens*. The plan was to complete the statue as the Ark neared the end of its voyage. As the ship finally approached Refusis, though, it was the head not of a human being but of a Monoid that crowned the statue.

THE COMMON COLD

The common cold is the most unexceptional of infectious diseases in humans. It is also the one for which there is no cure, not even with antibiotics, although many of the symptoms are treatable or manageable. It is an upper respiratory infection whose symptoms include a cough, a sore throat and a runny nose. These symptoms aren't actually your cold – they are your immune system's response to the cold.

The cold is first mentioned in Ancient Egypt in the 16th century BC (on a snot-soaked papyrus), but it had finally died out so long before the Ark left Earth that the human race had forgotten what it was like. The sudden reintroduction of it by

Dodo Chaplet (a teenager from the 1960s) caused a fatal reaction among the Ark's humans, who had lost all resistance to it, and the Monoids, who had never been exposed to it.

This fatal reaction to an unexceptional and seemingly harmless disease echoed events in the late 18th century, when many native Aboriginal Australians died from encountering colds, measles and other common European diseases. This may even have been done deliberately – certainly the practise of giving American Indians blankets from the smallpox ward was used in 1763 at the siege of Fort Pitt.

THE SECURITY KITCHEN

The Monoids are responsible for one of the most remarkable ways of containing prisoners in *Doctor Who*'s history, with Monoid One uttering the line: 'Take them to the security kitchen!' Other candidates for Most Unexpected Dialogue in *Doctor Who* include:

■ 'Eh-heh.' The Black Dalek clears its throat before issuing orders in *The Dalek Invasion of Earth*.

■ 'Compute time lag by Earth scale.' 'Er... one... er... forty... er...' A one-off experiment in presenting a stupid Dalek, in *The Chase*.

■ 'Nothing in the world can stop me now!' Professor Zaroff concludes Episode 3 of *The Underwater Menace* in extraordinary fashion. According to Anneke Wills (who

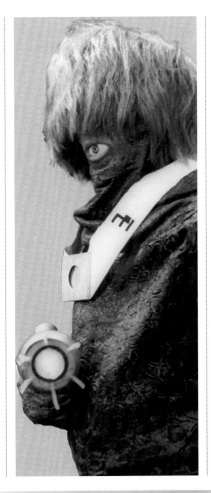

played Polly), at this point the studio burst into applause.

■ 'I could play for ever in my green cathedral.' Harrison Chase explains how much he likes to play music to the plants of his conservatory in *The Seed of Doom*.

■ 'And if you go further back, right in the Middle Ages, it came under the control of the Mother Superior of the Convent of the Little Sisters of Saint Gudula.' Romana discusses the ownership of the Nine Travellers in *The Stones of Blood*.

■ 'I must have forgotten to mention the other experiment I have been engaged in.' The miraculously resurrected Borad casually announces his experiments in cloning in *Timelash*.

■ 'You are elevating futility to a high art. There's nothing you can do to prevent the catharsis of spurious morality!' the Valeyard tartly informs the Sixth Doctor at the conclusion of *The Trial of a Time Lord*. This is shortly after his companion Mel has uncovered a 'Megabyte Modem' and the Master has been trapped in a 'Limbo Atrophier'.

■ 'The semiotic thickness of a performed text varies according to the redundancy of auxiliary performance codes,' a security guard confides to the Seventh Doctor. He is quoting from *Doctor Who: The Unfolding Text*, a 1980s work applying literary theory to *Doctor Who*. The passage in question roughly translates as '*Doctor Who* works better with incidental music.'

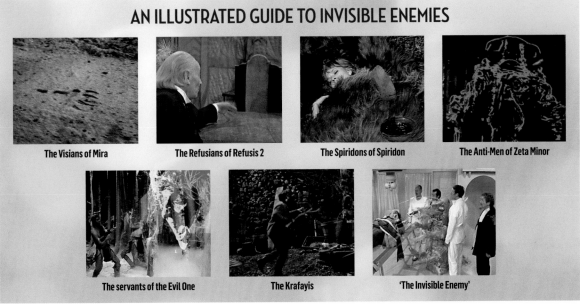

AN ILLUSTRATED GUIDE TO INVISIBLE ENEMIES

The Visians of Mira

The Refusians of Refusis 2

The Spiridons of Spiridon

The Anti-Men of Zeta Minor

The servants of the Evil One

The Krafayis

'The Invisible Enemy'

The Face of Boe

5,000,000,000

The expansion of the star Sol as it blossomed into a red giant in the year officially designated 5.5/apple/26 finally destroyed the planet Earth, and the galaxy's richest people gathered on a heavily shielded orbiting space station to witness the spectacle. The Earthdeath event quickly aroused feelings of nostalgia among humans across the cosmos and, when a similar planet was discovered 50,000 light years from Earth in the galaxy M87, a full-scale revival movement soon got under way. This planet was the same size as the Earth, with the same atmosphere and the same orbit. Its discoverers named it New Earth, and its colonisation began. After just a few years, New Earth was a viable world, with a population of millions. But, in 5,000,000,029, a virus mutated inside a new mood compound called Bliss, becoming airborne and killing everyone on the surface in just seven minutes. The last act of the Senate was to declare New Earth unsafe, and the planet was placed in automatic quarantine for 100 years. The walkways and flyovers to the Undercity were closed, saving the poorer population but leaving them trapped below ground.

The sponsor of the Earthdeath event was a 1.5-metre steam-driven, glass-fronted tank filled with fluids and smoke and containing a gigantic head. This was the Face of Boe, a legendary being from the Silver Devastation, who had survived the extinction of Boekind during the Fourth Great and Bountiful Human Empire and lived on for billions of years. Though he had long been assumed to be immortal, he became a patient in New New York's hospital in 5,000,000,023, slowly dying of old age. When the Bliss virus struck six years later, the Face of Boe wired himself into New New York's mainframe and sacrificed his own life force to maintain the motorway system and keep millions of people alive for the next 24 years. In 5,000,000,053, the Tenth Doctor arrived, and managed to restore the city's systems, but was unable to open the Undercity. The Face of Boe boosted the city's residual power with the last of his own energy, and the people were at last able to escape. This final effort proved too much, and the glass in the Face of Boe's tank shattered. The Doctor was with him as he died.

Superstitions and legends had surrounded the Face of Boe for millennia. One tale said that the sky would crack asunder at the time of his death, and this came true when the Undercity was

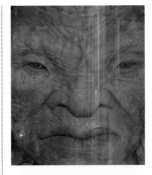

opened. Another legend was that, before he died, he would tell a great secret to a traveller. This prediction was fulfilled when the Doctor heard the Face of Boe's final words: 'You Are Not Alone...'

BOESHANE POSTER BOY?

The Face of Boe's origins are obscure. The Doctor, however, had his suspicions. His one-time travelling companion Captain Jack Harkness was made immortal by Rose Tyler channelling the power of the Time Vortex. Captain Jack once reminisced about his own origins:

> Used to be a poster boy when I was a kid back on the Boeshane Peninsula. Tiny little place. I was the first one ever to be signed up for the Time Agency. They were so proud of me. The Face of Boe they called me.
>
> *Last of the Time Lords*

When Martha Jones reminded the Doctor on Malcassairo of the Face of Boe's final words, Captain Jack was there and he didn't react at all. Perhaps he stored it up, and his 'poster boy' claim later on was just his little joke at the Doctor's expense.

And yet... when the Master used a Chameleon arch to become human, the naked infant was found abandoned on the coast of the Silver Devastation, home to the Face of Boe. Was it the Face of Boe who named the child Yana? Could it be that this was Captain Jack Harkness, protecting the timelines?

100

'Toclafane'

100,000,000,000,000

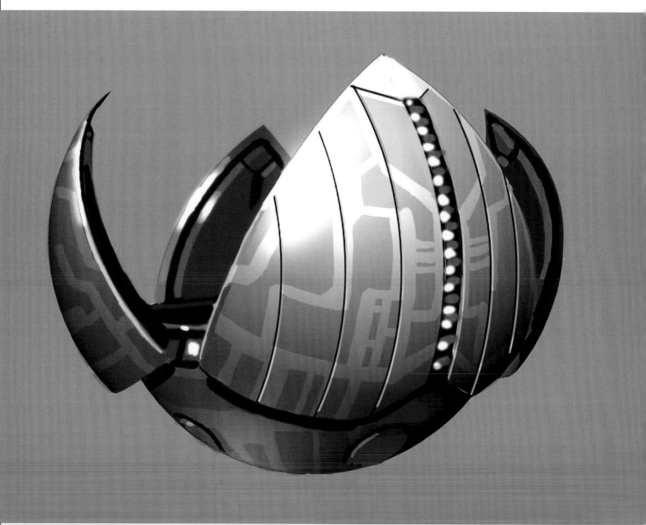

At the end of time, as stars burnt up and galaxies collapsed, every great civilisation died out. Just three species survived to the very end, and one of them was the human race. With the collapse of reality itself already in sight, an interstellar signal was detected emanating from a point far beyond the Condensate Wilderness, out towards the Wildlands and the Dark Matter Reefs. Its message was 'Come to Utopia.' It was a modulating signal, which meant it was not on automatic – someone was there. The Science Foundation established the Utopia Project to locate Utopia, learn what it was, and perhaps find a way to save humanity.

Humans had spent a million years evolving into clouds of gas and another million years as digital downloads called Digi-

Humans. Now, still struggling to outlast creation among the burning furnaces of Utopia, the remnants of the human race cannibalised themselves, reducing their organic existence to shrunken heads transported in heavily armed, magnetically sealed floating spheres. The Master discovered them and named them 'Toclafane', offering them a whole new future – in the past. Six billion Toclafane abandoned Utopia and passed through a tear in reality. The Master had created a terrible paradox, allowing them to emerge in the Earth of 2008 and slaughter their own ancestors, to become the new Lords of Time.

Moments later, the Toclafane reappeared in Utopia, the last, insane vestiges of humanity destined to watch helplessly as the universe finally ended.

WHAT MIGHT HAVE BEEN...

For a time in 2004, it seemed that the Daleks would not be appearing in the revived *Doctor Who*, due to rights issues. Writer Robert Shearman, commissioned to script the Daleks' return to TV, briefly found himself developing a story he called 'Absence of the Daleks', introducing an alternative enemy dreamed up by Russell T Davies...

```
The SPHERE is composed of an enormous eye. The
pupil a furious red / black, the iris constantly
shifting colour, insane. Ugly veined streaks. Metal
clamps seem to hold the eye tightly in place with
pincers.
DOCTOR: They rolled back through time, from
a billion years in the future. And attacked.
Every sentient species they could find, genocide
on a universal scale. Nestenes, Daleks, their
civilisations decimated, countless others
completely wiped out.
GUNTHER: Why?
DOCTOR: I don't know. Don't you see, we never knew.
My people trapped them on our planet, they had to
be stopped somehow. Mutually assured destruction,
we sacrificed ourselves to take them out. But it
didn't work, did it? There's still one down there,
it isn't over yet..!

                            'Absence of the Daleks'
```

THE END OF THE UNIVERSE

The universe has come perilously close to ending quite a few times, and has actually ended twice.

28 FEBRUARY 1981 The universe had long before passed the point of heat death but had been sustained by the Logopolitans. The Master's destruction of Logopolis saw large portions of the cosmos erased before the closed system was opened again.

1985 The Sixth Doctor once thought that the holistic fabric of time had been punctured while he was caught in an embolism and therefore outside the time flow and at the very epicentre of the engulfing chaos – the collapse of the universe had started, and nothing could stop it. He was mistaken.

2009 Davros and the Daleks' Reality Bomb was primed to collapse reality itself.

26 JUNE 2010 The TARDIS's explosion actually began the destruction of the universe, until the Eleventh Doctor used the Pandorica to detonate Big Bang 2 and reboot everything.

25 DECEMBER 2010 Rassilon intended to bring about the End of Time, becoming a creature of consciousness alone while creation itself ceased to be.

35TH CENTURY A potential second explosion in Terminus's engines threatened a second Big Bang, enough to destroy the universe.

37,166 The removal of antimatter samples from Zeta Minor came close to provoking the final cataclysm.

2,000,000 A potential black light explosion on Ravalox would have caused dimensional transference, making the universe unstable and destroying it.

100,000,000,000,000 The end of everything. Goodbye.

As the universe ends, James and Steve need to thank:

~ Paul Lang, for achieving so much, in so little time, with so little to go on

~ Peter McKinstry, for the astonishing creations that kept us above and beyond
what we'd hoped for

~ Gary Russell and Ian Grutchfield, for disappearing at just the right time

~ Derek Ritchie, Denise Paul, Matt Nicholls and
Edward Russell, for being there at just the right time

~ Albert, Nick, and the rest of BBC Books, for understanding and coping
with the flexible demands of dealing with time travel

~ Marek Kukula, for astounding insights into the Origins of Everything

~ Kate Webster, for helping us decode the secrets of Bletchley Park

~ Robert Shearman, for giving us a glimpse of what wasn't

~ and Russell T Davies and Steven Moffat, for... well, they know...

This book is dedicated to
Kieran and Lucy
Jacob
Vicci and Emily
Nellie, Charlette and Lucia
and everyone at Anton Junior School
plus everyone who's joined the Doctor, Rose, Martha, Donna, Amy and Rory,
Captain Jack, Sarah Jane, K-9 and all the rest, in all their adventures, and will be with
them for always